Anthology of Essays
on Deep Listening

Anthology of Essays on Deep Listening

Foreword by Pauline Oliveros

Edited by Monique Buzzarté and Tom Bickley

DEEP LISTENING PUBLICATIONS

Anthology of Essays on Deep Listening
Edited by Monique Buzzarté and Tom Bickley
Foreword by Pauline Oliveros
Copyright © 2012 by Deep Listening Publications
Second Printing

Cover design: Nico Bovoso
Cover photo: IONE

Deep Listening Publications
Deep Listening Institute, Ltd.
77 Cornell Street, Suite 303
Kingston, NY 12401
(845) 338-5984
www.deeplistening.org

ISBN: 978-1-889471-18-1
Printed in the United States of America

Listen Deeply, Beauty Surrounds You

David Gamper (1945–2011)

Tom Dougherty (1962–2000)

Joe Catalano (1952–1998)

Bill Jones (1962–1994)

Contents

Foreword

Pauline Oliveros

DEEP LISTENING WAS BORN in a cistern at Fort Worden, Port Townsend in Washington State in 1988. My long-time friend Stuart Dempster and I share an interest in reverberant spaces. What was supposed to be a visit to investigate the nature of this cistern and its 45-second reverberation time turned into a recording session. As an afterthought Stuart invited recording engineer Al Swanson to go along with us as well as my assistant Panaiotis.

The lengthy reverberation time of the cistern was very clear and smooth. Reflected sounds of instruments were difficult to discern from direct sounds (Dempster, trombone/didjeridu; Oliveros, accordion/voice; and Panaiotis, voice). Sounds also seemed to travel around the ovoid shape of the cistern in both directions.

We recorded that day for five delightful, timeless hours. The reverberation of the cistern supported our sounds, making the session magically tireless and the listening ecstatic. Al Swanson aimed his mics at our instruments and at the walls of the cistern to achieve a documentary recording released by New Albion in 1989[1] that is still available more than twenty years later.

Naming the recording *Deep Listening* and naming the *Deep Listening Band* came about because of the way that we had to listen in order to play in that environment. As described in the liner notes of the CD, we were listening to our own sounds and to the other's sounds and to all of the reflected sounds of the space as well. We were fourteen feet underground

---

1   Pauline Oliveros, Stuart Dempster, and Panaiotis, *Deep Listening*. New Albion NA022, compact disc, 1989.

i

so the pun was intended. We were listening deeply deep down under. We were also improvising without any pre-planning, using only our collective listening and responses to guide our music.

Since composing *Sonic Meditations* (1970)[2] my attention has been directed to listening and how to bring attention in others to listening. My intention is to compose, improvise and live in a heightened state of awareness of sound, silence and sounding.

My first Deep Listening Retreat occurred in summer 1991 at the Rose Mountain Retreat Center in Las Vegas, New Mexico. Twenty people interested in what *Deep Listening* might be for them came to the mountain, 8,000 feet up a bumpy road navigable only via four wheel drive, to camp out with no plumbing in a beautiful, natural environment and listen together.

This pilgrimage up the mountain to a pristine location that uses water captured from rainfall and electricity generated from solar panels, with no nearby distractions or noise, was very appropriate for a retreat.

I loved the idea of a retreat devoted to listening. Concepts from my *Sonic Meditations* and newly composed *Deep Listening Pieces*[3] helped to organize the activities. Listening meditations were held daily along with silence practice.

The first Deep Listening Retreat felt very successful and ended with all participants creating and performing their own pieces based on their listening experiences. All twenty pieces are published by Deep Listening Publications as *Deep Listening at Rose Mountain*.[4]

I am thankful to all the numerous people who have attended Deep Listening Retreats and workshops in good faith. They have been tremendous learning experiences for me. I have studied the difference between hearing and listening. I have learned that hearing can be measured and that listening still remains mysterious and is peculiar to individual perceptions and interpretations.

---

2   Pauline Oliveros, *Sonic Meditations* (Baltimore: Smith Publications, 1974).

3   Pauline Oliveros, *Deep Listening Pieces* (Kingston, NY: Deep Listening Publications, 1990).

4   *Deep Listening at Rose Mountain* (Kingston, NY: Deep Listening Publications, 1991). In addition to that collection of scores and writings by participants in the first Deep Listening Retreat, see also Marc Jensen, ed., *Deep Listening Anthology: Scores from the Community of Deep Listeners* (Kingston, NY: Deep Listening Publications, 2009) and Marc Jensen, ed., *Deep Listening Anthology Vol. 2* (Kingston, NY: Deep Listening Publications, 2010).

Listening consists of a complexity of emotional reactions leading to feelings, decisions and actions or lack of action.

Listening is experiencing what is heard inwardly. Sounding is expressing what is heard outwardly. Silence is the space between experiencing and sounding.

I have learned that listening can be focused, linear and exclusive and listening can be open, global and inclusive. Focal listening is concentrated, moment-to-moment attention to details, such as a phrase or phrases of music. Inclusive listening is receptive to all that can be heard in an ever expanding field of continuous simultaneous events perceived as a whole. Balancing of these two modes of listening may bring about homeostasis. Learning to recognize these ways of listening is important musically, technically, socially, professionally and humanly.

A receptive listening presence can bring about harmonious feelings with others.

Our powers of exclusive listening are hard-won and take repetition and practice.

Receptivity takes relaxation and openness. These opposites make us whole.

The essays in this book come from wonderful practitioners who listen deeply. They all have managed to connect, communicate and explicate a world of listening that may open all of us to unheard newness and creativity. They are sounding their experiences of listening.

Introduction

Monique Buzzarté and Tom Bickley

PAULINE OLIVEROS WROTE to Monique Buzzarté in mid-August 2010, proposing that she solicit and edit an anthology of Deep Listening™ essays. From that seed this work grew, germinating and blossoming into the collection of twenty-three essays now before you. Beginning with a call for abstracts of proposed essays (September–December, 2010), this project progressed in turn through peer-review of submitted proposals (January–February, 2011), essay writing (March–August, 2011), editorial feedback and author revisions (September–December, 2011), layout and proofreading (January–April, 2012), and finally the publication process itself (May, 2012). Along the way the editorial team was expanded to include co-editor Tom Bickley and layout editor Joseph Zitt. Authors of twenty-three of the thirty-eight proposals received completed the editorial process. Their essays form this anthology.

Ranging widely in style, subject and scope, what each essay shares in common is a relationship of the author to the practices of Deep Listening. Given that the inclusive community of Deep Listeners/deep listeners forms a marvelous mandala of conceptual, professional and personal links, it is no surprise that deep listening emerges beyond Deep Listening.

While each author's introduction to and connection with Deep Listening is unique, all of them have occurred through a direct connection with Pauline Oliveros, frequently in complex and overlapping ways in a variety of roles.[1] Some authors are musical colleagues who have performed and recorded

---

1   See http://www.deeplistening.org/essays for additional information about these connections, along with other supplemental material provided by the authors.

with Oliveros. Some are scholars, or taught with her at academic institutions where she was on the faculty or visited as a guest artist. A number have formally studied Deep Listening at Deep Listening Retreats (indeed, seven of the authors are Deep Listening Certificate holders) or in university settings, while others made their acquaintance with Oliveros through workshop or conference settings. A few have long associations with her, a handful have been correspondents, two co-led the Deep Listening Retreats, one has edited a volume of Oliveros' collected writings, others have been interns at the Deep Listening Institute, and have served on the board of directors for the Deep Listening Institute.

The possibilities for ordering the essays in this volume were as infinite as the practices of Deep Listening itself. After considering various options we settled upon an arrangement that leads through stages of life and the natural world, into somatic listening, through engagement in teaching and learning, and finally into the realms of the collective (un)conscious.

This anthology has been brought into realization through the dedication of many others in addition to ourselves, several who served in multiple roles. Particular gratitude goes to the anonymous peer reviewers; layout editor Joseph Zitt, who wrestled with myriad issues of spacing, page design and software; proofreaders Al Margolis and Lawton Hall; artists Nico Bovoso for his cover design and IONE for the use of her 2002 photo from a Deep Listening Retreat held at Big Indian, NY on the covers; the staff at the Deep Listening Institute, especially Label and Catalog Manger Al Margolis and Events and Marketing Coordinator Lisa Barnard Kelley for their logistical support; each of the authors, for sharing their unique understandings of Deep Listening; and the Deep Listening Institute Board of Trustees. Tom Bickley acknowledges his family (including Daifuku) and friends, particularly spouse Nancy Beckman for her patience and encouragement during intense periods of work on this project.

This anthology is a gift to Pauline in celebration of her eightieth birthday on May 30, 2012. Her commitment over a lifetime of creative work in conceiving, developing, and transmitting the practice of Deep Listening makes this volume possible. We offer this work in deep gratitude and with loving appreciation for all that Pauline is, from all of us. Our hope is that this volume will serve to more widely disseminate information about and awareness of Deep Listening in increasingly wider circles. Deep Listening is a truly revolutionary practice, one that fosters creativity, encourages, supports and nurtures creative work, and facilitates growth—inner and outer, local and global, personal and universal. In 1990, between the formation of the Deep Listening Band and the first Deep Listening Retreat, Pauline described Deep Listening:

> "As a musician, I am interested in the sensual nature of sound, its power of release and change. In my performances throughout the world I try to transmit to the audience the way I am experiencing sound as I hear it and play it in a style that I will call deep listening. Deep listening is listening in every possible way to everything possible to hear no matter what you are doing. Such intense listening includes the sounds of daily life, of nature, of one's own thoughts as well as musical sounds. Deep listening is my life practice."[2]

Monique Buzzarté and Tom Bickley
April 16, 2012

---

2   Liner notes from *Crone Music* (Lovely Music, Ltd. CD 1903, 1990, compact disc). "Album Notes: Crone Music," accessed March 24, 2011, http://www.lovely.com /albumnotes/notes1903.html.

Deep Listening
through Life

<u>Noises</u> Very Good *Kris*

I like noises of all the Beasts
from the mouse to the Lion.

I like the birds and the bees

to sing their happy songs.

I like the wind so nice with his
merry breeze to sing his *whistling*
ling Tone,

I like all the noises
in the whole world. It makes
me cry to hear them.

Noises: Deep Listening from a Child's Point of View

Kristin Norderval, singer, improviser and composer, has premiered numerous new works for voice and presented original compositions incorporating voice, electronics, and interactive technology at festivals and concert houses in Europe, Asia, and the Americas. A two-time recipient of the Norwegian Artist's Stipend, and a 2005 recipient of the Henry Cowell Award from the American Music Center, Norderval has also received support from the Jerome Foundation, Meet the Composer, Harvestworks, and Rensselaer Polytechnic Institute. Commissions include works for Den Anden Opera in Copenhagen, the Bucharest International Dance Festival in Romania, jill sigman/thinkdance in New York City, and the viol consort Parthenia. Norderval holds a DMA from Manhattan School of Music, a MM from the San Francisco Conservatory of Music, and a BM from the University of Washington, as well as a certificate in Deep Listening. http://www.norderval.org

Kristin Norderval

Noises
I lik[e] noises of all the Beests
from the mouse to the Lion.
I like the birds and the bees
To sing there happy songs
I like the wind so nice with his
merry brece to sing his wiss-
ling tone
I like all the noises
in [the] hole wo[r]ld. It makes
me cry to hear.

MY MOTHER FOUND THIS POEM a few years ago in her filing cabinet. It was something I'd written in second grade. I don't remember writing it. But here it was, an early expression of my sonic interests and my fascination with daily sounds; deep listening from a child's point of view. The sounds I listed in that poem are still sounds that I am attracted to.

I've used recordings of both birdsong and bee sounds in musical compositions—processing them as part of my electronic music scores. I've used wind as well, especially when the wind has been resonating objects and drawing forth various (whistling) overtones. I've used other sounds from the natural world—water, the crushing of leaves and sticks, animal sounds from turkeys to dogs to whales—as well as sounds from the man-made machine world. I do indeed like all kinds of noises in the whole world. And sometimes still "it makes me cry to hear."

The last sentence in the poem stands out to me. In Deep Listening a distinction is made between "the involuntary nature of hearing and the voluntary, selective nature of listening."[1] Perhaps I had some subliminal understanding of that difference as a young person. The sounds that I listed in my poem were identified as pleasurable, all things I liked. I don't ever remember having a response of crying in joy as a youngster. When I liked things I laughed, I listened, and I smiled.

In the last line of the poem I wrote "It makes me cry to hear." My teacher corrected it to "It makes me cry to hear *them*" (emphasis added) implying that it made me cry to hear the sounds I had listed. But I'm not so sure that that was what I was actually expressing at the deepest level. My sense now is that that formulation, that choice of words, may have been a subconscious way of describing the discomfort at hearing things that were disturbing to me, things that I had no choice about hearing. And that perhaps this was a contrast to the things I liked to focus on, sounds I could choose to listen to carefully. I wonder now whether this was a sonic equivalent of children who innocently draw disturbing scenes—a way to alert adults to violence or difficult events that they can't otherwise articulate. There were events in my young years that left sound imprints that continued to haunt my dreams for many years afterwards. These sounds I did not like. But other sounds in the world, and my deep engagement with sound and with music, was what got me through those early traumas.

---

1   Deep Listening Institute, "Mission Statement," accessed June 7, 2011, http://deeplistening.org/site/content/about.

The drawings at the bottom of the poem provide me with other clues to my early listening. In addition to the bird and insect figures, there are two four-legged "beests"—hybrid animals. One looks like it has the head of a dog or cat, an indistinguishable body with a long neck and long tail, and stick legs with bird's feet. The other looks like a cross between a horse, a sea creature and a dinosaur or dragon with flippers. I think what I may have been trying to draw was a Chinese Lion (dragon).

When I was five years old we had moved to Kuala Lumpur, Malaysia. There was a substantial Chinese population living there, and at the Chinese New Year there were parades. The major attraction of the parade was the Lion dance. I was fascinated by the Lion dance and by the sounds of drums and cymbals and gongs that would announce its arrival in our neighborhood. If you left money and offerings at the gate, the lion would enter and perform a private dance for the household. I don't remember any visits to a zoo that early, and I don't think I'd ever seen a real lion at the time I wrote the poem. But the Chinese New Year Lions had made a big impression on me. They were colorful, exciting, and they arrived with a great sound-score! Perhaps the drumming and gongs in those Lion Dances are the roots of my later interest in minimalism and my love of the sounds of metal.[2]

Insects, geckos and the sounds of street vendors and open markets were another part of the sonic landscape that made an impression on me in Malaysia. There were numerous insects in the rooms at night, as the walls were open lattice brick. Lying safely under mosquito netting, I would listen to the buzzing and flitting of many winged creatures, and the scritch-scratches of geckos as they climbed the walls. In the days I enjoyed the chaotic sounds of the market with its combination of vendors, bicycles, cars, and even snake charmers. Both subtle quiet sounds and loud chaotic sonic combinations are still fascinating to me. Recordings of crickets have made their way into several of my works, but so have recordings of loud street protests and motors of all kinds.

---

2 "2011 Malaysian Chinese New Year Lion Dance - 1/3," accessed November 1, 2011, http://www.youtube.com/watch?v=WKd8yOUB1mI&feature= related.

When we moved back to Minnesota after a year in Malaysia, the sound world there was quite a contrast. Even the sound of the wind was different. Maple and oak leaves rustling in the wind sound very different than rubber and palm leaves. Each place we lived after that acquired sound markers: site-specific sound memories. In Iowa, it was the sounds of the trains that I loved. In Norway at my grandparents, it was the gulls, the old ferry boat motors and the sound of my grandfather's voice. In Seattle it was the sounds of the boat horns out on the Puget Sound, and vendors again—this time the Pike Place Market. That attention to site has also been a recurrent theme in my work. I've created many site-specific performances, and even in works that are not tied to a specific location I try to absorb and respond to the sounds of the environment in performance.

My earliest memories are sonic memories. Listening carefully to the sounds around me connected me to the world, both to the industrial human world and to other living things. It formed a basis for what I might now call my animist/bio-Buddhist leanings. Trees were my allies, and all things had songs. The notion that everything is connected in our eco-system—even the things we call inanimate—was easier for me to understand through a sonic orientation than a visual or verbal one. I understood innately that everything vibrates, that each bit of matter had its own unique sonic properties, but was also part of the whole.

My early listening prepared me for deeper listening later, both joyous and difficult. When I came to study the Deep Listening practices at retreats with Pauline Oliveros in 1998, the emphasis on listening to the sounds in the environment was what enabled me to stay grounded and in my body during meditations. My earlier attempts with meditation had often resulted in dissociation, but through a listening focus I could stay present. Listening to "all the noises in the whole world" outside of me eventually allowed me to focus on all the noises inside my brain as well. Some of those noises were inner voices that condemned and undermined and needed some constructive backtalk. Some noises were unpleasant sounds of past events to be reckoned with. Listening gave me the key to dealing with these unpleasant sounds by allowing me to play with them, showing me the joys of tuning into a world in vibration. I have come to see that by focusing on what I truly like and exploring where my ear leads my attention, I have gained an ability to move away from being captive of destructive involuntary hearing. I can choose instead to selectively listen with love to that which is nurturing. It makes me smile to listen.

Training for Listening: A Lifelong Practice

Stuart Dempster

STUART DEMPSTER, sound gatherer, trombonist, composer, didjeriduist, et al. and professor emeritus at University of Washington, has recorded for numerous labels including Columbia (Sony), Nonesuch, and New Albion. The latter includes *In the Great Abbey of Clement VI* at Avignon—a "cult classic"—and *Underground Overlays from the Cistern Chapel* consisting of music sources for a 1995 Merce Cunningham Dance Company commission. Grants are several, including being a Fulbright Scholar to Australia and receiving a Guggenheim Fellowship. Dempster's book *The Modern Trombone: A Definition of Its Idioms* was published in 1979. He is a founding member of Deep Listening Band, which celebrated twenty years with a double LP on TAIGA *Then & Now Now & Then* (2008). Dempster soothes aches, pains, and psychic sores with his healing, yet playful, *Sound Massage Parlor.* Golden Ear Awards: Deep Listening 2006 and Earshot Jazz 2009; International Trombone Association Lifetime Achievement Award 2010. http://faculty.washington.edu/dempster/

IT WAS ABOUT THE AGE OF SIX that I began semi-consciously training for listening. By then my training was literal, with the earliest memories of serious (deep) listening that I can document (at least in my head) including family outings during World War II to Berkeley Station (at the foot of University Avenue) to listen to and watch trains. This was cheap entertainment (gas rationing restricted travel) and the sonic palette was fascinating with so many sounds emanating from passing steam engines and from the rails themselves not to mention the visuals of it all. This interest expanded in 1951 when our family made an extensive summer drive across the nation to the East Coast during which I heard many different kinds of trains. Further interest continued all through the fifties and sixties including when I was in the army in Europe and listening and watching—and traveling on—trains in France, Germany, Great

13

Britain, Ireland, and Italy. This interest continues to this day and, as I write some of this essay, I am looking in appreciation at the confluence of the Long Island Rail Road with New York City's 7 Flushing subway line crossing overhead in Woodside (Queens), New York.

Much of my early listening not only included trains but also sounds of nature in locations as diverse as the backyard of our home and local parks, as well as many trips to Yosemite National Park and regular trips to Kenwood (Sonoma County), California. Consciousness of natural sounds was among my earliest memories, along with fascination with automobiles of the era and the streetcar line that terminated on Arlington Avenue about a half block away from our house in Berkeley, just over the Alameda County line into Contra Costa County in an area now known by its neighborhood name of Kensington.[1] I loved the comings and goings of that streetcar and from an early age rode on it regularly to downtown Berkeley. Besides autos there were occasional horse-drawn wagons, two in particular including the block-ice deliverer as well as a wagon with a driver slowly calling out "bottles, cans, rags" in a singsong voice as he progressed along the street in front of our house. Even by then—age five, perhaps—I had become quite taken by the idea of recycling because of our family home practices not to mention roots in the Sierra Club dating back to about 1894, a story for another time.

By age six (1942) World War II was in full swing and gas rationing was a reality that nearly every family had to face. The aforementioned "training" at Berkeley Station occupied me regularly along with a continuing appreciation of streetcars. I was very impressed with bells on trains and streetcars and admired the diversity of not only how they sounded but also how they were "performed." The "performance" by engineers on train whistles is well documented even down to being able to tell who

---

1 "Ardmore Road & Arlington Avenue," accessed December 14, 2011, http://www.oberail.org/photo/290/26/g. This photo includes not only the number 7 streetcar at the end of the line, but also my childhood and young adult home (1936–1964), the house immediately behind the colonial (barn-shaped) house left of center. This photo likely was taken by Louis L. Stein who was proprietor of the corner drugstore less than a half block away to the right.

is doing the "performing" but I did not acquire an appreciation of that aspect until considerably later on. At Berkeley Station freights would pass without stopping and the Doppler effect thrilled me no end. My father, ever the scientist, was quick to explain the phenomenon to me, and did it in such a way that made me believe that I actually understood it; maybe at some level, I did. All passenger trains stopped—it was quite an important and busy station—and I remember being so excited at all the incredible noises as they came to a halt, waited, and then started up again. That and the conductor's "All Aboard" and waving of a red lantern stay with me to this day.

By this time I instinctively knew I was onto something special. None of my childhood friends were particularly interested in sharing this listening passion. I wish I had realized and appreciated the deep listening skills of my parents, particularly my mother, but that wouldn't come until later. However, I had also begun to study piano, and this served to accelerate my awareness of what now has a label of Deep Listening, coined in 1988 by Pauline Oliveros at the time of Deep Listening Band's first recording.[2] I was already, by 1942, seemingly listening to everything. The piano offered what I later learned to be harmonics, or partials, to appreciate and I wasted no time in playing around with those. Our house itself was especially creative in sounds it presented, such as creaking during change of seasons or windstorms, and peculiar traveling sound waves and attendant wobbles that would come during regular, smaller earthquakes from the nearby Hayward Fault. Our backyard hummed with lots of bees and insects and, should I eat my lunch outside in the patio, distant train whistles could be heard from several miles away traveling along the East Bay shoreline. At that time Arlington Avenue traffic was minimal enough that one could easily "hear through" it.

A little later I was old enough to go by myself and sit on an interestingly designed cement bench at the end of the trolley line and watch streetcars come and go. Eventually the motorman allowed me to put the trolley pole up in back and lower the one in front to ready the streetcar

---

2   Recorded in 1988. Stuart Dempster, Pauline Oliveros, and Panaiotis, *Deep Listening,* New Albion Records NA 022, 1989, compact disc.

for its return to downtown. I can still hear the delicate rumbling and clunking of the pole as it became secured in its bracket. Looking back, they were appealing because the streetcar acted as a resonator. Similar to "high iron" rails at Berkeley Station, I could listen to these rails "sing" and estimate how far away the streetcar was from where I was sitting. There was a curve fairly close to the end of the line and between rails singing and overhead wires humming, especially as it got closer, my interest was definitely engaged. The overhead wires offered harmonics akin to string instruments and I enjoyed—still enjoy—that sound of humming and buzzing and attendant harmonic glissandi when I am around trolleys or, more likely these days, trolley buses.

Whenever I visit San Francisco, I am regularly reminded and amazed at the range of sounds that the city has and had to offer. Coming from Berkeley I would take the "F" Key System train from the end of the line at the head of Solano Avenue—a big advantage because if I was lucky I would snag a front seat by the train operator. On the Bay Bridge these trains could go fast enough that they would lurch from side to side and an odd buzzer-bell would sound when we were (likely) going too fast. I remember San Francisco's Market Street in the 1940s with four tracks of streetcars, two in each direction. There was always the illusion if not the reality of streetcars "racing" each other. Not only that, but these early streetcars were incredibly loud. The electrical motor, doors, and track noise made for an astonishing "concert before the concert" when on the way to the Opera House with my mother for a children's concert. I loved those concerts too, actually, but I sure looked forward to those streetcars, and cable cars anticipating our trip home as my mother and I had a post-concert lunch at the "Golden Pheasant" in Union Square on Powell Street.

In 2009, performing a concert at Meridian Gallery, I was reminded of that youthful time as cable cars went up and down Powell Street hill ringing their marvelous old bells, beautifully mixing with my improvisations. "They're playing my song!" seems to be my answer to nearly all ambient sounds I encounter, especially if they are particularly noisy, cacophonous or surprising. Of course, bells get me thinking of carillons, such as University of California, Berkeley's, or the 2008 addition of a "change-ringing" set installed at University of Washington.

My family traveled a lot by auto during the 1940s and 50s, and when we would go over Donner Pass on then US 40 I would suggest—or ask or plead—that we stop to listen and watch multiple cab-in-front locomotives pull mile-long freight trains. There was little resistance to this stopping and we generally made a picnic out of it in order to allow time for trains to make their appearances. Cab-in-fronts were designed for use in snow sheds in order that smoke would not block the engineer's view. The sounds from these enormous engines were absolutely astonishing, and reverberation from surrounding hills only served to amplify the effect and my unfettered joy! Even in 1951 during our cross-country drive a relatively brief stop was made for lunch and "training." On one trip east, likely the one in 1949 to Yellowstone and Grand Teton National Parks, and Salt Lake City, we stopped overnight at a Nevada town, probably either Winnemucca or Elko. Of course, after dinner I wanted to go to the train yard and hang out. Dad, somewhat reluctantly, consented and went with me. From a postcard to Nana (my maternal grandmother):

> What a thrill we had last night! Dad and I went to the train yard to watch trains. After we got there an engineer invited us both into his steam switcher cab. Was that ever something -- listening to an engine from the inside! We heard and saw the coal being shoveled into the fire, and the heat from the fire was so amazing. . . The engineer was nice, too, answering all our questions. And he even let me sit in the cab window! Wow. . .

This was really something at that time—even Dad perked up! Can anyone imagine this invitation happening today in our litigious society and terrorism considerations? We had quite the time looking and listening—deep listening at that; it was a whole new take on what trains sounded like.

The 1951 trip was a major marker in my "training" practice, and little did I realize the sheer quantity and diversity of trains that we would encounter. In those days trains were usually side-by-side with highways and that made for ample opportunities to not only hear and see them but, also, "race" alongside. Generally, there was little enough traffic that one could pace driving to match train speed. My mother would, at the appropriate time, yell out "train!" and we would perk up, open car windows, and listen. I don't remember ever being disappointed; there was always something new to appreciate. From another postcard to Nana:

> I have been enjoying trains already starting 3 days ago with the cab in fronts. Today we drove through the Chicago area and there were train tracks everywhere. As we continued east along US 30 [now people would use I-80] we crossed one set of tracks after another, each angled like huge spokes toward the Chicago hub. We were stopped several times by train traffic as we progressed and could scarcely believe the number of trains there were!

Obviously, I was in "training" heaven. The variety of engines, whistles, bells, and rolling stock was beyond anything I could imagine, and most grade crossings offered unique sounds as well. As we continued east the density of rail lines only increased.

By the time we arrived in Pennsylvania, New Jersey, and New York areas I had been "introduced" to a large variety of trains running on electricity whereas in the west nearly all "high iron" (so named because mainline rails were larger and, consequently, "taller") trains were coal-fired or diesel. Coal was phased out completely sometime during the middle to late 1950s. Different kinds of electrics, mostly depending upon whether or not they were powered by "third-rail" or overhead wires, produced a wide variety of sounds. In this eastern area of the country at that time there was close to an equal balance of steam, diesel, and electricity but, depending upon the area, it might be nearly all electric, or all steam and/or diesel. Although these power sources collectively provided a rich variety of sounds, there were also quite a variety of sounds even within one power source.

In 1952 I found myself with a friend in the Southern Pacific (SP) yards in San Francisco. We had gone down simply to photograph trains and watch them come and go from the passenger station then located at Third and Townsend Streets. Before long we had gravitated to the adjoining switching yard and, lo and behold, another experience of being invited into an engine cab! This time it was a diesel switcher but no less interesting than the steam switcher experience in 1949. The engineer even let us take pictures in, and from, the cab and was willing to chat with us and answer any of our questions. This was an experience coupled with a trip across San Francisco Bay in a ferryboat run by SP. We left from what was then known as the "Oakland Mole" (all cross-country San Francisco bound trains terminated there). We went right under the Bay Bridge on the way to the Ferry Building in San Francisco. On the way back we managed to board a ferry with a "walking-beam" engine!

After I graduated from San Francisco State University in 1958 I was drafted into the Army. After basic training and band school I, through judicious letter writing and a successful audition, landed a position in early 1959 in the Seventh Army Symphony Orchestra based in Stuttgart, Germany. Over and above extensive travel associated with the Orchestra, I took every opportunity to hop a train to somewhere be it close (trams to Stuttgart suburbs or trains to, say, Baden-Baden and Freiberg) or far (Heidelberg, Munich, Paris, and Vienna, for instance). From a letter on 6 July 1959 to Mom and Dad:

> The grand and glorious 24-hour train ride [from Naples to Stuttgart] via second-class crowded coach was extremely tiring [and hot!] but very interesting. Sleeping? Well, I didn't do much of that but it seemed to work [likely because] where I had been before it was nighttime. Consequently I didn't miss anything. And say — the trip thru Italian-Austrian-German Alps was beautiful. The people I met were fantastic, mostly Germans who had been hiking in the woods and in the mountains. And talking to them was fascinating. . .

The above letter excerpt triggered my memory and I remembered the following that I, at the time, told to many people verbally:

> The single second-class "through" car is packed to overflowing, and the sounds of the passengers (and vendors at stations) are phenomenal. At what was apparently a transfer point, probably near Rome, the train pulled away leaving the one car I was

on seemingly marooned in the rail-yard. It was very freaky – and ominously quiet (no station and attendant vendors) and I thought, "Oh, Oh!" There weren't even any trains nearby. After nearly an hour a clanking and rumbling train backed up to the car we were on and, with quite a thump, hooked up. At last we were on our way again to great applause and cheers by all the passengers. . .

The best part of the trip was going through the Italian and Austrian Alps. Not only that, we could open the windows. I stood in the aisle and leaned out over the windowsill looking at the stunning views. That and taking in the soot that came from the coal-fired steam engines that was particularly prominent on the steep grades. Also, when the train was on curves we could see and hear the engine and feel the soot blowing directly in on us. The weather was glorious and the sounds were coming through without interruption; the sounds of wheels on tracks, the fast almost hyper huffing and puffing of the engine, the whistle at grade crossings (along with crossing-gate bells) and stations, the latter including bell sounds. Absolutely beautiful!

In Europe I had been dropped back into the steam age and there were so many different engine types along with various electrics to savor. Every train, and every country's rail system, seemed to have so many different sounds and I found myself listening critically, and deeply, all the time. Did the train sound differently on a curve? What was the influence of mountains on reverberation of whistles? Why so many different kinds of crossing gates? Even though trams looked alike, why did they sound different? Questions such as these occupied me on nearly a daily basis.

Back in the United States in 1960 I entered graduate school and for a time did not pay much attention to trains. This coupled with the extensive newly built interstate highway system limited my access to trains. Already in the 1950s, Key System (later AC Transit) trains that went across the Bay Bridge were gone with nothing afoot that would replace them except added buses. However, construction began on BART (Bay Area Rapid Transit) not long after we moved to Seattle in 1968. I rode BART whenever I could during our visits to the area. I was most taken then, as I am now, with the howling and yowling of BART trains when they cross in the Transbay Tube. Some of this has to do with higher speeds being possible on this stretch, but most of it likely is due to being in an enclosed tube, or tunnel. It is a most astonishing and fascinating sound but, while it seems loud, one can still converse over it. It is an amazing all-encompassing melange of high, screaming pitches that continually vary.[3]

Ever since the 1940s I have known about Dunsmuir, California, as a "railroad" town, it being a location of an engine yard for adding or subtracting auxiliary engines necessary for steep grades around nearby Mount Shasta and on into southern Oregon. This makes for the prospect of much switching yard activity at various times of day or night. Since 1968 my wife and I have lived in Seattle. Besides traveling by air, we also make regular automobile trips to the Bay Area for concerts and/ or family and friends. During these road trips we invariably stop in Dunsmuir to fill our water jugs with water right off the mountain. Our favorite is to go slightly north of town to Dunsmuir City Park where we can have our picnic lunch and enjoy the scenery—and hope to engage in a deep listening experience. From what I remember of a rather animated phone call in the early 1970s to my brother:

> Did we ever get lucky today! A train descended along the riverside track and provided us with the most incredible concert one could imagine. . . The track is curved, of course, and along with squealing brakes the sounds are dramatic. Descent is more interesting than ascent because of braking, and as the train descended from north to south we discovered that we were in the middle of a huge, wide stereo system. Actually, because the sounds reverberate from all over, it is a surround

---

3   The following video was done to show off the lighting in the Transbay Tube, but it is the sound that I find so very special. You can hear the sound in this YouTube video: "Trans Bay Tube West Oakland To San Franciso [sic]," accessed November 30, 2011, http://www.youtube.com /watch?v=H0x22U4d6XE.

sound experience. It is so amazing we often find ourselves looking around trying to locate non-existent piccolo players!

We have since found that this may happen about every third stop at the City Park.

It was the drive across country to New York in 1966 that finally had Renko and me listening deeply in New York City subways. This was a somewhat hastily arranged tour to present the pieces I had commissioned from composers Luciano Berio (*Sequenza V*), Robert Erickson (*Ricercar á 5*), and Pauline Oliveros (*In the Garden: A Theater Piece for Trombone Player and Tape*) along with earlier works by Larry Austin, John Cage, and Barney Childs. We arrived in Hollis (Queens) where we would be staying, just in time to catch the F train into Manhattan for a new music recital (I only had ridden the subways a couple of times, once in 1951 and again in 1960 when I mustered out of the army). Was I ever listening! This may have been an era when the subways were going downhill, but the sounds were as delicious as I had remembered. Always, my most favorite sound is the very soft clicks that, insofar as I can tell, signal (to me anyway) that a train is about two stations away. Actually, I have no idea what those little click sounds mean. The other sounds I especially like are vacillations between about Eb and F in the low piccolo range on some newer trains.[4] (How can they afford to hire all those piccolo players?) Lastly I am at the same time somewhat amused and yet thankful that there is at long last recognition of and research into the extreme subway noise.[5]

---

4   "LIRR : Port Washington And Penn Station Bound M3 & M7 Trains @ Flushing - Main Street," accessed November 30, 2011, http://www.youtube .com/watch?v=3EFL6HKAfj4&NR=1&feature=fvwp.

5   Regarding noise in New York City subway, and elsewhere in New York City, see Winnie Hu, "Subways Are Noisy, Study Finds, to the Point of Being Harmful," November 1, 2003, accessed November 30, 2011, http:// wirednewyork.com/forum/showthread.php?t=4197&page=1. Also, this video provides an example of the noise at 14th Street/Union Square station on the 4, 5, and 6 lines. Observe the moving platform. It is much noisier than it appears. "IRT Lexington Line: 14th St-Union Square," accessed

When we made the move to Seattle in 1968 for me to begin teaching at University of Washington I realized I didn't know much about trains in the Northwest except for the SP's Shasta Daylight which I had taken from Berkeley in 1962 to attend the Seattle World's Fair. A minimalist monorail was built for the Fair, but I found myself more interested in sounds of trains in the Interbay neighborhood where Burlington Northern and Santa Fe's locomotive maintenance yard is located, and also looking from Fourth Avenue down onto the trains passing below near King Street Station—the train pit, I call it. Union Station is nearby but is no longer used for train service although it does house various transportation administrative offices. Also nearby is the 1999 baseball stadium (Safeco Field) with very busy rail lines immediately to the east. This offers an amazing sound palette of train horns, rumbling freights and various passenger trains going by, usually four or more per game. Even the announcers comment on the beauty of baseball and trains, and how beautiful it is in that marvelous, reverberant ballpark. Another favorite train experience near Seattle is the variety of trains that cross the access road to the Edmonds-Kingston Ferry. I am particularly enamored with the combination of sounds as the ferry pulls away from the dock when I can hear the ferry horn and also see and hear often more than one train. There might be an Amtrak or Sounder passenger train, or a freight train nearby, and then, because from the ferry one can see fairly far to the north, one may spot up to two trains further up the track.

I first visited the Oliveros/IONE abode in Kingston, New York in 1989. To my good fortune I stayed in a small bedroom on the second floor with a window that faced out over Rondout Creek complete with two high railroad bridges, one fairly close and one much further away. To my utter delight, during both day and night one could hear trains reverberating in the canyon. I am always in "train heaven" when I visit there. Not to be outdone, in early October 2009 I was in residence at Lawrence University in Appleton, Wisconsin for concerts and teaching. I was immediately confronted with train tracks going through town in various directions—another train heaven! In my talk to a composition

---

November 30, 2011, http://www.youtube.com/watch?v=pgIUf2AMYeY& feature=related.

class a train whistled in the distance, I paused and went to the window to listen (deeply). I mentioned what an amazing town Appleton was for train sounds, often multiple trains in various directions, likely due to its relative proximity to Chicago. The students observed me in curious amazement, but were receptive to my taking notice of the trains and what that might mean. The next day, students were coming up to me mentioning how they had already adjusted their listening to and thinking about trains and what a beautiful concert they offered.

At this point it is important to recognize aforementioned Woodside (Queens) New York as something rather special. Although I am somewhat familiar with Manhattan trains, I had never had an opportunity to spend any significant amount of time in other train stations around Manhattan until 2010. Woodside presented itself because our youngest son lives there, so not only was I able to listen to and see—and also use—the Woodside Station, I was able to do so several times each visit. The main interests include the convergence of Long Island Rail Road (LIRR) with New York City's 7 Flushing subway line. Often multiple trains present themselves, some stopping and others "expressing" their way through Woodside. Additionally, due to the stations for both trains being outdoors, one can hear everything up close and at a distance. Other unique qualities are frequent occasions when one might be relatively close to an LIRR train, seeing but not hearing it due to other factors such as distance, traffic and/or wind masking the sounds. Woodside, New York LIRR trains offer pitches from an interval of a ninth,[6] about A to Bb as trains stop, and then start up again.

---

6   Listen to the soundtracks of these videos: "LIRR : Port Washington Bound M7 Train Departing Woodside," accessed November 30, 2011, http://www .youtube.com/watch?v=zC3Btxp2okc&NR=1&feature=fvwp and for two Woodside convergences see/hear: "LIRR : Thre7 Trains @ Wooside Station All Platforms," accessed November 30, 2011, http://www.youtube.com /watch?v=svARUTkJOh4&feature=fvwrel and "LIRR : M3 And M7 Trains Bypassing Woodside," accessed November 30, 2011, http://www.youtube .com/watch?v=Jc86cL-rtSQ&NR=1. The latter shows two LIRR trains bypassing Woodside. At the very beginning one can see a distant number 7 subway arriving at Woodside. At the end, one again sees the same number 7, this time departing Woodside.

Finally, my life embraces and encompasses eager listening with profound attention and keen interest in everything around me. During the early interest I discovered that, even though I liked some sounds more than others, I enjoyed listening to everything. Soon I realized that I was committed to listening to everything all at once—and all the time, as Pauline Oliveros would put it. I didn't have a label for it and, even after meeting Pauline for the first time in February 1955, it would be over three more decades before there would be Pauline's description of what I was feeling. I knew early on that, while my interest in deeper listening was different from other people, I also was surprised that more people didn't share my interest—perhaps obsession—with listening in this concentrated and critical manner. As a child, listening in this way didn't seem to be anything special but was simply beautiful and, albeit lonely sometimes, joyous fun! It was much later, 1960s, that I found myself in the company of others—mostly at the San Francisco Tape Music Center—who were of like mind. It was during this time that I began serious inquiry into trombone acoustical palette, continuing that into commissioning composers, and ultimately forming and performing with Pauline Oliveros in the Deep Listening Band (DLB) along with another founder in vocalist Panaiotis.

This Band has embodied all aspects of deep listening. For the last twenty years our third member has been David Gamper. As I complete this essay, it is just over a month after David's sudden death on 27 September 2011. This has hit DLB especially hard because he was so integral to what DLB does. Pauline and I changed our 29 October DLB concert at Lawrence University in Appleton, Wisconsin to be a tribute to David Gamper. One of the pieces included was "Landgrove,"7 a track from one of DLB's many recording sessions at the spectacular January 2011 residency at Town Hall, Seattle. Around the edges of this I realized my hope that I could find solace in this, my second visit to Appleton. I was not disappointed because I may have hit the jackpot in amazing train sounds. Various notes from my journal:

7　Slated to be released during May 2012 on Taiga Records as Side A of a double LP titled *Needle Drop Jungle*.

27 October 2011

During the night there were a couple of especially nice trains passing through. About 4:00 a.m. there was an enthusiastic whistle blower on an E minor chord that must have been on a diagonal track running near LU campus. It was so beautiful as it moved along with sound reflections ever changing as it moved further and further away. Later on, about 5:30, it was a much more polite C minor chord that could be heard, apparently on a different track, that was moving more equally from left to right. Appleton still offers an array of beautiful train sounds on a regular basis just like I remember from two years ago.

And later on 27 October

There is a train going by now [afternoon] as I am writing [in my journal]. The whistle is amazing in its F minor with an occasional added 7th. And then the whistle chord will occasionally slide down a half step and immediately move right back up again — very unusual — perhaps every fifth time the chord is heard. About an hour later I heard a train with a diminished 7th and was that ever beautiful!

29 October 2011

I left lunch at 11:50, took the three flights of stairs two at a time [out of the Warch Student Center], and walked briskly across campus to catch the 12:00 "concert." At 11:57 a distant train enters stage right. Already one carillon somewhere near campus was indicating the noon hour. As I got to the Music Conservatory I decided not to go in but rather proceed to the street and make my way to the back of the "Con." As I rounded the bend the nearer carillon started its noon cycle mixing with the train beautifully as the train moved towards center stage. I saw Brian Pertl [Dean of Lawrence University Conservatory of Music] sitting on the stairs recording the proceedings.[8]

    I positioned myself a little to the right of Brian so as not to

---

8 "Train Siren Carillon Convergence.wmv," accessed December 2, 2011, http://www.youtube.com/watch?v=1EbtvmxIvlA&feature=youtu.be.

disturb the recording by adding noise of any kind (although upon hearing it later there was significant wind noise). Soon the tornado sirens started (a regular Saturday noontime test) followed by the carillon beginning its noon renditions. By this time the train was center stage along with the tornado sirens and the mix of the three sound sources was absolutely amazing. As the train moved toward stage left it soon became apparent that the sirens were settling in for a lengthy test—some two or more minutes—as it turned out. Exit train stage left just before the sirens quit leaving the carillon finishing its second hymn.

The sirens were phenomenal with their tones not quite in agreement making for quite a "beating." Their rates of glissando both at the beginning and at the end were slightly different making for amazing "glide" or "slide" changes at the beginning and end of their performance. With the train well into the wings, and the sirens finished, one could hear various vehicles mixing with the carillon. Up to that point the noise of vehicles had been masked by sirens, unless a vehicle was quite close to us. It was amazing the undercurrent of sounds that were exposed when the sirens ended. All in all a very special "concert" and I am so glad I made the effort to attend.

How could I have possibly anticipated the delightful quantity let alone the quality of trains during my short three days in Appleton? To have that amazing convergence of trains with sirens and carillons on my last day there was one of those treasures of sound that I live for as I continue my "training."

Cupped Ears

Fred Frith

FRED FRITH is a songwriter, composer, improviser, and multi-instrumentalist best known for the reinvention of the electric guitar that began with *Guitar Solos* in 1974. He learned his craft as both improviser and composer playing in rock bands, notably Henry Cow, and creating music in the recording studio. Much of his compositional output has been commissioned by choreographers and filmmakers, but his work has also been performed by Ensemble Modern, Hieronymus Firebrain, Arditti Quartet, Ground Zero, Robert Wyatt, Bang on a Can All Stars, Concerto Köln, and Rova Sax Quartet, among many others. He continues to perform internationally, most recently with Lotte Anker, Evelyn Glennie, Ikue Mori, Mike Patton, and his latest band, Cosa Brava, whose first CD—*Ragged Atlas*—was released in 2010 on the Intakt label. Fred is the subject of Nicolas Humbert and Werner Penzels' award-winning documentary film *Step Across the Border*. http://www.fredfrith.com/

I MET PAULINE *when I began teaching at Mills College in 1999. I'm ashamed to admit I knew very little about her at the time, a glaring gap which my friend Willie Winant was quick to fill, plying me with scores, articles and recordings to bring me up to speed. I soon came to appreciate her greatly, not only as the radical musical and sonic pioneer that she undoubtedly is, but as a colleague who goes quickly to the heart of the matter—with humor, persistence, and imagination. Meanwhile we have performed, researched, read thesis papers, dined, laughed, and argued together, and while I still have no first-hand experience of Deep Listening, anyone who spends any time with Pauline will soon become a deeper listener! The following stories are snapshots taken with the aid of the notebooks that I have kept since the early 1970s, as well as memories that have grown indelible with re-telling over the years. Re-searching the memory bank has been a journey of discovery for which I'm most grateful.*

§§§

29

Improvisation Workshop notes, 1993.[1] "The qualities of a good impro-viser are not dissimilar to the qualities you would look for in a friend. A good listener, who knows when to speak and when to be quiet; someone who shares your basic values but who brings a unique perspective to bear when needed; loyal and supportive, but not afraid to be critical or have a different point of view; someone who brings out the best in you; above all, someone who's seen the worst of you but didn't run away! Patient, flexible, ready to have fun or be serious or both, and who knows that there are matters far greater and more important than either of you."

§§§

North Yorkshire Moors, 1950s. When I was a kid we would sometimes spend a day on the moors, a windswept and treeless desolation emerg-ing from the rolling farmland of North Yorkshire. Up in the vast expanse of heather I loved to fall backwards in a straight line, with eyes closed and arms outstretched. One minute the wind, anything from a whistle to a howl, the next a perfect stillness, accompanied by a drone of flies and bees and obscure crawlings. In this secret place I could still hear the occasional asthmatic bleat of sheep straggled sporadically to the horizon, or the cry of a curlew, the epitome of solitude.

§§§

Almost nothing, 1970. After previously having read John Cage's *Silence* and learned that any sound could now be considered music, I heard Luc Ferrari's composition *Presque Rien #1: Lever du Jour au Bord de la Mer,* an unadorned and beautifully spacious recording of a beach at dawn.[2] By the time I moved to New York almost ten years later,

---

1 I've been leading improvisation workshops for musicians and non-musi-cians of all ages since receiving an invitation from Ferdinand Richard and the Festival MIMI in 1986.

2 This recording was released as part of Deutsche Grammophon's Avant-Garde box set, an important part of my musical education at the time. It has since been re-issued on a number of different CD compilations, and available in three parts on YouTube: "Luc Ferrari - Presque Rien No. 1 (1 of 3)," accessed December 27, 2011, http://youtube.com/watch?v=z2aWEM1nnNg.

framing environmental sounds as music had become almost fashionable. Finding myself wondering why these "sound pieces" seemed to be mostly about nature, I wrote an article[3] attempting to describe the sounds heard around my Lower East Side neighborhood. The last sentence reads: "Oh, one thing I forgot. . . the sound of cockroaches scurrying when you turn on the light."

§§§

Working on the soundtrack for *Rivers and Tides*,[4] 1996. In one scene, Andy Goldsworthy is in Newfoundland in the early morning, creating a sculpture using icicles. Because his fingers are so cold, he keeps dropping pieces of ice, and sometimes when they hit the ground they make a resonant sound that reminds me of a marimba. Before long, sampled "ice marimba" takes its place alongside guitar, violin and berimbau. What you see is what you hear. . .

§§§

Less is more, 1986. Sally Potter[5] and Peter Mettler are two directors from whom I've learned a great deal about life in general and film music in particular. They have taught me, among other things, to pare down my contributions to the absolute minimum. Sally told me that, as with all other aspects of filmmaking, it's often about what you leave out—"the

---

3 The article was published in a magazine called *Musics* in the UK. I'm grateful to Clive Bell for digging out a copy for me after thirty years! See Fred Frith, "New York Sounds," *Musics* 23 (November 1979):27.

4 *Rivers and Tides* is a documentary film about the work of Andy Goldsworthy, directed by Thomas Riedelsheimer, which went on to win international acclaim. My work on the soundtrack started by listening to audio recordings of what was happening on location during the shooting. It was from this source that I derived not only the "ice marimba" but also much of the other material used in creating the music. Film: Thomas Reidelsheimer, *Rivers and Tides: working with time*, Burlington, VT: Docurama, 2004, DVD; Soundtrack: Fred Frith, *Rivers and Tides*, Winter & Winter 9100922, 2003, compact disc.

5 I have worked with Sally on every film she has made since *Orlando* in 1992. Long before that, in the late 1970s, she and I also performed together as improvising musicians (she's a great singer).

spaces you can create, the silences you can create paradoxically through music" as she put it. Once, working with Peter on *The Top of His Head*,[6] I had to improvise on guitar through a fairly long scene, and knowing his penchant for sparseness, I did so with the utmost restraint, carefully placing a few phrases at what I thought were the right moments. "That's beautiful" he said, "but I need you to do a lot less".

§§§

Richmond Station, 1958. Delicate, slow, cracking from slabs of dry ice on the railway platform, punctuated by the arrival and departure of steam trains in all their pomp, the hissing of pistons, eruptions of steam, roar of the furnace when the driver lifted me up into the cab and let me pull the whistle. On one occasion, driving the locomotive out of the station to reconnect at the other end of the train, the fireman dangled me by my legs out of the side of the cab. I can still hear my shrieks of nervous laughter mixed up with the rattle of points and the rhythmic acceleration of the engine as we picked up speed.

§§§

Zuckerfabrik, Dormagen, 2003. I first started playing barefoot as a member of Lars Hollmer's Looping Home Orchestra[7] in the early 1990s. Everyone else in the band played barefoot, so I did too. When I asked them why, there was no particular reason that I can remember. Later I also played barefoot for solo concerts. It was easier to move quickly

---

6   Starring Stephen Ouimette and Christie MacFadyen, *The Top of His Head* was Peter's first fiction film and my first soundtrack experience. We were given six weeks in the National Film Board's sound studio in Montreal, an unparalleled luxury which gave me a completely false impression of the "normal" conditions for recording film music, and allowed me to make numerous mistakes since there was plenty of time to fix them! Peter Mettler, *The Top of His Head* (Toronto: Rhombus Media and Grimthorpe Film, 1989, motion picture and 2007, DVD) and soundtrack by Fred Frith, *Top of His Head*, Made to Measure MTM21CD Crammed Discs, 1989, compact disc.

7   Lars Hollmer (1948–2008) was an extraordinary Swedish keyboardist and accordionist, founding member of Sammla Mammas Manna, The Accordion Tribe, Looping Home Orchestra, and other unique projects, and composer of some of my favorite music. He is sadly missed.

around my pedals, and I'd grown to like it. The truth hit me, however, when I first performed with percussionist Evelyn Glennie.[8] Evelyn has been profoundly deaf since the start of her teenage years, but aided by a stubborn streak and a supportive teacher, she was able to continue her studies and become the renowned performer she is today. Evelyn explains that "hearing is a sensation for which you need your whole body," that playing barefoot can also be an essential component of listening, listening not only with the ears but with every part of you, vibrations coming through the floor, through your fingertips, through your pores, sometimes continuing after your ears have stopped relaying information. I had some kind of intuitive understanding of this, I think most musicians do, but when I heard Evelyn explain it, and watched how her whole body acted like an antenna as she played, it made perfect sense. It's as if she's in a state of exquisite tension, her whole being acting as a "divining rod" for sound.

§§§

Elsässerstrasse, Basel, May, 2011. At the bus stop there is a mind-numbing level of noise from a construction crew using pavement-pounding equipment to flatten the road. The only thing anyone can think about is getting away from it as fast as possible. Suddenly the machine stops, and for a few seconds it's as if we've achieved a new sonic hyper-awareness: clack of high heels, curiously emphasized fragments of several conversations at once, wires humming, a passing crow. *Un son peut en cacher un autre.*

§§§

---

8   I was invited to perform with Dame Evelyn Glennie during the filming of *Touch the Sound,* (NY: Docurama, 2006, DVD and soundtrack Evelyn Glennie and Fred Frith, *Touch the Sound,* Normal, 2007, compact disc) Thomas Riedelsheimer's documentary film about her work, released in 2004. Our performances in the film actually constituted the first time we had ever played together, and culminated in the CD *The Sugar Factory,* released on the Tzadik label in 2007 (Tzadik 7623, 2007, compact disc).

A café in the village of Hérisson, France, 1992. Heike[9] and our nine-month-old son Finn,[10] who has not yet been diagnosed as hard of hearing, are sitting quietly with friends. Suddenly without warning Finn starts to cry, intense and urgent. Nothing seems to pacify him, so Heike takes him outside and he calms down immediately. Within seconds a violent altercation breaks out among some of the patrons at the bar, a fight that Finn had clearly "heard" coming, though none of the adults picked up on it.

§§§

Lower Tullochgrue farm, Scotland, 1959. In Scotland during the long summer holidays, I made friends with Johnny and learned to be quiet enough to creep up on deer—not to shoot them, just for the fun and the wonder. An engagement of all the senses—sound of wind and water, smell of swamp and cowpats, touch of trees and stones, getting close to deer without them seeing, hearing or scenting us. Everyday life as an adventure with endless variations, improvised without a guide, to see and hear for yourself: what's next, what just happened, what will happen next? Once we found the wreckage of a plane scattered across the slopes of Ben Macdui. Another time we were charged by a bull, saved only by crawling through the mud under a barbed wire fence. I watched eleven-year old Johnny head for home one evening down the long farm lane after another breathless day, shouting at the top of his voice to anyone or anything that wanted to listen, just for the joy of being alive. "Come on gurrls, here I am, I'm ready, come and see wha' I've got!"

§§§

The Manor, Oxfordshire, 1973. Henry Cow are in residence at Virgin's fancy recording studio, working on our first LP with engineer Tom

---

9 Heike Liss, whose work as a visual artist in multiple fields challenges and excites me on a daily basis.

10 Finn's ingenious ways of living with his hearing loss have been a constant source of inspiration. He has never once, to my knowledge, accepted that something that he wishes to do is not possible for him, and is currently studying (and making) music and films.

Newman,[11] who has determined that as far as possible we should take charge ourselves. This was unusual at the time, and has probably as much to do with preserving his own sanity as with any desire on his part to empower the musicians! The task is to mix down the studio recording from sixteen tracks to two, the stereo master. He has given us a quick rundown as to how everything works and each of us is assigned a couple of faders. After a few run-throughs we attempt a mix; then we listen to what we've done, identifying the many changes required. During the next take we make enthusiastic comments as we go along: "That's much better," "This is the one," and so on. Turning to Tom, we eagerly await his approval. "I hate to tell you this," he says, "but you weren't actually doing anything, just listening back to the same mix you did before!"

§§§

Mills College Faculty Village, 2002. I'm sitting in the garden reading a book on a sunny afternoon. I become dimly aware of the sound of some kind of motor coming from the direction of the main road. Turning my head I surprise a hummingbird hovering about an inch from my right ear.

§§§

La Monte Young rehearsing with the Ensemble Modern, Frankfurt, 1996. I'm taking a break from my own rehearsals, and am graciously allowed to observe. The musicians are arranged in a circle, with La Monte and Marian Zazeela in the middle, listening intently. There are four groups of four instruments, and the musicians have been instructed to play Bb. It is not going well. The composer stops the group and says: "If you can't play the Bb, better to stop for a while and then rejoin." They continue, apparently puzzled, struggling to find whatever precise Bb La Monte is looking for. Finally they hit a pure note, all together, and the whole room starts to vibrate, a ringing of the rafters, curved air, extraordinarily

---

11 It was Tom who introduced me to the idea of the "studio as a compositional tool." In his own music he was endlessly inventive, recording drum tracks by tapping a microphone with a pencil and simply changing the equalization, thus simulating the sound of the drum machine years before its invention!

beautiful. It continues for some time, but eventually they have to stop. "Good," he says. "After lunch I suggest we try C."

§§§

Montréal, 1988. In Scotland I had my first experience of a language I didn't understand, and puzzled over the sound of it: new music, alive and enticing. I have always loved the sound of people speaking, and as I've learned new languages have come to realize that the best way for me to do it is to become the person I am in the new language, which involves not just words but body and attitude, and most of all a sense of the melody of the language you want to learn. This was brought home to me again when working with René Lussier[12] on his masterpiece, *Trésor de la Langue*, a series of powerful reflections on language and culture based on interviews recorded in the streets of Montréal and its environs, as well as free access to the archives of Radio Canada. The music is entirely focused on the sound of everyday speech, full of unexpected twists and turns, pauses, repetitions, exclamations—challenging to play and wonderful to listen to. It's a great *hommage* to Québecois, revealing and revelling in the deep musicality of people talking. Since *Trésor* I've never been able to hear any language in quite the same way again.

§§§

Stuttgart, 1997. Three-and-a-half-year-old Luci[13] is singing her favorite song from the movie *Michel und der Suppenschüssel*,[14] behind the closed doors of her bedroom. Putting our ears to the door we hear a heartfelt

---

12 René Lussier, brilliant guitar player, highly original musical thinker, and one of Quebec's most famous musical sons, has been a central figure in my creative life since the early 1980s. We have worked on many projects together over the years, of which *Trésor* is a notable example (*Le trésor de la langue*, Ambiances Magnétiques AM 015 CD, 1989, 3 compact discs).
13 Luci is my youngest daughter. Her love of movies has led to her aiming for a career as actor and director. Her knowledge of Swedish has yet to improve.
14 *Michel und der Suppenschüssel* (Hamburg: Oetinger, 2007, DVD) is one of a number of Swedish/German co-productions from the 1970s, based on books by beloved Swedish children's author Astrid Lindgren. Pippi Longstocking is her most famous character, but there are many others, and these films are beautifully made and enduringly popular.

rendition of the Swedish of the original. It sounds curiously authentic without actually making any sense. "Fnü så plüd grå flö, snåte klü frå plö, klåv man-tel fråd fnödel rö " and so on. Lasse Hollmer would have laughed his head off!

§§§

Tokyo, 1987. I've been invited by John Zorn to play rhythm guitar in a one-off concert with a blues band, the other members of which are all Japanese. It'll be the first time I've played in a blues band since the 1960s, and I'm excited. We are playing some of the classics of Chicago blues, and the singer is a monster! His voice sounds like a cross between Willie Dixon and Muddy Waters and he sings every number with an authenticity and intensity that blows me away. Afterwards I walk up to him and tell him how much I loved his performance. He looks at me blankly. He doesn't understand a word of English.

§§§

Oakland, 2000–2006. For a period of six years (under–8 to under–16) I coached my son's team in the Jack London Youth Soccer League. Kids' soccer begins with twenty enthusiastic bodies clumping around a ball like a swarm of bees and following it up and down the field. Bit by bit the players learn to get away, to create space for the ball to be passed to them. Football has a lot in common with musical improvisation. You constantly adjust to events that are not quite what you expected. The patterns may be familiar, but the movement is unpredictable, and you have to work in the dynamic and ever-changing area between what you would like to happen, what you think might happen, and what actually just happened. Where is the ball, where would I like it to be, where is everyone else, and what are they doing? What do I expect them to do next, and what are they expecting me to do? The more experience you have the more options you'll be able to draw on, but you are also dependent on everyone else having the same degree of motivation, similar sets of skills, and the shared experience which has led you to avoid certain kinds of responses and embrace others. What's critical is listening to the process, to the unpredictable interlocutor who's keeping you in the moment by removing the security of whatever plan you thought we were following.

§§§

Oakland and Esslingen, 1990–2011. After spending more working hours in the studio during the last forty years than practically anywhere else, I have a deep admiration for recording engineers. The ones I've been lucky enough to work with can hear the tiniest details of timing, tuning, acoustics, and everything else besides without losing track of what it is we're actually trying to do. Careful to the point of obsession in their attention to detail and desire for perfection, patient in the face of the contentious clang of changing minds, always flexible in their approach, they have been integral to my compositional process. We continue to learn from each other, and I raise my hat and a glass (or two) in their direction. Peter[15] says: "Fred, if you want that to be in tune (or in time) you might want do it again!" Myles[16] says (as I'm overdubbing a violin part): "Fred, I know the name of a very good violinist, would you like her number?" These are the kinds of people you want to work with!

§§§

On the way to a workshop with Mark Dresser, Porto, June, 2011. Our car is stopped at a traffic light outside the Casa de Musica. Clacks and cracks of kids jumping on and off skateboards. An impossibly wrinkled old lady at the window asks for money with dignity and resignation. Flag slapping at the pole in the wind, car engine stuttering, dogs baying in the distance. Swifts swoop and shriek, someone is singing on a balcony.

§§§

---

15 Peter Hardt, award-winning engineer and owner of the Jankowski Sound Fabrik in Esslingen, Germany. Our association began in 1994 when I was invited to record some music for Richard Linklater's film *Before Sunrise*. The music was never used, but we have had a cheerful and productive working relationship ever since!

16 Myles Boisen, of Guerrilla Recordings and the Headless Buddha Mastering Lab, in Oakland, California. I've been working with Myles for over thirty years, ever since I asked him to cut up and reassemble pieces of tape for several days during a recording project commissioned by RAI (Italian national radio) in Rome in 1980.

Sussex, 1957. Springtime on the Downs, lying on the grass and listening to endless loops of skylarks. These small birds ascend almost vertically, with strenuous effort, until they're only tiny specks in the sky. There they hover awhile, singing their hearts out, before parachuting down to earth again in mesmerizing, slow circles.

§§§

Cambridge, 1970. My friend DJ Perry[17] has a job teaching English to foreign students in a language lab. The students are all seated in small soundproof cubicles, and, using headphones, the teacher can work with each of them in turn as they continue to practice their assigned words and phrases. One day David invites me to go in to work with him; he wants to show me something. I put on the master headphones, he presses a switch, and suddenly I can hear every one of the fifty students at once, a glorious cacophony as accents from what seems like every region in the world wrestle with the same short phrases, sometimes barely comprehensible, all out of sync, completely surreal—some of the greatest music I have ever heard.

§§§

Libya, 1940. My father[18] is reconnoitering in the Western Desert. He's left his unit behind him while checking out the terrain ahead for enemy activity. Turning, he finds himself entirely alone in a vastness of nothing, 360 degrees of identical terrain with not the smallest sound to help him. Without his compass to show him where he had come from, he might be there still. I have always been haunted by this story, which I

---

17 David "DJ" Perry was a fellow student of mine at Cambridge who collaborated on a number of projects in the early days of Henry Cow. As an employee of the BBC, his access to the renowned BBC Archives provided an endlessly fascinating source of material that found its way in various guises into numerous pieces.

18 My father was a gifted pianist, and one of my earliest memories is of sitting under the Bechstein he had bought for a song in the 1950s and happily bathing in the sound. Captain Donald Frith's job at the time of this incident was leading convoys carrying petrol to troops on the front line near Tobruk. After the long trip across the desert most of it had evaporated, leaving barely enough to make the trip back to get more!

heard many times over the years. I try to imagine the strange, blank, suddenly silent space and my twenty-one-year-old father, completely alone, standing in it.

§§§

St Etienne, France, April, 2011. A concert at the Festival des Musiques Innovatrices. The venue is in a complex of buildings surrounding an old coalmine, now a museum; guitarist Paulo Angeli[19] and I are to perform in a room called *La Salle des Pendues* (literally, "the chamber of the hanged"). A transfixing sight awaits us—above our heads (and those of the audience) are suspended the working clothes of miners, left as they were when the mine closed in 1973. To save space, the men would attach the clothes to numbered chains, along with helmets, clapper boards and mirrors, and hoist them high above to be reclaimed when they came back to work the next morning. The effect is eerie, having the air of an atrocity, silent "figures" swinging gently above us, as if the aftermath of a bizarre ritual slaughter. But "listening" to the room reassures us that far from being sinister, this was a place of solidarity and bonhomie, of a shared awareness of danger, of bonding between men whose families had sent their sons to work the mine for generations. The disjunction between what the image first suggests and what it actually represents was resolved for me through the act of listening, almost an invocation.

§§§

Kirchberg, Switzerland. Etienne Conod,[20] the wonderfully imaginative and creative engineer of Sunrise Studios in the 1970s and 80s once told

---

19 Sardinian musician and historian Paolo Angeli, inventor of a unique guitar that is played with both hands and feet, defying logical explanations as to how what he is doing could be possible!

20 Etienne Conod has had one of the most colorful careers of anyone I know. After obligatory military service, he has (so far) worked as a photo-journalist, sold wickerware, played keyboards in a rock band, founded and directed one of the most successful recording studios in Switzerland, and emigrated to the Australian Alps where he more or less singlehandedly ran a bed-and-breakfast and a pretty big farm. Eventually he returned to Zurich, where he studied psychology and social pedagogy. He now works for a charitable trust with particular focus on drugs and poverty (when he's not playing the Hammond organ).

me about a colleague of his who could recognize the details of a studio's architecture and construction by listening to a recording. "Wish they hadn't left that left skylight open," he would grumble.

§§§

Big Sur, 1991. Sleeping in a cabin high up in the mountains, I'm woken up by a mysterious sound—something large is very close by, and moving rapidly. It's pitch dark. A bear, I'm thinking, and sit bolt upright. I'm having a moment of slight panic. There's no bear, but what else could it be? Heike must be shaking the blanket outside to get rid of some horrendous beastie. I'd better get up and go find out. Then I notice that she is actually sitting next to me, shaking Finn's baby bottle. . .

§§§

Reach, Cambridgeshire, 1970. Fishing in a remote spot below the high bank of the Lode, watching the float drifting. After a while I'm invisible to the life of the place, motionless and spellbound. Slowly I become alive to details, to the gentle ripple caused by hints of a breeze on the water's surface, or the shiver as it passes through willows and sycamores, an interference of finches or starlings, a cow anxious to be milked in the next door field, a tractor sputtering, the dull continuo of traffic on the main road five miles away, an occasional chuckle of duck or coot or moorhen. Punctuations of rain, sudden flash of a kingfisher, the eloquence of warblers; suddenly, dry crackles become a roar of burning stubble in the field behind me; I have to walk home in the water.

§§§

Brèves, France, 1977. My band-mates and I are eating dinner after the concert. I have become hypnotized by the sound, heard through the window, of a nightingale singing. I leave the others and go outside to sit on the wall with my *cahier de musique*. I want to try and write down what I hear. I can barely manage half a phrase out of every six phrases or so, and even that is only the simplest of approximations. Eventually I give up and just listen, rooted to the spot for what seems like hours.

Years later I happened to see a film of Olivier Messiaen and Yvonne Loriod walking through the woods together, he with his notebook, she with a portable tape recorder. He listens intently to a bird singing and scribbles rapidly. Then she plays back the recording as he checks his notes. *"Oui, c'est ça."* He nods, and they continue their walk. I am speechless with admiration!

§§§

In the mountains near Stans, Switzerland, April, 2004. Rehearsals with Arte Quartett for *Still Urban*[21] are beginning today in the convent at Niederrickenbach, most easily accessible by cable car. No traffic, complete peace, nuns going about their business and leaving us to ours. As we walk towards our rehearsal space, a gymnasium, I notice a young sister at the end of a corridor, talking animatedly on a mobile phone. *"Lass von dir hören!"* she says.[22]

§§§

S-Bahn from Stuttgart to Rutesheim, July 2011. The train pulls into the station, the long tones of the electric motor making a slow glissando downwards, with a diminuendo that reveals a continuous, quiet, sixty-cycle hum. Hiss of compressed air, sliding doors, snatch of a different acoustic space from the platform outside, open and inviting, another hiss, slide and loud bang of the doors closing. A glissando upwards eclipses the hum in an even crescendo. The driver has forgotten to switch off the microphone, and starts to whistle in a cheerfully off-hand kind of way, accompanied by the whooshes and drones and clicks. This continues until the next station. The feeling in our carriage has changed. We are all listening attentively, and everyone is smiling.

---

21 *Still Urban* was commissioned by the Stanser Musiktage in Switzerland. It's a long composition for saxophone quartet and electric guitar that also incorporates recordings of West Oakland, and is a kind of meditation on urban life. (Fred Frith and the Arte Quartett, *Still Urban*, Intakt Records CD 155, 2009, compact disc.)

22 This would probably best translate as "stay in touch," but literally means "let me hear from you."

Deep Listening
in the World

The Warbler, The Cricket, The Whale: Three Ways Toward Deep Listening in the Natural World

DAVID ROTHENBERG is the author of *Why Birds Sing, Thousand Mile Song, Sudden Music,* and *Survival of the Beautiful.* Recent recordings include collaborations with Marilyn Crispell, Scanner, and the New Jersey Laptop Orchestra. He is professor of philosophy and music at the New Jersey Institute of Technology. http://www.davidrothenberg.net

David Rothenberg

ACCORDING TO PAULINE OLIVEROS, "*deep* listening is listening in every possible way to everything possible. This means one hears all sounds, no matter what one is doing. Such intense listening includes hearing the sounds of daily life, of nature, and of one's own thoughts, as well as musical sounds."[1]

I have spent many years trying to listen to the world of animal sounds, making music together with as many other creatures as I can interact with who play and sing. Without Pauline Oliveros' plea for discipline in the task of better listening I'm not sure I ever would have gotten into this. I started with birds, then moved on to more remote and more alien musics: next whales, then bugs.

---

1 Pauline Oliveros, "Acoustic and Virtual Space as a Dynamic Element in Music," *Women, Art, and Technology*, ed. Judy Malloy (Cambridge: MIT Press, 2003), 213.

45

I wanted to hear music in nature and people told me, "oh sure, birds are always singing" and I would say, "yes, birds, everyone's done birds, forget about them," but then I realized everyone thinks that birds have been listened to, celebrated, sung about, and imitated while we haven't really listened to them all that clearly. Birders listen to a bird only as long as it takes to learn what bird it is, then knowing what they've heard, chalk it up on a list and move on to the next one.

But naming doesn't do so much for real hearing. Listening, I started to realize, is forgetting the name of the thing one hears. One must inhabit the full extent of a sound without being satisfied with any explanation of it. That is why I begin many a concert by playing along with a slowed-down phrase from a hermit thrush or nightingale: the offerings of these master avian singers are full of order, possibility, and space, the hallmark qualities of any of the best human musical phrases. If I am surprised and provoked by what hear I will be inspired to join in. The birds get my own musical phrases going.

Even better to do this in the wild, jamming with shamas, mockingbirds, humpbacks, belugas, crickets, cicadas, all more-than-human musicians with unique repertories and an interest in all the sounds around them. The best creatures to improvise with live may be those who also practice a form of deep listening, being hip to the sounds in their lifeworlds, even the human ones, enough so that it sometimes sounds like they might even be interested in us. Here are three stories from these adventures to consider.

The Warbler

Without such a practice of deep listening, so many of nature's potentially available sounds will be missed. I am reminded of one of the world's most remarkable singing birds, the European marsh warbler, *Acrocephalus palustris*. This bird does one remarkable thing that no other songbird has achieved. Although many birds migrate from Europe southwards to spend their winters in Africa, only the marsh warbler learns a wide number of African bird songs during its winter vacation, and then flies back north every spring to sing these equatorial melodies one after another, at extremely high speed, like a birdsong identification tape played in fast-forward. It's an audio slide show of the joys of migration.

Françoise Dowsett-Lemaire first figured this out in the 1970s as a teenager. She was listening to a recording of an early morning male marsh warbler song and she started to pick out fragments of African bird songs that she recognized from a record of tropical bird songs that she had also heard. The similarities were unmistakable. She mentioned this discovery to some ornithologists who just scoffed at her, saying "impossible! No birds do anything like that, copying what they hear on migration. It's just coincidence."[2]

But Lemaire would not be deterred. She went to college, than graduate school, working on the song of the European marsh warbler. In several of the best academic papers ever written in musicial ornithology,[3] she meticulously documented the ability of this northern European wetland bird's ability to make use of African bird songs thousands of miles from where it hears them. Woven into the marsh warbler's extremely complex song she heard black-eyed bulbul notes, bleating bush warbler calls, along with such colorfully named singers as the blue-cheeked bee-eater and the fork-tailed drongo. The more common and noisy the birds in the warbler habitat, the more likely they are to be imitated. The marsh warbler turns out to have no original song syllables at all. It builds its whole repertoire out of others' material! The originality lies in the expert mimicry and virtuosic recombination of all the sounds in its vocal range. It even imitates birds it could only hear while en route to its winter grounds: passing through Tunisia it picks up tunes from the *Boran cisticola* and the vinaceous dove.

And though it is, as in most but not all bird species, only the males who sing this global song, biology assumes its main purpose is to dazzle the females with an extreme form of virtuosity. But this is not what

---

2 All quotes from Françoise Dowsett-Lemaire are from a telephone conversation in March, 2004. Quoted in David Rothenberg, *Why Birds Sing* (New York: Basic Books, 2005), 94.

3 Françoise Dowsett-Lemaire, "The imitative range of the song of the marsh warbler *Acropehalus palustris*," *Ibis* 121 (1979): 453–468. See also Françoise Dowsett-Lemaire, "Vocal behaviour of the marsh warbler," *Le Gerfaut* 69 (1979): 475–502.

Lemaire noticed. The females seem rather uninterested in its awesome complexity. Says Lemaire: "The larger the territory, the more potential nest-sites it contains, and the more likely the first female who comes in will stay. Besides, as the song is so complicated and it takes over thirty minutes of continuous singing to get the full repertoire, females would need to sit and listen for ages to evaluate a male's musical skill. Of course they do no such thing."[4]

As soon as a female appears, the male stops his singing. Concert over. He then devotes himself to helping her find the best nest site, giving only brief snatches of song along the way. "She may never get to hear what her mate is capable of."[5]

Females, Lemaire notes, occasionally sing the same kinds of songs as the males, but for no more than a minute at a time. She believes they have the same sound knowledge as their mates but have less need to use it. A similar pattern is found throughout the sexist world of bird songs. Females can sing if driven to do so, but most of the time they have too much else on their minds and not enough of the right hormones to pull them on towards music and away from practical life.

And on clear sunny days, Lemaire often observed ten to twenty males singing together in low bushes or fruit trees. She doesn't believe these group choruses are song bouts or challenges, but rather a kind of social play. Male marsh warblers "enjoy singing and must realize in some way that music is fun. There is no doubt about that."[6] No doubt, that is, until one tries to make that kind of statement in the context of science. Science has no idea what to do with the song of the marsh warbler—it is so out of line and away from the dominant paradigm of why birds sing. Best to just pretend we know nothing about this amazing song. Lemaire had discovered the one bird in the world who can recount its migratory path as a kind of songline, where the journey is mapped into the music itself. No one else has dared criticize her work, or even attempt to verify or disprove it, since what it suggests is so remarkable. Only deep listening got Lemaire these results.

---

4   Dowsett-Lemaire, quoted in Rothenberg, *Why Birds Sing*, 96.
5   Ibid., 96.
6   Ibid., 97.

The Whale

And the same might be said about the song of the humpback whale, one of the most incredible animal sounds on the planet, even more remarkable that no humans seem to know anything about it until the 1960s. The standard story is that we were unable to hear the songs of these whales until underwater microphones had been invented which makes the subaquatic sounds perceptible to our ears, but that really isn't true. Just swim a few feet down below the surface and anyone can hear them, faintly, but clearly, when there are enough whales in the water during any of the tropical mating localities, like Tonga, Hawaii, or the Silver Bank north of the Dominican Republic. The song is there, distant but clear. And yet no one heard a thing. Not until the Navy released their previously classified recordings to the world as *Songs of the Humpback Whale* in 1970, which became a surprise bestseller, the most popular nature recording of all time.[7]

But even without technology, we can hear these whales. Why did no one do it? It is as if no one thought to listen underwater, in the deep itself. We assumed, like Melville in *Moby Dick*, that this was the ultimate silent abyss, where sound is swallowed up. Actually sound travels five times faster in water than through air. But before technology taught us that, no one thought to open our ears while diving or swimming. You have to want to hear before the full range of sound will reach you.

With its extended, clear structure, humpback whale song is more clearly musical than the songs of most birds. And with the uncertainty about who the males are singing for, the song of the humpback whale is full of mysteries impenetrable to humanity. But for our species, a mystery means a challenge. As a musician, I wanted to hear for myself. Having spent several years playing my clarinet to birds, sometimes getting a response, sometimes not, I was eager to try this interspecies jamming with humpback whales. To my surprise, I got a very different result than whale scientists did. So different, that when I played my recording of a humpback whale/clarinet duet to several leading humpback scientists,

---

7 *Songs of the Humpback Whale*, recorded by Roger Payne, CRM, lp, 1970 (reissued on CD by Living Music, LMUS 0021) discussed in David Rothenberg, *Thousand Mile Song* (New York: Basic Books, 2008), 14–16.

they did not believe the encounter was real. But I assured them it really happened. What surprised my audiences most is that nearly everyone considered the sound they heard to be music: a music made between human clarinetist and humpback whale.

Making music with whales is not easy, since humans are above water, the whales down deep. It requires even more technology, an underwater speaker as well, to get my clarinet sound down into the world of whales. Here's how it's done:

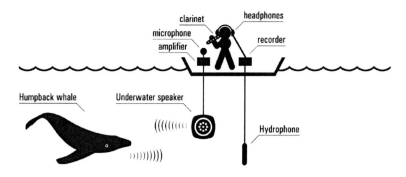

The chain of technology enables the clarinetist to talk to the whale, or, more accurately, use music to cross species lines. Why do I think this is even worth trying? Because music can communicate across cultures in a way language cannot.

Can I do the same with a whale whose name I'll never know? Humpback males usually suspend themselves motionless underwater in a curved posture, singing continuously in a solo trance. I am essentially interrupting a reverie whose purpose we do not know. In the musical moment I do not care about the purpose, but instead wish to understand the result. Can I prove the whale is responding to me in this single best duet, the most exciting several minutes of the many hours I tried to record? Many things can go wrong in such an experiment: the whale might stop singing and move away, a loud motorboat might come near and mess up the sound quality. Scientists might call my duet statistically insignificant, because it represents the one best case scenario rather than the probable result of broadcasting a clarinet underwater next to a singing humpback whale male. But even a single interesting improvised performance is worthy of musical analysis. I want to figure out why I like it, why even the skeptics I have played this to have responded to this sudden music.

The clarinet sounds are often high, held-out notes, more constant in pitch and thus closer to straight horizontal lines on the sonogram printout. There are usually at least a few parallel lines of overtones, more than usual for the instrument because the clarinet is being broadcast underwater, and the properties of underwater sound propagation seems to add overtones to the timbre, making the clarinet more bell-like, closer to a soprano saxophone (which, because of its conical bore, produces more overtones). Yet after some minutes, my clarinet starts to produce higher, shriekier, and more uneven, warbling notes, not exactly like the whale but somehow more compatible with the whale. And what does the whale do? Does his sound become more clarinet-like during the encounter? I am not really sure, but some of our high squeaks are quite hard to tell apart. And the clearest sign of communication comes when I stop, and he begins with a direct sense of response, in some cases continuing the very same note I just finished, and in other cases trying to join in, and overlap me with a complementary sound. Throughout this duet are several clear examples where the whale seems to match the clarinet. Two of my favorites are enlarged here [on page 54] in sonograms, where frequency is plotted against time using a simple Mac program called Amadeus.[8]

After four minutes of interacting, the whale dares to match my sound as I am playing it. He can't quite hold the pitch but he is wavering up and down around it:

---

8   "HairerSoft, "Amadeus Pro – Audio Editor / sound and voice recorder for Mac OS X," accessed November 30, 2011, http://www.hairersoft.com/pro .html.

Eight seconds later he joins in with my steady note by uttering a deep, complex boom, then after my riff of discrete pitches he comes in with a whistle that finally matches me truly in tune, then I end with that new whale wail I have learned during this performance:

To truly assess the musicality of this encounter, and decide for yourself whether this interspecies duet is music or not, you should first of all listen to it. An MP3 of this four-minute excerpt is available online.[9] Is this duet music: yes or no? There is a play-by-play account of the best part of the duet, including a complete sonogram, also online.[10] Whenever I listen to this recording, which comes entirely from the hydrophone, I am struck by something deeply alien about it. It does sound somewhere between human and whale, perhaps a music that neither species will completely appreciate until we and the whales are ready to suspend disbelief a little bit and truly attend to the possibility of sounds that the world reveals. Deep listening is the key to making such music, and to appreciating it.

---

9   "Clarinet / Humpback Duet | Thousand Mile Song," accessed January 18, 2012, http://www.thousandmilesong.com/clarinet-humpback-duet/.
10 David Rothenberg, "To Wail With a Whale: Anatomy of an Interspecies Duet," accessed January 18, 2012, http://www.thousandmilesong.com /wp-content/themes/twentyten/images/wail_with_whale.pdf [36].

The Cricket

I travel to Stockholm to meet Mr. Fung, a man of many names. Sometimes he is called Bolingo, and originally he was Lars Fredriksson. He is sitting at a café at the Swedish Natural History Museum, instantly recognizable. Or instantly un-recognizable, his visage is hard to place. He's wearing loose, worn clothing like a Chinese beggar-saint. He is completely bald, with a wispy white goatee. Except for his blue Nordic eyes I would swear he was a wandering Chinese holy man. In a way he is, a keeper of the ancient Mandarin tradition of keeping crickets in the home for the full enjoyment of their songs.

"I used to keep 108 crickets in traditional cricket-boxes in my tiny Stockholm apartment," Mr. Fung shrugs. "An arbitrary number perhaps, but an important one in Buddhist tradition. I liked the way my crickets would sing together and apart, different blendings of species, sounds one would never find in the wild. But now I sense that whole activity as something contrived. I have spent many years learning about this, perhaps it is true I know more about the whole tradition than anyone in China. You were right to come to me. Everyone else has a vested interest in the game. They all have something to sell. Individual crickets best for mating, fighting, singing. Some might cost thousands of dollars, just one bug, a prize for those who can afford it. They will only live a few months, but could produce a next generation that will sing even better."[11]

After listening to birds and then whales, I'm now in the midst of preparing a book and CD on the music of insects. The biggest challenge of this project is how to convince the audience, and myself, that insect sounds are really musical. That is why I have traveled to Sweden to see Mr. Fung. Not only is it closer than China, he may be a better source for what I'm looking for: someone who deeply listens to this ubiquitous kind of sound and truly appreciates it.

Fredriksson has invited musicians of world renown to join along with his insect orchestra, but over the years he has decided that captivity is not the answer.

---

11 This and all quotes that follow are from an interview with Lars Fredriksson, Stockholm, July 23, 2011.

DAVID ROTHENBERG

"I will travel to India, I will travel to Oceania, and back to the Far East, listening for the most beautiful insect sounds I can find. I can imagine the place, a misty hillside in late autumn, a thick fog, and a swirl of cricket choruses on all sides, perfectly arranged with me in the center, hearing the perfect sound that I have been seeking. I will smile, and find myself at the center of the world."

Cricket-rearing in traditional China is a bit of a hobby for those who have retired from day-to-day life. They sing in the autumn, a fitting metaphor for the final years of life. "Last night the chilly cricket did not cease its song," wrote poet Yueh Fei in 1130 AD. "It woke me from dreams a thousand miles away."[12] So many ancient cricket poems of the East are full of sadness and ennui, the fearful realization of human life creaking onwards toward death, while the strange music of the suborder Ensifera lasts as long as life goes on. This orthopteran soundtrack has little to do with human life but we always notice it, grasping frequencies that even the bugs can't hear. He does not think of these sounds so much as music, but as a signal of the balance of the world. "Crickets," Mr. Fung reminds me, "sing only when they are safe. Listening to them brings us a lasting sense of peace."

He pauses and looks longingly in the air. "I sometimes worry about these stories. You must know that I don't want myself to sound important, to boast that I know any special knowledge in particular. It's just something I have attended to over the decades. I have learned to listen."

I do know what Fung is talking about. I feel the same unease when I tell my own stories, which too often seem to have me as the center of attention. This is a danger. We need not be the heroes of our own lives, but should aspire to be witnesses to the beauty of the world. That is what deep listening is all about.

---

12 Chinese text and translation available at http://www.insects.org/ced3/dkmce_kevan.html, published in Douglas Kevan, *The land of the Locusts: being some further verses on grigs and cicadas, Part 2, English translations, paraphrases and adaptations of mediaeval verses (451 A.D. to end of 15th century), mostly with corresponding texts in the original languages* (Ste-Anne-de-Bellevue, Quebec: Lyman Entomological Museum and Research Laboratory, 1983).

Lars Fredriksson is a decade older than I. Pauline Oliveros is thirty years older than I, and I am now exactly the same age she was when I first met her. As a young student I found her inscrutable, a bit severe, deeply serious and awfully hard to approach. She and Linda Montano had us do an all-night performance at the Banff Centre for the Arts. In the middle of it she sat, Buddha-like, with a giant accordion pealing out endless sounds deeper than drones. I don't remember what the rest of us were doing but as dawn approached I collapsed, exhausted, into the arms of someone in the audience.

The last time I saw Pauline was after a performance I did in the autumn of 2010 at Rensselaer Polytechnic Institute in Troy, New York. "You said you were going to visit my class," she complained. "What happened?" "The soundcheck was more complicated than anyone expected," I apologized. "All right," she insisted. "Let's go talk somewhere now." It was 11:30 p.m. One place was still open in Troy. As she downed a tall pint of Guinness I laughed. "Get prepared," I told her. "In two years the world will be celebrating your eightieth birthday. There will be a lot of parties, a lot of music, a lot of listening."

I'm sure she's doing fine. After these thirty years I still feel a student in Pauline's presence, but also find her much easier to talk to. She's still at the cutting edge, one step deeper into technology than everyone else. I've seen her do performances in Second Life, be quicker with a response on email and Facebook than anyone else, and invent a way for one's nose to control a sound long before Microsoft's latest Xbox could. She shows us how to listen to the future, years before it ever happens. May she continue to teach us how to listen in ever deeper ways, to all possible sounds around us, even those which we will not hear for years to come.

The warbler, the cricket, the whale—all life in the world offers us an endless range of sounds to attend to, if we can ever find the time and the ability to tune in our senses. Try it for many years, then if you can imagine a way to join in, you are ready to be a musician. Only when you feel like there is space to make a musical announcement of your presence, go ahead, do it. Be a bird among birds, a whale among whales, a cricket among crickets. Then leave more space, listen again. Know that most musical creatures will only sing their own, stylized song. The best species to communicate with are those who share with humanity a curious interest in all range of sounds, and who have evolved to want to improvise, to try something new, to enjoy real play with sound. Take a stab at their style and twist the essence of what you do. You may be surprised, and just might effect a change in a musical world of which you cannot quite speak. Learn to appreciate more than what your own species has attuned itself to hear. Make a more-than-human music just past the edge of what you expect and could believe. A music greater than the sensibility of one species alone might show us a way to live a bit better with nature, and not destroy our planet with rampant human aesthetics, saving the Earth while there still is time.

Deep Listening Deep: On the Pursuit of Acoustically Unique Spaces

PAULA MATTHUSEN is a composer who writes both electro-acoustic and acoustic music and realizes sound installations. She has written for diverse instrumentations, such as *run-on sentence of the pavement* for piano, ping-pong balls, and electronics, which Alex Ross of *The New Yorker* noted as being "entrancing." Her work often considers discrepancies in musical space—real, imagined, and remembered. Her work has been featured at numerous venues and festivals, including Roulette Intermedium, Merkin Concert Hall, Diapason Gallery, Sonic Arts Research Center, Tanglewood Festival of Contemporary Music, the Aspen Music Festival, Bang on a Can Summer Institute of Music, ArtBots, Gaudeamus New Music Week, and SEAMUS. Awards include a Fulbright Grant, two ASCAP Morton Gould Young Composers' Awards, the MacCracken and Langley Ryan Fellowship, a Van Lier Fellowship, and the Walter Hinrichsen Award from the American Academy of Arts and Letters. Matthusen is currently Assistant Professor of Music at Wesleyan University. http://www.paulamatthusen.com/

Paula Matthusen

I AM STANDING outside the Basilica Julia in the Roman Forum, construction of which began around 54 B.C.[1] A mild breeze tempers the summer sun, while the gently rustling grasses in its wake create a subtle counterpoint to the footsteps on gravel and the pseudo shuttersounds from the digital cameras of tourists passing by. The breadth of the ruins is staggering, though what interests me most is one small doorway and a grate off the side of this former Basilica. An even cooler breeze emanates from the grate, along with an incongruous smell for the location. As I listen very closely, I hear the sound of water gently moving underneath. A small weather-worn placard on the side of the ruins confirms I am in the right place—one of the points along the Cloaca

---

1 Christian Hülsen, *The Roman Forvm: Its History and Its Monuments* (Rome: Loescher, 1909), 61.

Maxima, the sewer which helped enable the enormous infrastructure supporting Ancient Rome.[2] I continue to follow the path that the Cloaca Maxima took through Rome above ground (with the dream of one day being able to crawl underneath, fumes be damned). I end up at the Tiber River, and find a staircase leading me to the exit point of the Cloaca Maxima, which is remarkably less touristy than the Roman Forum. The water exiting into the large and swift Tiber sounds remarkably intimate and peaceful as the light trickle is gently amplified by the Etruscan-built drain, now over 2,000 years old. I record. As I exit the area, I examine the surroundings, and am amused by the various layers of graffiti, each of which in their own way mark the surroundings, saying "I am here."

This pilgrimage to honor, in this very simple way, the hidden veins of a city has grown from a longstanding fascination with trains. The desire to learn more about the Cloaca Maxima specifically stems from my work in conducting a number of recordings inside the Atlantic Avenue Tunnel—considered by some to be the world's first subway tunnel—in Brooklyn, New York.[3] This opportunity was made possible by the generous support of The Brooklyn Historic Rail Association, led by Bob Diamond who rediscovered the long-forgotten tunnel after it had been sealed for over a century. Through my interactions with Diamond, I learned that much of the tunneling technology used to construct this historic tunnel derived from Roman Aqueduct technology, including the original structure which encased the Cloaca Maxima. Upon first learning about both structures, I was immediately excited to hear how sound might behave in such spaces. There is an uniqueness to these structures, in part because of their historical and cultural significance, but also because they themselves have their own livelihood and singularity as chambers excited by sound. The pursuit of and interaction with acoustically unique spaces is an implicit element of Deep Listening. The careful interaction with space through sound is part of what binds us temporally with the events that precede and follow our

---

2 Peter J. Aicher, *Guide to the Aqueducts of Ancient Rome* (Wauconda, IL: Bolchazy-Carducci Publishers, 1995), 4.

3 Julia Solis, *New York Underground: The Anatomy of a City* (New York: Routledge, 2005), 133.

present moment—allowing us to creatively engage with and document our own interactions with the immediate moment and the spaces within which they occur.

The founding of the Deep Listening Band as well as the name Deep Listening itself is inseparable from acoustically unique spaces. The recordings of the improvisations of Pauline Oliveros, Stuart Dempster, and Panaiotis inside the inoperative and now famous Dan Harpole Cistern (formerly named Fort Worden Cistern) in Port Townsend, Washington, with its staggering forty-five second reverberation time, dramatically reveal how carefully interwoven performance is with acoustical space.[4] That Dempster was able to find resonant frequencies of the cistern with his trombone and obtain an even longer reverberation time of seventy-two seconds further illustrates how the trio sought out and played with the unique characteristics of the space.[5] This catalytic moment for Deep Listening evolved from longstanding interests of each of the musicians in acoustically unique environments. As Oliveros states:

> Generally speaking, the architectural acoustic space (concert hall) is assumed to be fixed, with relatively unchangeable characteristics. Harmonies, melodies, rhythms and timbres change in more or less intricate relationships, while the acoustic space does not change; it is the container of music. As my experience of numerous performance spaces accumulated, I began to wish for the possibility of changing the acoustic space while performing. I also wished that I could hear as if I were in the audience while I was performing for it.[6]

The collected interactions with various spaces played an integral role in Oliveros' pursuit of flexible performing environments. Through Deep Listening, Oliveros questions the assumptions about performance space—that it is "fixed" and "unchangeable." When we hear sound ricocheting off the walls of the cistern as the Deep Listening Band plays

---

4 *Deep Listening*, New Albion Records NA022, 1989, compact disc.
5 Pauline Oliveros, "Acoustic and Virtual Space as a Dynamic Element of Music," *Leonardo Music Journal*, 5 (1995): 22.
6 Ibid., 20.

with the reflections and inherent resonances of the space, the space in turn comes alive, a dynamic figure throughout the course of the sonic interactions.

The pursuit of acoustically particular and changeable spaces as part of Deep Listening coalesced with an openness and hunger for uncommon sounds. Thus, the exploration of the potential of live electronics evolved more or less alongside a curiosity about the relationships between sound and space. Pauline Oliveros describes her delight in the use of tape-delay techniques, as the acoustic of the instrumental sound would change as the delayed signal was played back in space.[7] The temporal play involved in these processes continued as Oliveros' original tape-delay techniques evolved into the Expanded Instrument System (EIS), a live-processing system written in Max/MSP that enables a variety of live effects to be utilized, including delays as well as sophisticated panning and room simulation techniques. As Oliveros states:

> Through the years I understood the Expanded Instrument System to mean "time machine"—what is expanded is temporal—present/past/future is occurring simultaneously with transformations. What I play in the present comes back in the future while I am still playing, is transformed and becomes a part of the past. This situation keeps you busy listening.[8]

Through this use of technology, both space and time are reconfigured creatively, as the past, present, and future interplay with one another in a variety of virtual and acoustic spaces. These interactions with musical time and space draw on another crucial element of such engaged sonic interaction: that is, memory.

The lens of memory enables the interaction with past musical events and helps us imagine what is to come. It is through memory and listening that we can listen to what is happening within the musical space

---

7 Pauline Oliveros, "The Expanded Instrument System: An Introduction and Brief History" (keynote address given at the Music, Technology, Innovation, Research Center Colloquium, De Montfort University, Leicester UK, November, 2007), accessed July 20, 2011, http://deeplistening.org/site content/expandedmusicalinstruments.

8 Ibid.

at the moment, and also creatively (re)imagine the past and present. Acoustically unique spaces remind us to question our assumptions about performance environments (i.e., that they are neutral, "fixed" and/ or "unchangeable"), and to imagine the lives these spaces have on their own. I believe this is part of what makes us excited when we find unique acoustical spaces originally intended for purposes other than performance. The Dan Harpole Cistern is interesting not only because of its sonic characteristics, but also because it has transcended its original purpose and taken on another life of its own. Formerly part of military developments in the Northwest, the chamber has since become heralded as an "instrument" in its own right.[9] In this way, its original purpose is reimagined. New memories surround the space in counterpoint with the past as the cistern lives on in this new form.

Memory—its construction and fallibility—is intertwined with our own sensory apparatus as well as the documentation methods used in an attempt to fix it permanently. Perception and the technology used for documentation can be creatively played off of one another as well. As Oliveros states in her discussion of field recording:

> Field recording is a great way to become more sensitive to sounds. Headphones tend to focus attention on sounds that ordinarily are not in your awareness. . . . Try different placements of your microphone as well.[10]

The Deep Listening Exercises this description surrounds ("A Study in Mixed Environments" and "A Study in Pulses"[11]) not only invite one to listen differently, but also to consider the impact audio technology has on what one records and is capable of sonically reproducing. In a different context, Alvin Lucier invites performers to seek outside environments, document them "by any means" and then recreate them "at any later time" by means of their voices and/or instruments in his

9 "Fort Worden Cistern Renamed Dan Harpole Cistern," accessed July 29, 2011, http://www.centrum.org/fortworden/2007/06/fort-worden-cis.html.

10 Pauline Oliveros, *Deep Listening: A Composer's Sound Practice* (Lincoln, NE: iUniverse, 2005), 28.

11 Ibid.

piece *(Hartford) Memory Space*.[12] By requiring performers to recreate their documentation completely acoustically, Lucier foregrounds creative engagement with the usual methods (memorization, notation, recording) used for affixing sonic memories. Moreover, by introducing a time delay between the documentation and the performance of the documented space, the variations that occur by virtue of separation in time and space become a necessary part of the creative rendering of the act of reproduction. In this way, the technology becomes part of the life of the space and sonic interaction, as the characteristics of the microphones, speakers, and recording medium impart their own signatures upon the recorded sound and excite certain parts of one's own remembrances of spaces.

The flexibility and sonic engagement Deep Listening invites—that is, the consideration of time, space, technology, and their interplay with one another—is part of what led me to the Atlantic Avenue Tunnel to create the piece *navigable*. Highly motivated by Lucier's seminal work *I Am Sitting In A Room* (1969) as well as the Deep Listening Band's self-titled album (1989), the piece functioned as a theme and variations in recording the resonant frequencies of the tunnel using a series of different recording scenarios within the tunnel. Over the course of several months in 2010, I would descend into the tunnel, and record and re-record fragments of natural sound also originally recorded within the tunnel. The resonant frequencies that emerged were deep, pulsating, and surprisingly rich. Through each of the different recording sessions, I employed different microphone placements and used different microphones in an attempt to see how these variations impacted the evolution of sound throughout the process of rerecording. Unfortunately, midway through the project, the space was closed and rendered inaccessible.[13] The subsequent uproar with regards to the closing bespeaks a desire among city dwellers to not forget such historic sites. The work of visual

12 Alvin Lucier, *Chambers* (Middletown, CT: Wesleyan University Press, 1980), 43.
13 Jen Carlson, "Diamond Wants Tunnel Reopened, Plans Lawsuit Against DOT," accessed July 30, 2011, http://gothamist.com/2010/12/27/diamond _wants_tunnel_reopened_plans.php.

artists and urban explorers Miru Kim,[14] Julia Solis,[15] and Steve Duncan[16] beautifully document historical and hidden infrastructures that too often are made unreachable and removed from public consciousness. Nevertheless, the creative engagement with these spaces seems inevitable, and artists often take a sense of responsibility as they approach these unique spaces. As Miru Kim states, "I feel an obligation to animate and humanize these spaces continually in order to preserve their memories in a creative way before they are lost forever."[17] And as Julia Solis notes in *New York Underground: Anatomy of a City*, these historical and singular sites are becoming increasingly inaccessible.[18]

This is part of the underlying impetus for the pilgrimage to the mouth of the Cloaca Maxima. By listening to and recording (even at a distance) these sounds and the spaces they reverberate in, they become accessible even while the spaces remain off limits. While standing and listening carefully to the sounds occurring underneath me, it is hard not to be impressed and awestruck by the reverberant structure that contributed to the development of an enormous empire. In recording these sounds, I hope to interact creatively with this space. Each time I visit a spot to record within the Roman Forum, I am struck by the sudden and random droves of people that surround me. Looking at what I am doing and then deciphering the placard on the Basilica Julia, the onlookers slowly and quietly exclaim, "wow, the world's first sewer!" By interacting with these spaces sonically, they come alive and are remembered. Through such moments of interaction with spaces and, above all, by listening to them, we engage powerfully with a space that has outlived the concerns of the times within which it was built. The space takes on new life each time someone seeks it out in these various creative capacities. As such,

---

14 "Miru Kim," accessed July 30, 2011, http://mirukim.com.

15 "Julia Solis," accessed July 30, 2011, http://www.solis.darkpassage.com.

16 "Undercity.org: Guerrilla History & Urban Exploration," accessed July 30, 2011, http://www.undercity.org/.

17 "Miru Kim's Underground Art," accessed July 30, 2011, http://www.ted.com/talks/miru_kim_s_underground_art.html.

18 Julia Solis, *New York Underground: The Anatomy of a City* (New York: Routledge, 2005), 225.

it is moving when musicians and artists seek out these spaces and listen deeply, and in so doing remind us that this history, and these spaces, like us, are here.

Acknowledgements

I thank Bob Diamond and Greg Castillo of the Brooklyn Historic Rail Association. Their knowledge and encouragement of creative activities in the Atlantic Avenue Tunnel—including my own—has been continually impressive. As of this writing, I hope the space at some time becomes accessible again. For more information on the tunnel, please see http://www.brooklynrail.net/proj_aatunnel.html. Also, many thanks to The Friends of the Old Croton Aqueduct (http://www.aqueduct.org/), for their continued support of my explorations in this area.

From the Ordinary to the Extraordinary: Plants and Deep Listening

MIYA MASAOKA resides in New York City and is a classically trained musician, composer and new media artist. Pioneering the koto in contexts of improvisation, computer processing, new music and sound installations, she has expanded the koto to include lasers (Laser Koto), and has expanded the traditional costume while playing the koto— the kimono—to include responsive and wearable technology with thousands of hand-embroidered LEDs. She creates works that hover the boundary of music, sound, movement and light and that both investigate and reveal these fluid relationships. http://www .miyamasaoka.com/

Miya Masaoka

IMMEDIATELY FELT AT HOME with certain tenets of what I perceived as Deep Listening practice and philosophy in that the underlying assumptions resonated with training that I had received from various Japanese music masters, both on the Japanese koto and in gagaku, or Japanese orchestral court music. During koto lessons, I was told to "become the fourteenth bridge," (there are thirteen bridges on the koto, and the player sits in the location where the imagined fourteenth bridge would be located). Similarly, in gagaku training, I was instructed to "become the drum" when playing the kakko, a drum in the gagaku ensemble. In this respect, the musicians were encouraged to not have a separate identity from the instrument, but instructed to become something of a transmission vessel, a conduit for the music, from an energy force outside ourselves and through the musical instrument. It was also assumed

65

that the actual instruments have a soul, and were themselves sacred. This concept of minimizing the individual personality of the musician aided in an integration of the player into the entirety of the sound environment that was being created by all the musicians in the ensemble. In addition, rhythm in gagaku has a long arc, and build up of this arc can span forty-five minutes or longer, in which the very slow pacing of the sound events of the orchestra gradually increase to a faster pace and rhythm. This extended sustain resembled Pauline Oliveros' continuous and at times slow-moving accordion playing, which to my ears sounded hauntingly similar to a sho, a reed instrument in the gagaku ensemble.

It was only much later, after more exposure to Deep Listening, that these overlapping concepts came more clearly into focus. Performing with Pauline Oliveros for the first time at Bard College, and later spending several days with her in the recording studio and performing with the poet IONE in the Oracle Bones Trio, I became closer to understanding this multi-faceted practice and philosophy, or praxis, of Deep Listening.

I had first come to know of Pauline Oliveros from playing her compositions in an ensemble while a student at Mills College. (Pauline did not hold the Darius Milhaud chair at that time, 1992–94, and unfortunately she was not there while I was a student.) During this time, I had written her a letter, asking particular questions about a composition she had written, and was happily stunned that she had found the time to write back. That such a renowned composer and pioneer would make herself so accessible to someone who was not her student was quite a revelation. Later, I published an interview with her, and in the following years I also came to contemplate some aspects about *Pieces for Plants* (a ten-year body of work of mine) that had some relevancy with the Deep Listening operatives. From the mid-1990s I have had the privilege of knowing Pauline Oliveros as an amazing thinker, pioneering artist and humanitarian.

Plants + Deep Listening

In oddly similar and dissimilar ways, house plants and Deep Listening seemed to be harvesting the potential of something so basic, mundane and ordinary, yet also so fundamental to our way of existing in the world, that it can be easily overlooked or discounted or mistaken for nothing at all. Yet, this intangible connection was something I was compelled to further investigate.

On Sunday mornings in New York City, I often ride my bike to the local Jodo Shinshu Buddhist temple on Riverside Drive, which is a few minutes away from my home. The service typically begins with thirty minutes of slow, long-tone chanting which is realized by everyone reading a simple graphic notation for non-musicians with lots of lines and steps, and half-step intervallic medieval-sounding modes. This group chanting activity relaxes the body and the mind, and puts us in a frame of mind for listening to the sermon, which is usually about some obscure observation about life, naturally from a Buddhist perspective. In Deep Listening, the long tones that are sung (or "sounded" using Deep Listening parlance) during certain exercises and pieces produce a similar relaxing state, but here there is a critical departure. In Deep Listening, the participants are free to choose their own pitches, vary the pitch, and, while listening to the environment, continually change pitches, or even choose to be silent. There is a sense of profound integration with the environs, and a non-hierarchical approach to perception of sounds in the space. The participants become free and creative agents. Magic is afoot.

But What Exactly is Deep Listening?

The entity and praxis of Deep Listening is not easily categorized, and involves a spectrum of narratives over a span of decades. For the purposes of this essay and in an effort to avoid redundancy I will try and focus on some areas that have not yet been written about, beginning with two subtly changing definitions of Deep Listening found on the Deep Listening website about six years apart.

What is Deep Listening?

Deep Listening® is a philosophy and practice developed by Pauline Oliveros that distinguishes the difference between the involuntary nature of hearing and the voluntary selective nature of listening. The result of the practice cultivates appreciation of sounds on a heightened level, expanding the potential for connection and interaction with one's environment, technology and performance with others in music and related arts. The practice of Deep Listening provides a framework for artistic collaboration and musical improvisation and gives composers, performers, artists of other disciplines, and audiences new tools to explore and interact with environmental and instrumental sounds.[1]

In an earlier 2004 definition posted on the site, Deep Listening is described in the following way:

Deep Listening involves going below the surface of what is heard and also expanding to the whole field of sound whatever one's usual focus might be. Such forms of listening are essential to the process of unlocking layer after layer of imagination, meaning and memory down to the cellular level of human experience.[2]

And again in 2010,

Deep Listening includes all sounds expanding the boundaries of perception. In this concept is language and the nature of its sound as well as natural sound and technological sound. And too, Deep Listening includes the environmental and atmospheric context of sound.[3]

All told, the description of the environment and its unbiased mingling of natural and technological sounds, and the stated intent of Deep Listening to mentally refocus aural attention and shine attention upon what is usually not given the aural spotlight, is the crux or vortex for this discussion. (The human ear can listen like a laser beam focused on a particular target, even through a din of unwanted noise, such as a noisy cocktail party. This particular ability of the human ear to choose to listen to selective sounds is very complex, and the mechanics are not

---

1 Deep Listening, "*About*," accessed August 25, 2011, http://deeplistening .org/site/content/about.

2 Judith Becker, *Deep Listeners, Music, Emotion and Trancing* (Bloomington, IN: Indiana University Press, 2004), 2.

3 Pauline Oliveros, *Sounding the Margins*, ed. Lawton Hall (Kingston, NY: Deep Listening Publications, 2010), 78.

fully understood. This phenomena continues to be an ongoing standing conundrum for artificial intelligence, as computers are very poor at this task). The lightning-speed decisions for the listener/improvisor, determining what to listen to and not listen to, and selecting what to respond to and not respond to are tantamount to improvisation, and to the execution of the works of Pauline Oliveros. When engaging with Pauline Oliveros as a fellow improvisor, or performing pieces from her immense body of work, these processes, which function in both an intellectual and emotional way, are accessed in the conscious and unconscious realm of our creative selves as musicians and improvisors. Her enormously influential works, such as *Sonic Meditations*,[4] with specific and lengthy instructions, isolate, refine and advance some of these processes, which include memory, choice and imagination. I have found, as an educator, that when students perform *Sonic Meditations*, it is not merely the execution of a composition, but also a powerful means to change how students listen, think, and respond to sound and each other in an environment. Oliveros' specific instructions on listening succeed in focusing attention on various procedures of our senses, choosing what to listen to, when to listen, and what to do accordingly. In Deep Listening, the conscious act of shifting one's patterns of attention to different sounds in an environment is tantamount to an ability to discern what is happening in the sonic space, and how to respond to that particular sound is the next point of consideration. These observations about the connections among Oliveros' music and the innumerable unconscious decisions we are continually making every moment dovetail with the mostly unnoticed biological response of our houseplants to humans.

Pieces for Plants

Enter *Pieces for Plants*,[5] a body of work I created over a ten-year period which, in part, draws ideas from the fields of ecology, biology and evolution, otherwise known as evolutionary ecology.

---

4   Pauline Oliveros, *Sonic Meditations* (Baltimore: Smith Publications, 1974)
5   For video of *Pieces for Plants*, see the video media files at http://
     www.miyamasaoka.com.

Consider the lowly houseplants. They do not make unwanted deposits on the rug such as a cat or dog. Nor can they get you evicted for loud barking sounds. Houseplants are seemingly very good at doing what they do—sitting still, adapting to their environment. They are somewhat passive (not asking you to clean your dishes in the sink), yet elegantly active, in a slow, time-based kind of way. These seemingly mundane, ordinary, mute, prosaic creatures are capable of some of the most complex tasks required for human existence, such as photosynthesis.[6]

> "[Plants] are more sophisticated in sensing than animals. Just to give you an example, every single type of root is able to detect, monitor and compute continuously at least fifteen different chemical and physical parameters. . . This underestimation of plants is always with us."[7]

Similarly, the act of human listening and its complex associated tasks are sorely underestimated.

These physiological, psycho-acoustical processes of listening and responding occur, according to Oliveros' definition of Deep Listening, "on a cellular level," and become, in a broader sense, the actual conceptual material of a music composition, which can be manipulated, expanded upon, molded and captured to create and re-create music/sound experiences. Similarly, in *Pieces for Plants*, patterns of attention are fluid and can be traced with various software which tracks the electrical data activity. The "player" of the plant can choose to move towards one plant, then another, and activate the plant with their movements and focus of attention on particular interactivity with the plants. A somewhat familiar yet alien interactivity is achieved, as if talking to

---

6 Photosynthesis: synthesis of chemical compounds with the aid of radiant energy and especially light; *especially*: formation of carbohydrates from carbon dioxide and a source of hydrogen (as water) in the chlorophyll-containing tissues of plants exposed to light, *Merriam-Webster Dictionary*, accessed August 30, 2011, http://www.merriam-webster.com/dictionary/photo+synthesis.

7 "Stefano Mancuso: The roots of plant intelligence," accessed January 22, 2012, http://www.ted.com/talks/stefano_mancuso_the_roots_of_plant_intelligence.html.

ANTHOLOGY OF ESSAYS

an old friend or relative you have known for a long time, but never conversed with. In early versions of *Pieces for Plants*, musical scores were created with the visual graphic raw data created by the plants. Other versions were created by superimposing the data waves onto the grand staff of music notation.[8] In my studio, with the electrodes on my plants, I became aware of patterns of plant activity with individual interactions with the plant, and the larger arcs of patterns over a period of days and weeks. New directions of mental and aural attention became possible with this ability to ascertain the response of my houseplants.

In *Pieces for Plants*, banal everyday activity, such as walking or moving closer to the plant is performed by the passerby/listener/activator. This simple activity engages the biological electrical activity of the plant, which is then expressed in electricity and sent through several configurations of software applications analyzing data and converting the data into sound.

To achieve this, I attached electrodes to the leaves of the semi-tropical houseplant *Philodendron* (the plants' leaves are not injured during this process). People are instructed to walk towards or away from the plant, and the plant responds fluidly to the activator/listener. Plant activity is mapped to sound parameters by way of an interface and computer through a mono-channel loudspeaker. EEG, or Electroencephalogram, electrodes are attached to the leaves of the *Philodendron*, and the electrical response in micro-volts (one-millionth of a volt) is then sent to FFT (Fast Fourier Transform). IBVA, or Interactive Brain Visualization Analysis software, is a product developed by friend and colleague Masahiro Kohata. The electrical response from the plant, as read by the EEG sensor, is read in micro-volts. Then, in Max/MSP software, the data is scaled and mapped to various sound parameters. This system can analyze data in real time, and express the ongoing raw data of the changing states of the plant response and activity throughout the day. (I have also used similar systems for sonifying data from brain activity, and have extracted data from my own brain volunteers in the audience

---

8   Alex Waterman, Debra Singer and Matthew Lyons, eds., *Between Thought & Sound, Graphic Notation in Contemporary Music* (New York: The Kitchen, 2007), 54–55.

for my piece *What is the Sound of Naked Asian Men*.) Real-time, raw and ongoing-activity data is then analyzed and sent continuous incremental changes that take place within the organism, the split-leaf *Philodendron*. Notwithstanding the fascinating yet scientifically unconventional Cleve Backster's work with plants, chronicled in *Primary Perception*,[9] plant research carries on.[10] Some fifty years after Backster's experiments, Stefano Mancuso, founder of neurobiology, states in his TED lecture, "It's much more easy to work with plants than with animals. They have computing power, they have electrical signals, the connection with the machine is much more easy, much more even ethically possible."[11]

Now, if I may back up a bit in this discussion. The passerby (or one who passes by the plant), whether at an outdoor installation or gallery space, might possibly be more socially open than an average person, as they are in a public space and interested in new encounters with contemporary visual sculpture, art, or sounds. In an installation setting, passersby approach the plant, and sometimes unknowingly engage the response of the *Philodendron* as they walk by. They may turn around and do a double take, and repeat their action with an intent to try to produce the same sound with their movement. But then, the sound will be different since most likely they are standing in a new location. Then they move, and begin to get a sense of what kinds of movements on their part produce what kind of reaction in the plant. But herein lies the rupture, where a change occurs in the internal state of the passerby. An innocent passerby becomes confronted with sound interpreted by a

---

9 Cleve Backster, *Primary Perception: Biocommunication with Plants, Living Foods, and Human Cells* (Anza, CA: White Rose Millenium Press, 2003), 54.

10 These plants on the treetop canopy are able to move significant distances in search of the optimal nutrients and sunlight. Plants can cut off the food supply to the old roots, which then dry up and die, and the plant moves on the canopy of the treetops to a new area, and sends out new roots in the new location, and stays there until it decides to move again. Mark W. Moffett, *The High Frontier: Exploring the Tropical Rainforest Canopy* (Cambridge, MA: Harvard University Press, 1993), 97.

11 "Stefano Mancuso: The roots of plant intelligence."

computer from a plant responding to them, and they are gently forced to rethink their sense of how they view the world, their state of being and thus their environment through a completely altered lens. Of course, they can choose to ignore this interruption, this affront, but they will at least have been given the opportunity to engage with the plant.

A few things are required for certain engagements with these two musical endeavors of Deep Listening and *Pieces for Plants*. Availing oneself to engage with some kind of communication or interaction with a houseplant, and availing oneself to enter a trancelike state (which may or may not occur with Deep Listening) are activities that require us to relinquish the rational, detached, objectified self. The surrender of our rational selves, of the plausible, of our inheritance of the Enlightenment is not easily effectuated. As participants, we are being asked to rethink the discreet categories of plant, animal and humans as delineated by Aristotle. Our deeply rooted assumptions about the world, about ourselves, once so simple—plant, animal, mineral—have, like the tectonic plates of the earth, been shifted.

From the ordinary, from the perfunctory, from the routine acts of breathing, listening and hence responding to the environment, from the discreet act of walking toward a plant, and paying attention, or not, from choosing to make a sound with others, or not, emerges something potentially extraordinary. What is that? Listen! Or not!

Deep Listening in Carbonoproyecto

Fabián Racca

FABIÁN RACCA was born in 1966 in the La Pampa province of Argentina, where he lives today. Primarily self-taught, by 1989 Racca began to explore several languages and possibilities at radio broadcasting in La Pampa's capital city of Santa Rosa. In subsequent years his interests widened to include recording and research of varying types of soundscapes, sound art, musical improvisation and experimentation with diverse sound sources and deep listening, among other practices, along with composing for theatre and creative advertising soundtracks. Racca founded Carbonoproyecto in 1998 as an experimental space for the support and development of deep listening, free improvisation (musical and poetic), radio art, ecoacoustics, and sound experimentation. http://carbonoproyecto.wordpress.com

Introduction

BASED IN LA PAMPA, Argentina, the Carbonoproyecto project has developed as an ever-growing space for sharing and disseminating improvisation, Deep Listening practices, sound art, field recording, as well as related ideas and concepts. The project, which emerged in 1998, includes as part of its background my earlier life experiences and intuitive listening practices since childhood, either in the small-town rural environment of La Pampa (a province in central Argentina), or the cities of Buenos Aires and elsewhere. It was only in the late 1990's that I came across the concept of Deep Listening, and began to understand the implications of the process that had developed over those years.

This essay is devoted first to characterizing the types of practices I intuitively developed before learning about Deep Listening. Secondly, I examine the ways

75

in which Deep Listening improved and influenced Carbonoproyecto practices and ideas.

Sound Memories of Childhood and Adolescence

My attraction to sounds and music began during my childhood, a period in which it is very natural for children to explore, play music and enjoy listening and communication with sounds in general. While it may be complicated to identify the multiple factors that converge in each individual process, there are some that I consider important because they marked distinct stages in my experience.[1]

I was born in Alta Italia in 1966, a small rural town of La Pampa province. In the early 1970s my parents moved to Realicó, another town north of this province where I grew up and lived until I was nineteen. The members of my mother's family were rural workers, descendants of German, Russian and native peoples, who emigrated to the towns of the region in the late 1960s and early 1970s after losing their jobs in the country (due in large part to the emergence of new technologies). My father's family, of Italian descent, had also peasant origins and had lived in Alta Italia for quite a while. In the early 1970s my father was a clerk in a flour factory in Realicó and my mother was carrying out different tasks as a weaver, hairdresser, and cook, among others. It was thanks to their tremendous effort that we could have our own house and my brother and I could attend school.

At that time television broadcast only a few hours each day and we didn't have our own TV set until 1978. The main media was AM radio, around which we sat to listen to soap operas or news. Among the music that was broadcast on the radio there was pop, commercial melodic songs of the time, popular cumbia rhythms and folk music. Such music was also heard at family gatherings and dances with orchestras in town. At parties and dances in the country, there were traditional folk rhythms such as polkas, milongas, rancheras, pasodobles, and waltzes. I was very attracted to watching the musicians performing; this was a moment unlike any other. By then I used to gather almost daily with my uncle,

---

1 Photographs available at http://www.deeplistening.org/essays.

who in his youth in the country had learned by ear some folk songs that were played and sung daily before sunset; and if I was lucky enough— which was not so often—he lent me his guitar. I was enthralled by singing and by making the guitar sound.

Our house was on the outskirts of town, near the railroad tracks, fields and the flour mill where my father worked. I remember falling asleep listening to the incessant drone of the mill at night and waking up with the horn announcing the change of shift for workers, who passed walking in front of my house, chatting loudly, every four hours all day. In suburban neighborhoods like ours, the sound environment was a mixture of rural and urban sounds. The soundscape was marked by different sounds that indicated important events such as the arrival of the milkman shouting from his cart, the horn of the kerosene seller arriving in the neighborhood, the flute of the knife grinder, the announcement of the man who repaired mattresses, the horn and grinding of the train's wheels on the rail, the trembling of the earth and the vibration of doors and windows when the trains approached; that is, each job or daily experience had its own sound mark. Since the market was not able to supply all food at an affordable price, in the yards of most houses chickens and other farm animals were raised: one of my grandfathers lived with us, and he was in charge of this, all the while singing fragments of old songs repeated in Italian. My other grandfather, having been a great farmer in previous years, kept a garden that supplied the family and taught me to grow vegetables while reciting gaucho verses learned in his rural work, or told me tales filled with much humor and unexpected outcomes of his experiences working as a farmer laborer in various parts of the country which I listened to with delight. His wife, my grandmother, who came from a Russian-German family of extremely poor herders of sheep and goats traveling as nomads in the arid vastness of La Pampa, always agreed to my request to sing in German one of those unknown countryside songs of oral tradition, or to say phrases in that language, which were very funny because these were naughty stories that she translated whispering them to me as if telling me a secret.

When I was seven years old my parents, who watched how I spent hours singing and hitting buckets as if drumming, sent me to a guitar teacher in the neighborhood who taught me music theory and how to play some scores. Once a year, a teacher from a conservatory in Buenos Aires came to town to give exams to move up into the next year. After two years I started studying with another teacher in similar conditions. At that point I felt every time less drawn to the study and generally ended up doing everything by heart, up to the point that nowadays I cannot understand how I could ever read and play those scores that today I find strange. What I liked best was playing and singing songs, and by nine years of age I had learned a repertoire of classic folk songs and even tangos. I used to play these songs at family gatherings or on the sidewalk of our house while my brother also sang and danced: smiling neighbors peered out to listen and watch the show! However, as I progressed in the years with the exercises I was assigned, my boredom grew and I preferred to make up songs or spontaneous rhythms, away from the tones that I knew and seeking out other sounds. The pleasure I felt with this made playing exercises for the conservatory more tedious. I could hardly concentrate and started making excuses for not attending classes. I even ran away from several until at age eleven I dropped out. My parents always respected my decision. In subsequent years I stopped playing guitar and forgot much of what I had learned in my time of formal music education.

When I was thirteen my father bought a radio-tape recorder, which I still keep with me. Being able not only to listen to but also record music was a fantastic possibility. Since blank tapes were very expensive back then, the same cassette was recorded over and over until the tape was no longer usable. This meant that I could not keep more than the memory of those enthusiast recordings; e.g., I remember having walked around the town and countryside, recording ambient sounds and my footsteps on different surfaces. Since I did not have headphones I could only listen to the results back at home, and it was a delight to sit in the courtyard to hear the recordings, drinking *mate* in the evening. I also compiled techno music recordings as well as rock and pop music that could be heard in the disco of our town, where we used to go when we were teenagers. These were the years of the military dictatorship that had seized the government in 1976 until the beginnings of democracy in the country by late 1983.

When I was fifteen I was diagnosed as having cancer, had to quit school and moved to a sanatorium in Buenos Aires because there were no trained doctors in town for treating such diseases those days. Time was pressing and if I did not undergo an emergency treatment I had no chance of survival. I spent a year between surgery and chemotherapy sessions, regularly being admitted fifteen days a month. Hospital days were long, they were a separate reality with many troubles and many virtues, but facing the prospect of death itself also accelerated my maturity process and increased the value of life, feeling it like something unique and unrepeatable, not to be wasted. I was interested in talking and listening to life stories of people who went there all the time, nurses, cleaners and other patients.

During the breaks between sessions of chemotherapy I lived with relatives at the Dock Sud, a port district of Avellaneda, a city near Buenos Aires. This was a suburb between factories belching smoke-stacks a few blocks away from the Riachuelo river, polluted for years by the dumping of industrial wastes. It had half-submerged old ships, and shanty towns. Despite this depressing atmosphere, I enjoyed those days away from the hospital; everything was a sign of life for me. As the treatment progressed the pleasure obtained through the senses became more intense, and I was glad to feel the warm air and the sounds of a subway station, traffic noise, horns, grinding of brakes, engines, murmuring voices of the human tide that moves across the metropolis. Tough as it was, I think this experience meant an awakening to a deeper awareness of life.

Once I was discharged after succeeding in controlling the disease, I returned to my family in Realicó and within a couple of years I finished high school and headed for college, which according to my family's income could only be at University of La Pampa, where art studies are not included. Besides, I had become a great lover of rock music, which was the somewhat "different" thing that could be heard in those years around here. I also liked writing poems and stories and reading literature (Poe, Lovecraft, Quiroga, Argentinian *costumbrismo* writers) and all kinds of comics. Since I also felt a great affinity with nature related issues, I finally moved to Santa Rosa to study geology for a career known as Use of Renewable Natural Resources.

Radio Broadcasting, Sound Art and New Horizons

In 1989, I approached the BDC FM radio 107.1 MHz in Santa Rosa, the only local radio to broadcast exclusively different styles of rock, progressive, and jazz, and I was immediately fascinated to know that there was such a whole world of music to discover.

My first incursion into this arena took place through a radio show with a group of college friends who started leaving this activity at different times while I became increasingly fascinated by the possibilities of radio.

I learned to operate a mixer, to mix music, voices and sounds, and thanks to an office job I had gotten, bought my first home recording equipment consisting of tapes, two tape decks, a microphone and a mixer. From that moment on, recording and the opportunity for sound modeling became my primary research tool. I spent many hours experimenting and listening to the results obtained either by overdubbing, sound collage, improvisation with radio language, small soap opera pieces with unpredictable situations, while at the same time I composed jingles or advertising identificatory pieces where I applied all these experiences. Through these practices, sound was becoming my best mirror to see my expressive peculiarities and those of other people who joined these experiences, and this in turn posed a thousand questions about the implications of each detail. This led to extensive and critical listening sessions of each element that sounded within a recording: I used to re-record as many times as necessary until I felt the piece flowed naturally and forcefully. Apart from some specific programs, most of the day the radio broadcast a combination of music and these productions, and eventually those became the trademark of the FM station.

My participation in this radio station grew to the point where I became responsible not only for its artistic production but also for the coordination of general administration and economic support issues.

The project became my life for those years, though only in spiritual terms, since it was impossible those days to survive on the meager income of such a non-commercial project. Beyond the obvious complications, I was aware that radio was the only means at hand to keep seeking and educating myself in a place always conditioned by its remoteness from the central circuits of culture and within the context of a very conservative society. However, we could do it here and live it fully, sharing adventures with people who due to their social, educational or economic background could never have afforded to attend arts college.

Over the years, the daily practice of sound exploration and production made me feel more comfortable with longer developments and trying to "control less and coexist more" with sound manifestations.

The radio station was on the air sixteen hours a day, seven days a week, and without any computers everything took place in real time. In such a context, during my live transmission shifts I used to experiment with different mixtures of pre-recorded materials. These included field recordings of ambient sounds, voices, sounds of our daily activities, sounds of the television, radio, vinyl, improvisations with any available instrument such as synthesizers, guitars, percussion objects, and all this was mixed with real-time possibilities of sampling, equalization effects of the radio mixing desk, and my own spoken interventions when I improvised a story, a character or thought, or did some reading. I found it wonderful to hear the new worlds that were generated from these sound combinations and sequences, which were pure intuitive exploration.

However, these searches, plus the increasing spread of experimental works of different authors, began to push the limits of the relationship with much of the local audience who perceived this as something disturbing and demanded that we go back to more conventional stages of rock, pop and jazz broadcasting. But for me there was no point in going back after so many intense changes in a few years. By late 1996, the radio station shut down, ending this stage after several consecutive years due to financial problems and the wearing out of the group.

Getting Acquainted with Deep Listening

Around 1994 I started to receive a journal that was written in Buenos Aires, *Esculpiendo Milagros* [Sculpting Miracles], which included dossiers on experimental music, free improvisation, sound collage, kraut rock, psychedelic, and other genres; ideas of artists like John Cage, Cornelius Cardew, John Oswald; and stories and ideas of the avant-garde. I contacted the editors and critics of the magazine, and they started sending me all the published issues to try and sell to the audience on the radio. Despite its interesting educational content, only seven or eight copies were usually sold in Santa Rosa, mostly among people who worked at the radio station. Most of our audience did not share the interest in other pursuits beyond rock, jazz and genres that had given rise to the radio.

There was a section in the magazine devoted to journals edited worldwide. Intrigued to have access to these sources, I sent letters by post (we had no Internet access back then) to different addresses, and one of the quickest responses I received was from the Canadian-based *Musicworks*, which sent me a catalog of all previous issues. I promised myself to gather enough money to buy it later.

Along with information came the need to listen and know about that music, which was expensive and very difficult to obtain since there were no local editions available and compact discs had to be imported. Luckily I came across a couple of music stores in Santa Rosa and Buenos Aires who dared to import those materials, in which I invested my meager monthly savings.

Both through these readings and listening I started to realize that these practices came from a long time ago, and many of them had been studied at music schools in addition to expanding the concept of music and having political and social implications, such as the ideas of John Cage. Although these were works coming from eminent performers or professional musicians, trained in remote and more receptive environments than mine, it was very refreshing to find common ground with those intentions and processes, learning that they were not just crazy, or delusions (as they were considered locally), but rather things of a great importance.

By the end of 1996 we had our last FM transmission, and in my case it meant the end of an uninterrupted period of eight years in which the radio had become a life meaning, but it had been increasingly difficult to maintain due to lack of human and technical resources. But this moment also meant the beginning of a deeper learning time and the building of a life plan with my partner and wife Claudia.

From that moment on I had more time to read, listen, experiment and observe how important these practices were for me as a spiritual need, without the pressure of preparing for an audience.

One of my activities then was to begin to listen, identify and organize a large number of tapes into a database that had few if any of its content previously tagged. By late 1992 I got my first portable recorder, a stereo Walkman used by reporters. I could start collecting the sounds of natural or rural environment, daily life in my parent's house, on the radio and from the neighborhood. Within a wide range of sonic possibilities I explored sound from different objects, conversations, voices and ways of speaking in different kinds of places and meetings. Some of them had been used during my radio performances, but I had not had time to listen to some of them carefully beyond the time of recording. This process lasted several years, because more tapes or recordings were added with new field experiments each month.

Moreover, attentive listening to everything happening at once revealed a sonic complexity that was wider than the object to be recorded itself. On several occasions the coexistence of different levels, timbres, volumes and sequence of sounds referred me to a kind of musical harmony, unexpected, strange. In everyday life the connection with these practices was very fluid, something like a permanent state of research and observation.

The practice of recording was increasingly important. Whatever the life situation you could always get a sound document to listen to attentively and then explore its possibilities. I also recorded jam sessions with friends who visited me as well as long sessions in which I played guitar without worrying about tuning, moving my hands freely. Listening to all this was pleasant work although some hours could pass without something "interesting" actually happening. Anyway, I was increasingly convinced of the relativity of this term when it comes to improvising or experimenting. In any case what I did not find interesting were some moments of poor concentration and not listening while playing, but over time I started finding them also necessary as a way to break free from the pressure of the search, and move more freely over the next few moments of concentration. What mattered was the process, the flow. . . if that was there, the outcome (understood as an enjoyable musical experience), appeared, unique, unrepeatable, not as you wanted, but rather as you experienced it.

The Significance of Deep Listening in my Experimental Practices

In subsequent years I shared these practices with people of different social and educational backgrounds. In each place I lived I always had a space for my circuit and sound recording, even if it could only be a small corner. My family or friends knew that it was a non-isolated study in which I spent several hours a day, and whenever they visited me they could accompany me in listening to what I was producing at the moment, or talk about what was being heard, or take part in improvisation sessions. These sessions were not scheduled, but rather I started to play some instrument or a tape, or checked the sounds of voices on the microphone and invited others to participate, or offered them to take the instrument they preferred, and make it sound. My work consisted in mixing it all, so that everyone could hear themselves, and control the return through an amplification system that was very effective so that the mix could have enough space for all the voices or sounds. On the contrary, when it was acoustic, we had to make agreements in advance, and in the case of people without musical training, such situations often inhibited them or they had difficulties in listening to everything simultaneously. In contrast, the amplification controlled by loudspeakers or headphones ensured that the mixture would always be clearly heard, and besides, as it was not a common experience for people who are not artists, they found it more attractive. I remember once that my grandmother, eighty years old, wanted to improvise singing as I played the guitar. Due to her age and history of rural life, I thought that the amplification system could be somewhat aggressive to her, so I started improvising on the acoustic guitar hoping she would do the same with the voice, but it was only me playing solo. When I asked her what happened she said: "But ain't you going to connect the microphone and electric guitar?!"

Children participated in several sessions, for example my niece Iliana, with whom I shared many experiences since she was a baby. When she was six months old I prepared a microphone with a delay, and tried it out a couple of times for her to see how it worked. When she approached, she started by letting her voice out, listening to the repetitions of the delay until the end before letting her voice out again. I found such attitudes and responses amazing, and they showed me the importance of listening for children as a way to acknowledge the world and to recognize oneself as a creative part of it, ie that modifies it and is modified by it.

Around 1998 I decided to group both individual and collective practices in an independent project, as a space to keep learning, developing and disseminating these activities called Carbonoproyecto [CP]. Throughout all these years in the CP, I lived many experiences with different people, both musicians and non-musicians, each of which has a different story related to these searches, which could not be included in a single essay. All of them helped to explore new potential to enrich my thinking and make sense of a way of life where the main objective is spiritual.

By 1999 we were living in a semirural area in Toay, a town next to Santa Rosa, where we built our house and live today. By then I had bought the whole *Musicworks* collection, and in many of the papers I found points in common and very useful knowledge for research for the CP. But it was in interviews or texts by Pauline Oliveros on various aspects of the concept of Deep Listening, that I found the greatest connection with my experiences of all those years. While I could never attend Deep Listening retreats to grasp more accurately the scope and its methodological issues, what I could read in articles in journals and on the Internet and listen to in music by Pauline was of great help to interpret some processes and rethink the value of these practices in our place.

There were many questions I used to ask myself, to which the ideas of Deep Listening provided almost always interesting answers, for instance: Why did all these coexistence or sound harmonies take place while improvising freely without following each other, and listening to all in this mix? The key was concentrated listening of what you were doing, what others do and everything that sounds at once; this continuous feedback leads us to moments where all the elements gather together in a kind of sound construction, which is perceived as music or pleasant relationship between sounds.

In the case of people with no intention of making music, what can this practice be useful for? Deep Listening can function as a type of sound meditation, a way to connect with the space which we are part of, an awareness of our sound within the sound, and how our interaction with this practice can create or perceive another reality within the reality we perceive. Or it just can be useful to learn how to appreciate information that comes from listening attentively to everything that happens, beyond the natural fact of "hearing" sounds in everyday life.

Does the fact that the experience arises without effort mean that it does not require any commitment on our part? It requires our attentive listening, voluntary, concentrated. Indeed I have participated in meetings where several people with instruments improvise at once, but most are concerned with things as drinking, eating, trying to fit into what the other plays, or seek their approval, and other distractions that do not allow concentration. The result can only be lack of communication or de facto deafness.

Final reflections

At some point, all the valuable information I had obtained and spread in my community about these practices and professional concepts developed in core cultural circuits did not contribute to the local valuation of my work, but rather reinforced the idea that they were only possible in urban cultural circuits and by academic musicians. I truly needed a concrete opinion of someone with real knowledge on these issues.

My enthusiasm for Pauline's writings led me to contact her via mail in late 1999 in order to get her opinion about my work and some ideas related to it. Fortunately she showed much interest in my views and the recordings I had sent her, and expressed her willingness to help me spread this music around the world. From then onwards, a friendship with Pauline began, one maintained over distance and time. Her feedback has been a very important encouragement to continue my work, which tries to pave a way from a place that is far away from big centers, but with infinite human possibilities as elsewhere in the world.

Deep Listening and the Peripatetic Life of an Improvising Musician

Thollem McDonas

THOLLEM MCDONAS is a perpetually traveling musician, sharing his time between North America and Europe, performing/recording as a soloist and in collaboration with many other individuals and groups, as well as leading large ensemble improvisation workshops. His music is diverse, approaching each album and concert uniquely, often resulting in dramatically new and different outcomes. Not long after birth, Thollem began studying keyboard repertoire from the medieval to the twentieth century. After graduating with degrees in both piano performance and composition, he dedicated his time to grassroots political movements and ecological restoration projects, eventually returning his full focus to music. He has performed piano concertos with symphony orchestras, played in West African drumming troupes, Javanese gamelan ensembles, punk bands, free improvisation groups, and as a "comproviser" for modern dance and film. He is the founding director of Estamos Ensemble, a Mexican-American cross-border ensemble for musical exchange. http://www.thollem.com

I AM WRITING NOW in Ponta Delgada, San Miguel, the Azores, Portugal, having begun this particular trek from the Baltimore/Washington International airport in the United States. Four horses pulling a carriage just passed beneath the hotel window, reminding me of how much everyday sounds, as well as the sounds of travel, have changed in a relatively brief span of time.

Yesterday morning I awoke to the sounds of geese flying above me, crickets below and an airplane far above faintly cruising by. As I made my way to the airport, the sounds of planes increased in intensity and occurrence and transformed into the sounds of aircraft landing and taking off. Knowing that soon I would be hearing primarily Portuguese of which I speak and understand very little, in the terminal I began listening to people speaking in English as if it were a foreign language. The words lost their literal

89

meanings and the sounds morphed into tonal inflections and rhythms. Eventually, I became one of the passengers, hearing the plane much differently from the inside than out, the engines roared as the plane began to roll. Then there was a sudden jolt as the engines increased. All of this is muted, in comparison to anyone standing on the tarmac.

Once in the air, the engines were a constant hum, a musical ground of our travel soundtrack to diverse sonic locations, far above the migrating geese. I meditated on the engines that were now being heard by people far and wide, a sonic connection from 35,000 feet to the ground below. Many, no doubt, blocking the sound out habitually, others being startled awake and perhaps some listening to us intentionally, actively, deeply.

§§§

This is the most interesting time to travel as a musician. More and more people around the planet are meeting in egalitarian and open-minded musical settings. The spirit of both free improvisation and Deep Listening have expanded the possibilities for musical interaction world-wide, allowing musicians to transcend each other's respective cultures and meet equally in a sonic world created together in the moment.

Although I have not undertaken formal training for certification in Deep Listening, it has been a great influence on me. I see Deep Listening as a way of life, an artistic practice and a meditation on waking up to the world at large, with or without a traditional musical instrument. This is an activity in which I consciously participate: focusing on the stimulation my ears transmit to my brain and that my mind perceives as a sonic experience. It is a process that is evolving within myself throughout my life as I develop myself through this practice, sometimes in culturally profound ways, sometimes evoking spiritual or mystical experiences and sometimes in ways that are simply free spirited and playful.

While amazing technologies for communicating, recording and collaborating now expand our reach across continents intellectually, these tools can never replace the physicality of traveling across and through socio-political and cultural borders. As a musician who travels perpetually, I find that the experience of being in physical motion encourages my mind to stay in motion as well. I'm exposed to unique sounds in diverse environments that continually inform the way I hear and interact. I experience the unknown sometimes around every corner, encouraging me to keep extra aware of my surroundings and therefore putting me into a continual state of non-habit. I feel the direct connection of the flow of my body through space with the flow of ideas through my mind as new experiences are constantly stimulating new ideas.

Perpetual travel enlightens both the traveler as well as those with whom they come into contact. I believe that traveling musicians/artists/ creative and free thinkers are necessary as non-governmental cultural ambassadors, because they represent their communities and countries and fill an important role as artist liaisons in the relations between diverse peoples. As a musician, I have the ability to participate in the immediate living culture of every place I visit, especially through my workshops. Traveling as a musician is an endlessly rich and authentic way to experience living cultures.

When I teach active listening, I always begin by asking the participants to close their ears as well as their eyes and to focus on the private concert inside themselves where they are simultaneously both solo performer and sole audience member. After this, I perform a brief private concert with each person by making a sound directly next to their ears that is quiet enough so that nobody else in the room is able to hear. The next step is listening to the sounds that are generated in the room, in the building or, if conducted outside, in closest proximity. Following this, I open the doors to the outside world. The goal is to hear everything in a fresh way that is otherwise normally taken for granted. I call my workshops active listening workshops in respect to the fact that I have not participated in the three-year Deep Listening certification program, though I always reference Deep Listening as my foremost influence.

During a workshop in Palermo, Italy I opened the doors just as a procession of a fifty-piece brass band passed less than a hundred meters from our door. During *Venerdi Santo* (Good Friday), there are processions throughout Palermo and in many cities and towns in the south of Italy, all with big brass bands playing behind large crowds of people walking solemnly through the streets. Many are helping to carry statues of the fallen Jesus and weeping Mary. It is the day that all individuals believe they have a direct communication with Mary and can both ask her for their needs in the coming year as well as curse her for not fulfilling their needs the previous year. To me, as an outsider, it seemed like total chaos in many ways, but clearly with a very strong underlying order that had existed for hundreds of years. At times I could hear more than one brass band from different directions bouncing off the old walls. I could feel the reverberations of those walls from all the years of these dirges intermingling throughout generations. It was some of the most dramatic and gut-wrenching music I've ever experienced. On that day, opening the doors from listening so intently to themselves and then to the room, the participants received an injection of Deep Listening. Even though I had heard recordings of this music, there was no way they could prepare me for the sonic hallucination that enveloped us.

Since this occurred in the beginning of the three days together, the experience definitely influenced the way I facilitated the rest of the workshop. It was an affirmation for keeping my workshops flexible improvisations that are based on the participants' needs/interests and the cultural context in which the workshops take place.

This particular event was sponsored by an anti-Mafia group and they had asked Jacopo Andreini and me to conduct this workshop with an emphasis on anti-war and social justice issues. We were on a three-week tour of Italy with our political band Tsigoti, with the tour itself sponsored by anti-Mafia organizations.

It quickly became apparent that to participate in an improvisation with others about war and injustices and crimes associated with war is very difficult, especially since not one person present had actually been in a war. Everyone agreed that we didn't want to rely on how war is depicted by others, especially in movies and the news. So, we decided to focus primarily on sounds that we conjectured would exist in the varieties of environments in which war exists. This began a process of listening to what we imagined these sounds would sound like. After a lot of trial and error, we then decided to concentrate on sounds that did not create a melodramatic effect as none of us wanted to belittle the suffering of others. For the most part we concentrated on what sounds we believed would describe the moments after and before heavy fighting: the airplane sound decaying in the distance, rubble falling, debris crackling underfoot, refugee sounds of walking, running, swimming, boating, faint calls in the distance then another oncoming plane and preparing again for fighting or bombardment. We all traveled in our minds through this workshop, to imagine sounds in a different part of the world, completely aware that we were not presently in a war zone, but that it is possible that someday we may be.

Improvisation is a means to express and practice Deep Listening spontaneously in the moment, with or without other people, both in response to sounds generated inside and outside our bodies and by redirecting sounds that are again generated both inside and outside our bodies. I believe improvisation is a necessary practice to fully realize the potential of Deep Listening. Improvisation is a real-time activity responding immediately to the sounds in the environment whether or not man-made. It is a practice of hyper-awareness of subtle and not-so-subtle sounds and their significance in the overall context of the moment, one's overall life, and the span since the inception of the universe.

I performed a solo piano concert in Palermo the night following *Venerdi Santo* and found myself repeatedly being automatically and very naturally influenced by the music and overall mood of the previous day. I played much more melodically than I normally do, and it was a somber and dark performance. Reflecting what I had experienced on *Venerdi Santo* was not my intention. However, I did not get in the way of what was naturally coming out of me in response. When I finished, I could sense that I connected deeply with the listeners. Many told me later that they had the impression of listening to their culture through the ears of an outside observer. They appreciated the way in which I communicated my experience of their deep culture back to them.

Friends often ask me to describe people and musicians in this country or that. I find that artists are more similar to artists in different countries than they are to people living on their same street. The activities that individuals are involved in shape their character equally as do the customs and languages of their respective countries. Though improvisation is rapidly becoming a global phenomenon, and truly, a universal communication device, it has fortunately not been codified overall. Free improvisation is a process, not an end result, and every individual and each community form their own approach based on their personal life experiences and cultural context. Though improvising music communities in different countries may share many things in common with others, they still have their own cultural musical expression that is unique to them and much of this I believe is based on their respective verbal language.

I am fascinated by the phrasing and dynamics of people's speech in different cultures. In my travels, I generally understand what someone is trying to communicate, given the specific context and the cultural framework even when I have no idea of the "meaning" of the specific words or grammar.

On my first morning waking up in Thessaloniki, Greece, I heard what I thought was perhaps a political demonstration of some sort. From a distance, the sound of a megaphone amplified the yelling of a man who was getting closer. I didn't speak or understand Greek at the time so had no idea of what was being said nor did I have any context since I couldn't see the source of this sound. Finally, a small pick-up truck came around the corner, driven by a man calling for people's recycling materials. Not long after this I heard a call from another megaphone that was coming from a family in a pick-up truck selling fruit. Another followed who was offering his services sharpening knives door-to-door. Over several days, I was able to differentiate these calls, not because I learned the literal meaning of the individual words or phrases, but because I was able to decipher the sounds of the words and phrases themselves.

When I am immersed in a language other than English, I have the fortune of listening to it completely differently than a native speaker of that language, without the meaning of the words getting in the way of the sounds. Sometimes it can lead to funny moments. For a time, there is very little or no specific significance of the meaning of the words being spoken and often no immediate need. I will begin to understand the inflection of the voices before grasping aspects of the vocabulary or grammar. It is much easier to abstract the sounds I am hearing and disassociate myself from any need for specific verbal significance. After a while, I notice that I can decipher individual words and that I hear some words repeated regularly. Over time I begin to sense more nuance as to a speaker's mood through the inflections of their voice. As I speak some words or phrases of a new language, my ears are as equally hard at work as my tongue, matching the sounds coming out of my mouth to those of the native speakers.

Marcel Proust observed that the real voyage of discovery consists not in seeking new landscapes but in having new eyes. Consequently, I have often begun to see a familiar place in a fresh way when seeing it through someone else's eyes. I brought Tsigoti to the United States for a cross-country tour in 2010. I don't know how many times I have driven across the continent. This was the first time I have brought folks from another continent and introduced them to the entire span. Since that tour, I have driven again several times each way and now see it completely differently than ever before, as my outsider band mates informed my perspective of the continent on which I was born.

Taking the lead from Proust, the real voyage of listening deeply is not in listening to new music but in developing new ears. I have been thinking for awhile to give listening walks in parts of the world in which I am a stranger. Since I have a completely different association with the sounds than the locals, I can help redirect people's ears in ways they may have otherwise never listened before.

I am in Lisbon now and I have been walking around Jardim da Estrela. I can see practically all the sounds I hear. Because I have functioning ears on both sides of my head, I can clearly hear specific direction and distance of where these sounds are coming from. I turn my head and point my eyes at the source of their sound: children playing in the playground, mothers laughing, a gardener raking, ducks swimming and the breeze through the leaves of the trees. There are airplanes taking off over the city today and are omnipresent in the air as they pass, filling the entire sky with their sound, often completely masking all other sounds.

THOLLEM MCDONAS

Most often the sounds of an airplane, an entirely modern phenomenon, are an annoyance at best. The sounds themselves and the way they interact with the environment are fascinating, however, and drastically unusual given their dynamic range, frequency, duration, and variety of effects based on distance and where the plane is in its respective process: taking off, cruising, or landing. Today, I find myself meditating on the sounds of the airplanes themselves, the ways in which these sounds interact with the pre-modern sounds and the final decay of each individual plane's sonic presence. The decay of a plane's sound as it disappears into the horizon is one of my favorite aural experiences. Paying attention to the point the plane disappears from sonic view connects my mind across the sky, expanding my mind into that sky to be penetrated once again by the following airplane. There exists the sounds of travel themselves, as well as the variety of sounds in all locations on, in and above this planet: migrating birds, horses and carriages, rocket ships, trains, buses, cars, airplanes, sailboats, rowboats, steamboats, bicycles, skateboards, rollerskates, wheelchairs, pogo sticks, stilts, feet and slugs.

I believe it is necessary as an artist, as well as a person, to challenge myself continually and traveling is the most effective way for me to do so. Interacting with new musical communities continually pushes me to explore new possibilities by responding to the individual musicians and environmental/social stimuli. This focused way of living is an important aspect to my practice of being a musician and a more complete human being. With Deep Listening at the core of my approach to traveling and improvisation, I am able to more fully develop the response to my experiences for myself as well as for those with whom I come into contact.

Listening From The Inside Out: Pauline Oliveros and Deep Listening

DANA REASON is a Canadian-born pianist, composer, improviser and musicologist. She has recorded over eleven CDs and has toured extensively throughout the United States and Canada. She holds a BM from McGill University; MA in composition from Mills College (where she studied with Pauline Oliveros and Alvin Curran); and a PhD in critical studies/experimental practices from the University of California, San Diego (where her teachers included George E. Lewis, Aleck Karis and Anthony Davis). Reason is currently the founder and artistic director of "Between the Cracks: A Forum for Music, Arts, Science and Ideas" (2008- present). She regularly performs as both a soloist, with her trio (featuring Glen Moore on bass and Peter Valsamis on drums) and with the Sonic Possibilities Ensemble (dedicated to new and improvised works). Reason is currently the Director of Popular Music Studies at Oregon State University. http://www.danareason.com/

Dana Reason

In the utter silence
Of a temple,
A cicada's voice alone
Penetrates the rocks.[1]

PAULINE OLIVEROS is a pioneering American composer admired and respected for her development of Deep Listening, a compositional and improvisatory practice and body of work that encourages performers, participants and audiences to connect to community through individualized free-choice practices. The practices of Deep Listening serve as an aural and sonic, rather than cultural and historical, ethnography of sounding and listening in the twenty-first century. Oliveros' music questions, provokes and awakens passive forms of listening and

---

1   Matsuo Basho, *The Narrow Road to the Deep North and Other Travel Sketches*, trans. Nobouki Yuasa (New York: Penguin Classics, 1966), 123.

97

sounding, which reverberate through the examination of community-music practices, and contemporary music-cultures.

Bang on a Can

As a freshman in college, I took trip to New York City, stumbling across Bang on a Can: a twelve-hour festival dedicated to new music. The music centered on new developments in twentieth century classical music.

I found my way to the non-traditional concert space (a building with a poster saying go to the 8th floor for the festival). I was shocked that the elevator opened right into the concert space because you had no time to acclimate to the environment. All you saw were chairs and a space for the performers. Bernard Holland's *The New York Times* review describes the festival: "The space was an eighth-floor loft fitted out with folding chairs. The elevators opened directly onto the performing space and overhead fans hummed away, but no one seemed to care."[2] Also present was composer Pauline Oliveros, a colleague of Steve Reich's (who, in 1961, was a graduate student at Mills College at the same time Oliveros was involved with the San Francisco Tape Center).

At Bang on a Can Oliveros facilitated the performance of her composition *Tuning Meditation* (1971), a radical and courageous departure in twentieth century performance practice whereby she privileges audience participation over professional musicianship. When Oliveros took the floor at the festival, the audience shifted from traditional roles of receiving the musical experience to the responsibility of creating the musical space with the composer. The work provides specific textual instructions for the performer(s). Below is a similar version of the piece called, "The World Wide Tuning Meditation" from 2007:

---

2   Bernard Holland, "Music: The Bang On A Can Festival," *The New York Times*, May 14, 1987, accessed April 19, 2011, http://www.nytimes.com/1987/05/14/arts/music-the-bang-on-a-can-festival.html?scp=3&sq=bang%20on%20a%20can&st=cse.

The World Wide Tuning Meditation (2007)[3]

Begin by taking a deep breath and letting it all the way out with air sound.

Listen with your mind's ear for a tone.

On the next breath using any vowel sound, sing the tone that you have silently perceived on one comfortable breath.

Listen to the whole field of sound the group is making.

Select a voice distant from you and tune as exactly as possible to the tone you are hearing from that voice.

Listen again to the whole field of sound the group is making. Contribute by singing a new tone that no one else is singing.

Continue by listening then singing a tone of your own or tuning to the tone of another voice alternately.[4]

At the 1987 performance, Oliveros instructed the audience and initiated the first sound. At first, the audience was tentative; holding back when producing a pitch (what sounded was timid, quiet and a series of unsure crackly voices). Oliveros' sound, however, was present and encouraging, and thus, more people braved the silence (partly because this was a New York contemporary music audience) to sound their

---

3 Pauline Oliveros, private email correspondence with author, June 20, 2011.
4 Pauline Oliveros, *Tuning Meditation* (Deep Listening Publications, 2007). Oliveros also provided additional instructions for this score which I have included here:

Commentary:

Always keep the same tone for any single breath. Change to a new tone on another breath.
Listen for distant partners for tuning
Sound your new tone so that it may be heard distantly.

Communicate with as many difference voices as possible.

Sing warmly!

Pauline Oliveros

own voice, which slowly amassed into a large sound texture that was astonishingly beautiful.

The experience was electrifying and different from anything I had ever encountered or participated in. Oliveros' music resembled a thick chord that at times moved quite unexpectedly; sometimes the textures would thin out or be quite barren. The sound floated around in waves, similar to inhaling then exhaling. *Tuning Meditation* was completely different from the previous works in the program—a series of compositions that celebrated standards of technical agility and virtuosic excellence championed by new music composers, performers and patrons. Oliveros essentially provided guided instructions whereby people had the freedom to discover what "sounded-in-them."

This was not just an expression of "sounds-within," but an opportunity to sound as a collective, too. Each person was at once acutely aware of their "individuality" (every time a sound or response was initiated by an individual, it seemed to them as if a huge fortissimo sounded, even if the dynamic range was small or soft) and yet there was a comfortable space created in that another person was there to "catch" your sound. You knew you were part of a transformative sonic community and that your individual voice mattered in the collective. Similarly, this work, by the very nature of its compositional structure, eliminated attitudes of having to demonstrate clever or wry and musical or virtuosic elements. It was human just to be able to sound or to remain silent. Period.

Oliveros unveiled to the audience a conception of the potentiality imbedded in composition—a potentiality that left open individual details, yet to be colored by the particular participants themselves, but that framed the sonic canvas in such a way that the experience was new, the sound refreshing and an inclusive environment formed. Essentially, all forms of musical or theoretical knowledge were suspended. This was innovative music, and compositionally different than the music of John Cage, Karlheinz Stockhausen, Iannis Xenakis, or Pierre Boulez in both how musicians performed and audiences received these works.

At the festival, iconoclastic composer John Cage walked about. Many composers toiled with Cage's provocative ideas around silence and noise. Ideas that were considered as radical as the twelve-tone theories his teacher, Arnold Schoenberg, had touted earlier in the twentieth century.

Cage's philosophy on music and sound created a resonant pathway for several generations of composers, including Oliveros, to rethink how and what constituted music and sound as well as the possible methodology used to execute creativity.[5] For Cage "the function of music is to change the mind so that it does become open to experience, which inevitably is interesting."[6] However, Cage was less interested in the function of music being used to communicate something in particular like an emotional or psychological state, whereas Oliveros creates music as a way to mediate the inner sounding space of an individual with the outer world of technology, aurality and humanity. For Oliveros, "sound impacts [her] body and resonates within."[7] The resonance creates a dialogue through which a narrative is spoken or activated. It is not just an isolated or intellectual happening but rather an embodied, visceral and collective experience. The articulation of the experience completes the compositional process.

Many of Oliveros' Deep Listening compositions have a feedback portion written into the compositional instruction and process itself. Essentially, she creates a context for a participant to make experiences with sound, then invites them to talk about what the event perhaps triggered for the individual. Take for example the piece *Sounds from Childhood*. The instructions are as follows:

---

5 Pauline Oliveros, *Sounding the Margins: Collected Writings 1992-2009* (Kingston, NY: Deep Listening Publications, 2010), 228–245. At the time, I was attending the University of Florida as a piano performance major on the "classical concert music track." Oliveros discusses the element of people being on the right "track" in her article "My American Music" published in *American Music* 25, no. 4 (Winter 2007). She uses the analogy of a train track and if we are put on a track, it essentially limits the ability to pursue other areas that we may not know of or about which we are curious.

6 Richard Taruskin, *Music in the Late Twentieth Century. The Oxford History of Western Music* (Oxford: Oxford University Press, 2010), 61.

7 Oliveros, *Sounding the Margins*, 23.

Can you imagine a time in your childhood when you loved to make mouth noises?

Can you imagine freely making those sounds now?

In the next five or more minutes, make as may of those sounds as you want in spaces you hear and claim as your own.[8]

Immediately upon reading the instructions, it is plausible that a rush of images and sound sources spring to the fore. The questions begin and so does the narrative: What sound should I start first? Did I ever make sounds with my mouth as a child? How do I feel about those sounds? Perhaps you are around young children and can easily recall the kind of sounds they like to make with their mouths. Now, does the reflection on the childhood sounds stir feelings about the experience of making those sounds in the past? If you are skeptical, consider experiencing this sonic meditation for yourself, right now.

The case could be argued that a participants' experience is an inherently important aspect of the work, thus lending unique accounts and a compositional environment where similarities and differences can be expressed and valued. This element of reflection is important because it enables the participants to recognize that a variety of perceptions and understanding as to the success and outcome of the piece are unique for each individual.

Oliveros was certainly aware of Cage's legacy and innovation as a composer, but she took his philosophy of sound and silence in another direction, one that involved community access and participation.

Certainly, composers throughout the twentieth century have fluctuated in their philosophy and politics towards audience reception. Pauline Oliveros holds a particularly interesting position regarding audience participation and receptivity because she creates accessible and playable music that often requires no formal musical training. Oftentimes, one need only be able to read instructions. Oliveros remarks that "musicians accustomed to reading notes and rhythms are often shocked by the bareness of the notation compared to familiar conventional scores,

---

8 Ibid., 31.

which direct their attention to predictable, repeatable, specific pitches and rhythms."[9]

However, the music that results from her directions may surprise a participant unfamiliar with contemporary art-music vernacular, techniques or sonorities especially when "participants take a share in creating the work rather than limit themselves to merely interpreting pitches and rhythms. . . These forms and guidelines, when appropriately applied, give the participants a creative opportunity to compose and perform simultaneously and to expand their musicianship."[10]

The paradox is that the participant need not be sophisticated in music reading or performance but the resultant sound is non-populist and requires an acceptance or understanding of contemporary extended techniques, microtones and open form practices and the resultant sound. Here is an example of her work from 1992 called *Sound Fishes*, which Oliveros performed with an ensemble at Mills College.

Sound Fishes (1992)
   for an orchestra of any instruments.

Considerations

Listening is the basis of sound fishing.
Listening for what has not yet sounded—like a fisherman waiting for a nibble or a bite.
Pull the sound out of the air like a fisherman catching a fish, sensing its size and energy—when you hear the sound, play it.
Move to another location if there are no nibbles or bites.
There are sounds in the air like sounds in the water.
When the water is clear you might see the fish.
When the air is clear, you might hear the sounds.
- November 1992[11]
Fairbanks, Alaska

---

9 Oliveros, *Sounding the Margins*, 4.

10 Ibid., 4–5.

11 Pauline Oliveros, *Deep Listening: A Composer's Sound Practice* (New York: iUniverse, 2005), 50.. Sound Fishes is available on: Pauline Oliveros, *Pauline Oliveros and the University of Michigan Digital Music Ensemble*, directed by Stephen Rush. Deep Listening DL-DVD-3, 2010, DVD.

Oliveros creates stillness and a visual picture from which to start sounding. She uses instructions "to start an attentional process within a participant and among a group which can deepen gradually with repeated experience."[12] You imagine yourself fishing, the water source, perhaps a sunny day, and the quiet.

In many respects, this works like haiku by Matsuo Basho through which the performer is attuned to the potentiality of sounds. In the case of Basho, there are different levels of reading his poems: a surface or descriptive quality, as well as a symbolic quality. Basho refers to the symbolic quality as *sabi*, which is the color of the poem. In many respects, reading and performing one of Oliveros' instructional pieces evokes similar symbolic and embodied responses, much like a Basho poem:

> Silent a while in a cave,
> I watched a waterfall,
> For the first of
> The summer observances.[13]

In both Basho and Oliveros, the reader is transported to the imagined place to experience the qualities of the poem or sound piece. There is a physicality that takes place in both works. However, if you are new to the experience of being a participant in the creation of non-conventional sound sources and experiences (i.e. you are not playing or singing a familiar tune or song), then the title of *Sound Fishes* and the images that reading through the directional score may initially generate may seem like a paradox when compared to the sounds you hear and subsequently respond to.

So what, if anything, does *Sound Fishes* create that seems different to our cultured perception of music, sound and listening? Pieces like *Sound Fishes* and many others that Oliveros has created frame naturally occurring sonic episodes (environmental, musical, technological) and revitalize them through the lens of human interaction, initiation and freedom. Thus by structuring seemingly random sonic arrangements

---

12 Oliveros, *Sounding the Margins*, 5
13 Basho, *The Narrow Road*, 101.

and formations from the "environment" we as both participants and audiences are able to actively appreciate and engage with the sounds in a personalized and communal sound-space. Oliveros' definition of "music" is naturally expanded because she directs our attention to the act of listening as well as hearing: "listening is processing what we hear, for meaning, understanding, and direction or action."[14]

Instead of the barking dog next door annoying us, we might listen to how the dog interacts and sounds (or communicates) with its sonic environment. With a new perspective or reinvestigation of sound, pieces like *Sound Fishes* not only revitalize our expectations and assumptions of how the piece ought to sound, we open ourselves up to experiencing more of the joy of various sound sources, frequencies and environmental and human sound.

The music of Oliveros can be relatively simple to perform, but the resultant sound serves as gentle auditory disruptors to conditioned listening or atrophied listening practices. Once we move beyond surprise or perceptual limitations, our heightened attention and awareness is freed to perceive the sounds in a new and refreshing way. In this way we become liberated from the constraints of previous musical experiences, histories and attitudes. The work of Oliveros is an invitation to listen differently, and in a way, ahistorically. Our expectations of linearity or a guided narrative as historically predetermined by our past listening experiences must be relinquished and instead our goal should be to experience the freshness of what the sounds trigger in us, whether representational (grounded in a musical narrative of sorts), or non-representational, like those moments found in abstract art or modernism.

Oliveros' own performances and research incorporate the use of microtonality and electronic music into her compositional palette. She plays around with the overtone series and non-Western tuning systems, using her knowledge of looping, splicing, and non-linear forms of music composition to shift our attention away from conditioned music materials such as melody, harmony and rhythm. She prefers "organic rhythms

---

14 Oliveros, *Sounding the Margins*, 28.

rather than exclusively metrical rhythms. I prefer full-spectrum sound rather than a limited scalar system."[15]

The combination of these performance techniques and compositional strategies serve as auditory disruptors which trigger the audience to remain alert throughout the performance experience while she provides the navigation for new listening experiences.

Compose-Her

Oliveros describes her process and Deep Listening "as part of a personal, and now communal, quest for peace."[16] Oliveros' quest for community and peace are an integral part of how she conducts her musical career, choosing to place the audience as a central component of the creative work. Here the audience is not necessarily separate from the performance process but a blurring of the two often occurs, whereby the participants are often central to her work. This is especially the case with her workshops and seminar/performances involving Deep Listening in that the participants spend time both actively listening as well as performing.

Oliveros' works challenge the ideology that new music (performance) is only for a small group of highly trained musicians. Her seminal Deep Listening work enables the abilities for both musician and non-musician to create a sonic work together, and as community in which all levels of ability are respected and encouraged. This is a remarkably divergent approach to more hierarchical structures in music based on ability, training and talent, or the polarity between insider/outsider common throughout formal and codified applications of music-culture. This group experience embraces a definition of music that ethnomusicologist Bonnie Wade argues:

> Is not only a thing—a category of organized sound, or compositions—but also a process. Every known group of people

---

15 Oliveros, *Sounding the Margins*, 4.

16 Pauline Oliveros, "My 'American Music:' Soundscape, Politics, Technology, Community," *American Music* 25, no. 4 (Winter 2007): 401 (available also in Oliveros, *Sounding the Margins*, 228).

in the world exercises their creative imaginations to organize sound in some way that is different from the way they organize sound for speech.[17]

Oliveros uses her knowledge of historical music practices to form new ensemble experiences that are inclusive, while at the same time pushing the boundaries of innovation and exploration in the world of sound and listening practices. Oliveros' musical practice problematizes the insider/outside paradigm in the field of new music by developing participatory and community music practices.

Oliveros' public performances demonstrate how to sound and listen, and embody attitudes, states, philosophies and understanding through the vibration of sound and intention. The very act of reading through one of Oliveros' Deep Listening exercises shifts the mind/body dialectic. For example, read through an excerpt of Oliveros' composition *"Earth" Sensing/Listening/Sounding* (1992):

> Can you imagine allowing yourself to express the sound of your breath as you continue your global listening and deeper breathing?"[18]

The reader shifts from thinking about making a sound to internalizing ideas about making a sound. Examining the instructions, it is evident that Oliveros wants the participant to make a shift or take a leap. Oliver Sacks reminds us in *Musicophilia: Tales of Music and the Brain*:

> [C]onducting a mental practice [of a musical event] seems to be sufficient to promote the modulation of neural circuits involved in the early stage of motor skill learning. . . and to this end "expectation and suggestion can greatly enhance musical imagery, even producing a quasi-perceptual experience.[19]

Oliveros is clearly aware that her pieces trigger changes in attention or awareness. The paradigm for musical analysis and meaning shifts under

---

17 Bonnie Wade, *Thinking Musically: Experiencing Music, Expressing Culture* (Oxford: Oxford University Press, 2003), 6.

18 Oliveros, *Deep Listening*, 32.

19 Oliver Sacks, *Musicophilia* (New York: Vintage Books, 2008), 35.

the creative framework of Oliveros. Historians will need to include new frameworks and analysis in order to examine the meta impact and significance of Deep Listening as a composition and performance tool and art form.

Hearing Nature in Technology

Oliveros regularly remarks upon her early childhood in Texas and the soundscapes that are etched in her aural history. Growing up in the 1930s, Oliveros' deep love and appreciation for sound in the environment is captured here:

> In those days [referring to her childhood] what you could hear in terms of the natural world was just amazing: very, very dense sound that varied according to the time of day or night.[20]

She often refers to the frogs and the cicadas in her writings or brings a conch shell to a live performance and holds it to her ear. In a recent article she mentions how, with the changing environment, the "once seventeen-year cicadas cannot emerge from their underground gestation through cement and asphalt."[21] Oliveros is keenly aware that our environment sounds different than it did in the 1930s. Oliveros' active engagement with the natural world started when she was a small child, and yet, she has maintained and developed her commitment to "hearing and listening" through her own music by creating opportunities for audiences and participants to develop a discipline for listening.

Her awareness of environmental soundscapes, both rural and urban, are profoundly intertwined in her work both as an acoustic performer and electronic composer and musician. She is comfortable at the intersection between the technological space as well as the acoustic and natural environment. She uses her body and her just tuned accordion and various technologies (both electronic and human) to mediate the sounds and to humanize technology in such a way as they recall the ambience and locality of place. Oliveros' understanding and acceptance

20 Oliveros, "My 'American Music,'" 390.
21 Ibid., 391.

of sound(s) are transmitted to the audience as part of her Deep Listening practice. To watch Oliveros perform is to witness the profundity of listening deeply. Deep Listening speaks to our humanity and the connections we have to ourselves, others and our environments.

In the twenty-first century, as people become more and more technologically reliant, Oliveros' work serves as a reminder of our sense of audibility and perhaps a biological need to listen deeply to our own ethnographical heritage.

Her practice of Deep Listening provokes the practitioner and audience to revisit inherited listening patterns, the evolution of hearing based on survival and evolution. Is there a biological need to be able to listen attentively and carefully that escapes twenty-first century living practices? The fact that Oliveros has developed a repertoire that actively engages the ears and listening qualities in humans is a remarkable accomplishment and serves as a way to preserve the geographical nature and anthropology of listening.

Several composers have written about the nature of sound and ecology. Many Canadian composers have developed research in this field of composition, perhaps because the vast open spaces and the limited human population make one acutely aware of the power of nature and sound. In his book *The Tuning of the World*, Canadian composer R. Murray Schafer remarks, "The blurring of the edges between music and environmental sounds may eventually prove to be the most striking feature of all twentieth-century music."[22] This blurring is not only in the materials selected, including environmental sounds, technology and traditional instruments, but ideologies regarding choices and uses of sound.

Composer John Cage (1912–1992) proposed that "sounds be liberated, and essentially left alone, without the ego of the performer or composer."[23] Oliveros, however, encourages an embodied and visceral engagement with both sound and listening. She liberates them from

---

22 R. Murray Schafer, *The Tuning of the World* (New York: Alfred A Knopf, 1977), 111.

23 Taruskin, *Music in the Late Twentieth Century*, 64.

isolation, acknowledging that they are not just empty signifiers but places from which stories are told and narratives shared. The responses to the sounds are alive and in the moment, attached to the human receiving or making them in every possible way.

Oliveros wants us to hear the sounds as though you could look at them, hold them in your hand, or turn them inside out. Her Deep Listening pieces require you to become intimate and comfortable with your ability to create meaningful and moving sounds while responding to sonic landscapes.

Oliveros redefines and rearticulates the role of the composer in society by placing the responsibility and freedom to experience and organize sound that is personalized by the performer or participant. With the use of instructional scores and group experience as one of the central aspects of organizing her music, Oliveros is able to transcend many of the limitations a purely notated score would create. It is through a sense of community that the work emerges and comes alive.

Sonic Meditations and subsequently, Deep Listening, have served as a composer's ethnography and laboratory through which Oliveros has studied how groups of people process, act upon and are affected by listening and hearing, attention and awareness, through both group and individual activities. This is different than an ensemble of trained musicians learning a score (following a set of notations) and then "sharing" the experience as an ensemble. In many respects, the open-ended set of instructions that Oliveros presents to the participant encourages the individual to interpret not necessarily Oliveros' conception of the instructions but the participant's unique understanding of them. There are many levels of interaction that could occur. For example:

1. People interpreting the directions the way they understand them;
2. People responding to other people's interpretations of the directions;
3. People responding to the sound impulses and content and adjusting to those aspects within the confines of the specific directions.

The space is dynamic and communal. The level of musical experiences varies. What is unique here is that the individual is always asked about himself or herself directly or indirectly. Oliveros speaks about "not instilling [creativity]—[as] that would not be free. It's not about "design-ing" creativity —I don't think that energy can be designed. I believe that facilitating a listening, caring and sharing environment is an invitation to creative work."[24] It is not only the act of participating that shifts the individual in the community, but that a community-driven ensemble is what generates creative action and responses.

Oliveros conducted a variety of Deep Listening pieces at the Sound Symposium in Newfoundland, Canada, in the 1990s, in which I was able to participate. One of the group activities was to sing or say your name the way you might like to hear it said back to you. The group was large. Perhaps fifty or more of us. The group was instructed to lie down in a big circle with our heads pointed to the center and our feet pointing outward. Already, that was something new.

Next we were instructed to sing our name out loud to the group and the group would sing it back. It was a curious feeling to hear forty-nine other people (that you have never met) sing your name. The response seemed to carry more meaning than just uttering your name, but it seemed to suggest an emotional message, one that translates to some-thing like: "You spoke and we were here to listen; you spoke and were heard." The musicality came in the form of uttering back people's names, one after the other. Everyone was present. In this way, the work was generative: dialogues were started because sound was made. Yes, this was a workshop, but it was an honest performance too. The distinction between audience and performer blurred.

Future Listening

The first challenge for people new to the philosophy and compositional methodology of Oliveros is that of moving beyond the Western binaries that exist between music and noise; music and nature; professional and novice; student and teacher; composer and audience; composer and interpreter. The former binaries have been institutionally reified and reinscribed in music education and scholarship throughout the twenty-first century. Oliveros talks about not being interested in her music

---

24 Oliveros, *Deep Listening*, 57

being categorized and this is an important step if we move toward an organic understanding of sound and listening practices.[25]

It is my hope that Oliveros' Deep Listening works inspire individuals of all levels and abilities to adopt elements of Oliveros' Deep Listening strategies and methodologies in order to develop a "conscious aurality" which can be utilized in all aspects of musical expression. By examining various exercises and approaches that Oliveros pioneered, I believe her Deep Listening practice, ideology and philosophy can be implemented in a variety of musical practices to provide meaningful and enriching opportunities for understanding ourselves and our communities.

As a performer/composer/philosopher Oliveros brings an acute virtuosity to the hearing and listening experience. In many respects, when she performs, she teaches the audience how to listen and perhaps hear for the first time. Oliveros' music brings us closer toward sounding and listening from the inside out.

---

25 Pauline Oliveros, email correspondence with author, June 14, 2011.

In Too Deep, Listening

Renée T. Coulombe

RENÉE T. Coulombe, PhD, is an artist and musician of considerable breadth. Composer, improviser, media artist, DJ, producer and scholar, her works have taken her across the globe. She is a founding member of the genre-bending free funk ensemble *Erroneous Funk*, which performed at venues from the Viper Room to the Roy O. Disney Hall, as well as the digital installation collective *Adaptable Girl*. As scholar, she publishes widely on topics from feminism in punk and blues, post-colonialism in drum and bass, and the use of audio in paranormal media. She taught for ten years at the University of California, Riverside and founded the UCR Free Improvisation Ensemble that performed at festivals across Southern California. In 2010 she left the University to found her own media company *Banshee Media*, and production company, *Improvised Alchemy*. An accomplished upcycler of vintage clothing and accessories, her designs are available at Banshee's House of Make. http://www .reneetcoulombe.com .

Overture

WHILE I WAS WRITING THIS ESSAY there was a word-of-mouth event by a group I particularly enjoy at a new venue in the high desert (quite close to the border between Arizona and California). The organizers had scouted this very remote location because it was a deep, narrow canyon—the kind that becomes a river when sudden rain hits, and which has been carved over millions of years by this rain. The dance floor area was about thirty-five feet across, with twenty-foot canyon walls rising on either side that gently curved forty feet in front of the temple-like DJ booth (complete with flowers, offerings, LED candles, icons of Buddha, etc.). Most of us arrived at the canyon before the sound system because the first truck hauling it out broke down (not an uncommon occurrence at such events) so all was quiet in the desert for a while before the music started. People gathered in their

113

camps and chatted, caught up with each other, made new friends—some climbed up canyon walls to listen to the desert in solitude and commune with the night. When the system arrived and the music began, some three hundred yards from where many were socializing, a kind of electricity shot through camp. Immediately I could hear the care taken in the placement of the sound system, especially the sub-basement speakers, as the super-low frequencies seemed tuned to the sandy canyon floor, and traveled from the speakers through the sand to our feet, vibrating them inside our boots and shoes. My family, my tribe, "my herd" was listening to the subsonic frequencies, receiving the news that our celebration was beginning. A spontaneous cry erupted and we were drawn toward the dance floor. There the low-level uplighting on the canyon walls gave the impression of being in an ancient amphitheater—looking to one side and seeing millions of years of geologic history exposed by ancient waters, hearing the mathematics of the Minimal Techno multiplied and divided under the so-close-you-could-touch-them stars and the completely visible band of the Milky Way galaxy, brought me to a new sense of awe and wonder— one that skipped right over reality and joyfully embraced surreality. Just as this sense broke over my body like a wave someone dancing a few feet away from me threw her hands into the air and shouted at the stars "I am one with the absolute!" I smiled and thought, "yes, sister, in Lacanian terms you are certainly rocking the Real. . . now metrically modulate for me one more time, brother DJ. . ."

I remember the day I heard in a story on National Public Radio that new research had uncovered elephants' ability to communicate across great distances using "rumbles" or extremely low frequencies not perceivable within the human range of hearing. More fascinating still, they could hear these rumbles through specialized organs in their feet, finally explaining to biologists why whole herds would suddenly stop, lean forward on their toes, close their eyes and remain still for minutes at a time. This research has developed in recent years and determined that elephants can distinguish rumbles from friends and family apart from strangers. I have always felt a deep, personal connection to elephants: their matriarchal family structures, their intelligence and complex emotional lives, their foreknowledge and grieving of death. This news of even more complexity in their communications set my imagination buzzing; I desperately wanted to know what it would be like to hear through my feet, rumbles so low they would literally vibrate my whole world. . .[1] To me, this was powerful evidence of Deep Listening in the natural world, liberating it from one particular context and demonstrating its relevance far beyond the Deep Listening Institute, its community of participants, or even just those who know the term. It is also a model for me of the kind of Deep Listening I longed for: one which went far beyond my ears to listening with my whole body, a quiet mind, and my whole spirit. This is listening as if one's very life depends on it, and certainly in the elephants' case, it does.

Written almost a quarter-century after the formation of the Deep Listening Band, and just over a quarter-century after the founding of the Deep Listening Institute, this essay arises in a very different moment in Western cultural history. With so much value now placed on multi-tasking and multi-channeled communication rather than intense focus on any one sense or sensory input, one must wonder how Deep Listening as both a practice and a community of practitioners has adapted or evolved in the digital age. What does the practice of Deep Listening offer the contemporary digital citizen—and is it only one practice or a host of practices that might include theory and analysis, musicology, performance practices, etc.? Is it a simple antidote to visual weariness and the speeding up of culture, or something more? Marshall McLuhan once observed: "[i]n any cultural arrangement, trouble always occurs when only one sense is subjected to a barrage of energy and receives more stimulus than all the others. For modern Western man that would be the visual state."[2] While McLuhan's remark is profoundly prescient

---

1   There are many sources for further information on this topic. I recommend: Caitlin O'Connell-Rodwell, *The Elephant's Secret Sense: The Hidden Life of the Wild Herds of Africa* (Chicago: University of Chicago Press, 2007).

2   Marshall McLuhan, "Visual and Acoustic Space," in *Audio Culture: Readings in Modern Music,* ed. Christoph Cox and Daniel Warner (New York: Continuum, 2004), 69.

of the digital age, this positions Deep Listening as an even more radical act. Images and noise in the age of YouTube, smartphones and televisual advertising screens cropping up everywhere from supermarkets to gas pumps—and continuously competing for our split attention. This contrasts sharply with Deep Listening; to listen deeply we must deny the primacy of the visual, and give our whole selves over to the act of listening, listening into rather than to. Deep Listening is more than just actively listening: it powerfully engages memory in what Pauline Oliveros calls "memorial/associational" listening, as well as the imagination, in what she has termed "imaginal" listening. Both join the listener and the "listened" in a complete embodied practice.[3]

This essay will interrogate Deep Listening as an embodied practice in contemporary (digital) culture through the prism of a performative and communal practice in which Deep Listening functions powerfully at multiple levels, from the sonic to the social. It will examine Deep Listening's potential role in constituting "reality"—a self-referential term in culture that is, in Lacan's words, "a fantasy-construction which enables us to mask the Real of our desire."[4] That there are many unfamiliar with the Deep Listening Band, community, or Institute, and yet who practice deep listening reveals that as an embodied practice it neither conceptually nor theoretically belongs to a single community, or, as the elephant example above demonstrates, species. This has powerful implications for the importance of Deep Listening conceptually as a set of practices, as well as the possibility of theoretical discourse and analysis of cultural phenomena based on Deep Listening.

The embodied practice of Deep Listening chosen for this essay is the growing movement of small, word-of-mouth, remote desert events (what might have been called "raves" ten or twenty years ago) organized around listening and dancing to various forms of post-techno

---

3 Oliveros has developed these terms over years of addresses and Deep Listening workshops and retreats.

4 Jacques Lacan, Jacques-Alain Miller and Alan Sheridan, *The Four Fundamental Concepts of Psychoanalysis (The Seminar of Jacques Lacan, Book 11)* (New York: Norton and Company, 1981). Paraphrased in Žižek, *The Sublime Object of Ideology* (London: Verso, 1989), 45.

electronic dance music (or EDM). Attendance at these events is by invitation only—one must know someone who knows someone—not for elitist purposes, but to ensure that the participants are deep listeners and responders in the context of the events, and attuned to fellow attendees as well as the natural environment. The smallest of these gatherings might see fewer than fifty people, the largest can attract upwards of five hundred; nonetheless these events are not ticketed, and therefore not public. The "success" of these events depends on all participants being equally committed to the form and function of the gathering. All those who participate are expected to "act right" both in respecting the location, the performers and the spirit of the event. From the outset let me say that in this essay I will not address larger, public, and more widely known (notorious?) events and festivals like Burning Man, Lightning in a Bottle, Symbiosis, etc., as these events are quite rooted in the visual, and have been well-documented in previous studies.[5] While they may have formed early models for outdoor events like the ones I will be addressing here, their sheer size and public profile make them theoretically quite different. Part of my interest here is geographic; having lived in Southern California for two decades now, it is fascinating to me that the West Coast of North America is the global center for such events, which many believe indicate an emergent culture that will have an enormously transformative impact on the planet and her people. While there are such events occurring in Europe, Asia and many other

---

5   Burning Man is mentioned in Barbara Ehrenreich's *Dancing in the Streets: A History of Collective Joy* (New York: Metropolitan Books, 2006), 259. But Burning Man also forms the main subject matter of many books over the previous decade, including books by festival organizers, like Holly Kreuter (*Drama in the Desert: The Sights and Sounds of Burning Man* (San Francisco: Raised Barn Press, 2002) which features hundreds of images, with writings from festival founder Larry Harvey as well as many other staff members). There are a host of others, including those which examine Burning Man's role on the rest of culture, including the very recently published Steven T. Jones, *The Tribes of Burning Man: How an Experimental City in the Desert is Shaping the New American Counterculture* (San Francisco: Consortium of Collective Consciousness, 2011).

regions, the West Coast of North America remains dominant in this emergent phenomenon.[6]

As the smaller word-of-mouth events are not widely known, a brief description will prove useful as all aspects of this socio-musical practice become relevant to the analysis. In many California deserts from Anza Borrego to the Mohave (geography chosen because of my own location, but I am aware of many other regions in which similar events take place) small, loosely-coalesced underground organizations of producers, DJs and other volunteers organize events using various forms of social media including private Facebook pages, text blasts and email lists. They acquire (or have acquired) and deploy extremely sophisticated audio creation and amplifications systems (particularly Turbosound[7] or Funktion-One[8] systems) and organize DJ lineups to perform (usually for free) burgeoning EDM genres for anywhere from one to four days. Participants are expected to adhere to the social and environmental protocols of the organizers (usually loosely based on rave culture's PLUR: Peace, Love, Unity and Respect). Unlike traditional concerts or festivals, organizers have little to no interest in generating money and admission is by donation only—indeed at most events no one is turned away for lack of funds, and requested donations are often only enough to cover costs of production.

Removing the incentive of an accumulation of capital from these events helps to reinforce an equalized power dynamic—while the DJ performers do occupy a place of performer during their sets,

---

6   For an informal but reverent presentation on this emergent festival culture, and many great visual images, see "TEDxVancouver - Jeet Kei Leung - Transformational Festivals," accessed August 30, 2011, http://www.youtube.com/watch?v=Q8tDpQp6m0A.

7   For more information and system specifics see "Turbosound | Professional Loudspeaker Systems," accessed July 12, 2011, http://www.turbosound.com/.

8   More information and system specifics can be found at "FUNKTION-ONE: OFFICIAL WEBSITE," accessed July 12, 2011, http://www.funktion-one.com/.

all participants can occupy a similar place. DIY,[9] flowing into these events from Punk, Third Wave Feminism, Burning Man and modern Eco-warriors, rules supreme. Spontaneous performance art erupts everywhere at these gatherings—from accomplished fire performers (spinning flaming staffs, fans, hoops or poi), (hula) hoopers, and belly dancers—in the general area of the "dance floor" or what we sometimes call "downtown." Space is held for "sharemonies" and "prayer-formances"—linking the sacred back to the landscapes of its birth. Participants bring drums and other acoustic instruments to contribute to the sonic experience, and they often dress in fantastic and unique costumes they have constructed themselves. Artists create sculptures or other forms of visual art from the materials at hand—sometimes right in the center of the action with others dancing around them. Particularly at small events, every participant takes responsibility for the production and performance, and agrees to leave no trace behind on the landscape. Like a gathering of nomads, a small tent city arises overnight with occupants decorating themselves and their camps—creating social spaces as well as performative ones—and then disappear just as quickly without leaving behind evidence of their presence. We come together for one purpose: to listen and respond deeply, completely and bodily to the music, each other and the environment. This is nothing new—almost every culture throughout history has had some form of ecstatic social ritual to bring about altered states of consciousness through dancing, or chanting, fasting or ingesting medicinal plants to renew the tribe and its members. This is something Western culture lost a long time ago, so what surprises me is not that there is an emergent neo-tribalism using sophisticated sound to bring about altered states of consciousness and catharsis, but that more people aren't doing it.

Further, a central aspect of this analysis posits that many genres of techno and post-techno EDM are extensively mimetic: generating and cross-pollinating sonic *and* social memes—Dawkins term for "units of cultural transmission" that are self-replicating and move through

---

9 "Do It Yourself"

culture like genes through the gene pool.[10] Yet, to fully experience this aspect of the music and the culture that it transmits, one must practice embodied imaginal and memorial/associational listening. In this context, Deep Listening is not just practiced with the ears. The memes are multi-dimensional: rhythmic, timbral, melodic, historic, social and, more often than not, all of these at once. EDM, perhaps more than many other genres of music in Western culture, generates memes so rapidly that entire new subgenres (subspecies?) of the music appear on the scene with startling frequency. For the producers, performers and audiences of EDM, a cultural memory of music technology and the sounds of various synths and signal generators, extensive knowledge of EDM genres and examples, as well as a working knowledge of signal processing provide the very deepest levels of sonic and cultural "quilting"[11] of meaning for the performer/audience. This music is thick with sonic, musical and cultural layering; it rewards the deep listener with a banquet of cultural and musical memes with extensive powers of self-identification or imitation. EDM serves powerfully as a central cultural "meme bank," able to create and transmit dense sonic, historic, social and cultural information at such a rapid rate that nostalgia is literally sped up—coming quite close to the unique condition that Frederic Jameson calls "Nostalgia for the Present."[12]

Some of these events are organized around specific EDM genres, which lend somewhat different atmospheres and appeal to different populations, but many events combine multiple genres within sets and/or lineups and often feature disparate DJs known for specific genres. As the sonic practice of many post-techno musical genres is represented at these events, it would be impossible to analyze them all. I have chosen two for this essay, Minimal Techno and Dubstep. Both have emerged relatively recently as wildly popular EDM genres (though new subgenres of EDM seem to emerge and evolve every day), but their roots

---

10 Richard Dawkins, *The Selfish Gene* (Oxford: Oxford University Press, 1989).

11 See the "Rigid Designator and *object a*" subchapter in Žižek, *The Sublime Object of Ideology*, 95–97.

12 Frederic Jameson "Nostalgia for the Present," *South Atlantic Quarterly*, 88.2 (1989): 527.

go back to the early 1990s and beyond. While most post-techno EDM genres share structural elements, samples, rhythms, etc., these specific genres have been carefully chosen to yield insights into new approaches to musical structures and functions, as well as new ways to theorize performative and mimetic agency.[13] That is to say, they yield important insights if one is willing to listen deeply enough. To analyze these events according to Deep Listening practice is to engage the social and the sonic not as separate and distinct elements, but as mutually interdependent co-creative aspects of this cultural phenomenon. It posits that Deep Listening is not only the physical act of focused, imaginal or associational listening, but also the active negotiation between listener and the sound in the human attempt to constitute "reality." It posits further that everything from the genres of music being performed, the quality of sound production, the natural acoustics of the chosen desert locations, to the spirit in which those present gather to deeply listen and respond to one another represent forms of embodied Deep Listening practice with profound theoretical, cultural and spiritual implications. These implications are no by-product of the practice, but rather a central function of Deep Listening in contemporary culture.

To draw out such implications, and substantiate their discussion in the context of Deep Listening, the Lacanian "Orders" of psychoanalysis are particularly relevant here, especially the Real, the Imaginary and the Symbolic, as they have been refined by the Slovenian philosopher, Slavoj Žižek.[14] While all three concepts come into play, it is particularly relevant to this discussion how these events mediate between the Real and the Symbolic. In Lacanian terms the Real is not what we casually call reality; instead it is that which cannot be adequately contained within language and is built around a fundamental "kernel" of trauma (things like birth, death, disease, decay, the vastness of the universe—reality

---

13 Oliver Bown, Alice Eldridge and Jon McCormack, "Understanding Interaction in Contemporary Digital Music: from instruments to behavioural objects," *Organized Sound* 14(2) (2009): 188–196.

14 While these concepts are covered in many of the writings of Slavoj Žižek, I draw here particularly from *The Sublime Object of Ideology*, cited earlier, and *Interrogating the Real: Selected Writings* (London: Continuum, 2005).

which is "never fully constituted"[15]). The Symbolic in Lacanian terms is linguistic—how we attempt to verbalize and represent such experience to one another and ourselves. As Žižek notes "the Lacanian notion of the Real being that rock which resists symbolization is extremely useful. . ."[16] and particularly useful here, because for Žižek, while the Symbolic as a category is characterized by the failure to adequately access the Real, the "symbolic order" fills this Void with language, objects, practices, etc. to grant us limited access.

This failure is useful here in avoiding the ideological "trap" of asserting that the experience of Deep Listening in the desert somehow constitutes a more "Real" or natural reality than other kinds of practices. This is not my argument. Indeed it is the dynamic tension between our inability to grasp the Real and our great desire to symbolize it that lies at the heart of many musical practices. Therefore Deep Listening is not just an active form of listening, but always already (in the Derridean sense) an active negotiation between our sonic environments and our internal systems for constituting "reality," often by carefully documenting individual moments as representative of the larger whole:

> As I sit here trying to compose an article for *Source*, my mind adheres to the sounds of myself and my environment. In the distance a bulldozer is eating away a hillside while its motor is a cascade of harmonics defining the space between it and the Rock and Roll radio playing in the next room. Sounds of birds, insects, children's voices and the rustling of trees fleck this space.[17]

Yet, to theorize music or sound or events organized around listening as part of the symbolic order, negotiating the trauma of the Real is somewhat problematic. Yes, it is true that in many symbolic orders (particularly religious or secular rituals) music and sound are often integral parts of the power the symbolic order holds to mask the Real.

---

15 Žižek, *Interrogating the Real*, 81.
16 Ibid.
17 Pauline Oliveros, "Some Sound Observations," in *Audio Culture: Readings in Modern Music*, ed. Christoph Cox and Daniel Warner (New York: Continuum, 2004), 102.

Yet, to use Lacan's concepts to analyze Deep Listening as a negotiation of the Real must be justified, as Lacan himself has stated that modern science touches the Real in a way totally absent in premodern cultural discourse.[18] He is not alone in this thinking. *The Third Culture* authors believed that theories of culture (literary, feminist, queer, etc.) were a misuse of the very concept of theory. Richard Dawkins rants, "[t]he very word 'theory' has been hijacked for some extremely narrow parochial literary purpose—as though Einstein didn't have theories, as though Darwin didn't have theories."[19] (I say "rants" because the inclusion of Einstein and Darwin reads as inflammatory). Dawkins and other authors from *The Third Culture* believed that theories of culture (literary, feminist, queer, etc.) were a misuse of the very concept of theory. Thus using Lacan and Dawkins theories to formulate an analysis based on Deep Listening practice might be considered questionable—does this mean I am leading us down a theoretical cul-de-sac?

While it is true that there is no way to come to any absolute knowledge of how Deep Listening functions with respect to Lacan or Dawkins at these specific events or indeed within the broader culture, Žižek forcefully counters both Lacan and *Third Culture* authors by deconstructing the ideologies of their discourse. He challenged the notion that scientific discourses were inherently closer to the Real first by noting that contemporary mathematical and quantum discourses have become almost spiritual in their vocabulary and syntax—so complex and abstract as to be almost indescribable without the use of metaphor. He questions the ability to come to any constitutive reality—instead the process of symbolization and its resistance by the Real, through many evolving and simultaneously conflicting discourses, is not a problem, but a cure[20]—one that drives many of our practices. Deep Listening practice scrupulously avoids the creation of a single interpretation or meaning within listening, does not require symbolization (description

---

18 Žižek, *Interrogating the Real*, 88.

19 Richard Dawkins, "A Survival Machine" in *The Third Culture: Beyond the Scientific Revolution*, ed. John Brockman (New York: Simon and Schuster, 1996), 23.

20 Žižek, *Interrogating the Real*, 39.

or speech), and encourages imagination, association and memory. Many responses to Deep Listening bypass the symbolic order entirely—creating art, making sound, movement—allowing direct access to the Symbolic.

The particular embodied Deep Listening practice I have chosen to discuss (post-techno desert events) engages Lacan and Dawkins (as well as other contemporary theories of culture) both sonically and socially in such a way as to make the use of their concepts both relevant and quite fruitful. This analysis should therefore be considered a limited, strategic intervention into Deep Listening practice. Minimal Techno and Dubstep are quite reliant on mathematical operations in time and rhythm as a central constitutive elements in the music's structure, aesthetic, and purpose. This is not to say that other forms of techno and post-techno do not—simply that these are two genres that are particularly dependant upon these processes for coherence and structure within the DJ set. There is a central aspect to these particular musics that speak deeply to mathematical relationships and operations within their structure as significantly and centrally as any numeric "art music" theory. But while no one (at least no one I know) "gets down" in the desert to Babbitt's *Semi-Simple Variations*,[21] the combinatorial similarities with Minimal Techno are considerable. Therefore I am saying both that Babbitt would be ripe for a remix and that the use of Lacan's psychoanalytic orders (as refined by Žižek) for analysis actually do get us closer both to the music, the embodied Deep Listening experience of the sonic, and its relationship to the Real.

Moreover, Dawkins' memes bring us back around to Lacan's Orders—this time to the order of the Imaginary and the Symbolic. First, the Imaginary, or what we might broadly refer to as culture—those things not continuously caught up with the trauma of the Real or its Symbolization. As Žižek notes: "This imaginary level—it is supported by the illusion of the self as the autonomous agent which is present from the very beginning as the origin of its acts: this imaginary

---

21 Milton Babbitt, "Semi-Simple Variations," *Contemporary Piano Music by Distinguished Composers* (Bryn Mawr, PA: Theodore Presser Company, 1957).

self-experience is for the subject the way to misrecognize his radical dependence on the Big Other, on the symbolic order as his de-centered cause."[22] Thus our misrepresentation of our own existence is responsible for culture as we know it—including art, music, literature, even, I would posit, our ideologies of science, mathematics, etc. It is this fundamental misrepresentation that memes speak to, engage with and replicate over and over again. As Žižek further elucidates: "we could say that in imaginary identification we imitate the other at the level of resemblance—we identify ourselves with the image of the other at the level of resemblance inasmuch as we are 'like him,' while in symbolic representation we identify ourselves with the other precisely at a point at which he is inimitable, at the point which eludes resemblance."[23] Thus two forms of active identification are functioning here: first, our mimetic imitation of that which resembles us, from fashion and musical tastes to the mannerisms of our self-selecting fellow participants. But further than that, we identify with our lack, our lack of ability to adequately symbolize the Real, and thus create a symbolic order to cope with our impotence in the face of the audio and environmental stimulus.

The final theoretical remainder yet to be accounted for in these events is the role of pleasure, or particularly in our case *object petit a* and the notion of pleasure for pleasure's sake. While Lacan notes that *jouissance* is a surplus of pleasure resulting in a peculiar kind of pain, music's non-verbal status can keep *jouissance* from losing its agency—in Žižek's terms, from becoming castrated (how terribly Freudian) by the process of signification.[24] When one takes pleasure and subjects it to the process of signification (putting it into words, attempting to describe reactions, etc.), *jouissance* disappears; attempting to hold on to pleasure makes it slip from one's grasp. In the context of these desert events, music's agency in keeping pleasure from signification cannot be understated— the very concept of Deep Listening's agency in allowing pleasure to go unsignified and therefore to continue to exist is revolutionary. The

---

22 Žižek, *The Sublime Object of Ideology*, 104.
23 Ibid., 109.
24 See the great chart for this: Ibid., 121.

very nature of Deep Listening, of giving oneself over to a "surplus" of listening (to borrow from Marx), relies on the very nature of sound to avoid signification. In other words, Deep Listening becomes pleasure's co-conspirator in allowing participants to experience the sonic and the social without assigning specific meaning, to keep signification slippery and unfixed and without agency to bind the pleasure of Deep Listening to any specific function. Even in the more social aspects described at the close of this essay, signification remains slippery and unfixed—meanings are purposefully playful and often contradictory. Thus, even when listening to language—the ultimate signifier—Deep Listening has the power to move the listener beyond signification to a place where meanings are constantly negotiated and renegotiated: never fixed, never painful, and never without play. The repetitive nature of EDM, and Techno in particular, has usually been explained by scholars and critics for its appeal for a drug-addled and dance-centric audience, but not as a genre that powerfully encourages this movement beyond signification. Each repetition of a motif, a rhythmic pattern, a musical or verbal meme is a fresh opportunity for the play of significations for the imaginal, or memorial/associational deep listener. It is by virtue of this repetition, not in spite of it, that the signification remains slippery, and responding artistically keeps significations unfixed. It is this that makes EDM one of the most important musical genres for direct negotiation of the Real, and accounts for its appeal far more accurately than the casual desire to dance or "party."

But beyond the performative and mimetic there are other sources of agency relevant here. As the McLuhan quote indicates, culture has become more and more visually stimulating—removing oneself from the visual stimulus of contemporary culture is not easy. Traveling to remote desert locations is particularly effective in this regard, and offers added benefits to the weary digital-ager. As anyone who spends time in the desert will tell you, one's visual perspective is uniquely challenged in desert landscapes: things that look close are in fact quite distant, things that are distant appear quite close. The visual stimulus of this ecosystem is unique, and central to the analysis of embodied Deep Listening in this context. Such visual distortion can be dangerous for those unfamiliar

with this effect, as misjudging distances or getting lost in desert locations can be deadly. As Žižek notes "the Symbolic is above all a place,
a place that was originally empty and subsequently filled with the bric-
a-brac of the symbolic order."[25] The relatively "empty" desert landscape
(relative to the urban or the suburban), filled momentarily with people,
with music, with temple-like DJ booths complete with altars of natural
and artistic offerings–bundles of sage, crystals, images of the Buddha
or other icons, stones, art, candles, are excellent examples of the "bric-
a-brac" of the symbolic order. The harsh desert environment is always
already (again in the Derridean sense) a locus of physical discomfort
and "Real" risk. This risk heightens the event's ability to function as a
place for the symbolic order to negotiate between the individual listener
and the Real, as well as to Lacan's "fantasy-construction," reality.

Masking the Real of our desire seems to be a driving force behind
these events. One of these underground groups has events during every
full moon—frigid cold in winter and sweltering heat in summer does
not dampen the groups' desire to come together during the full moon,
and participants are not dissuaded by the very real physical discom-
forts and risks posed by being in remote locations (sometimes at high
altitudes) during harsh weather. Even when the environment is favor-
able participants push themselves psychologically and physically in
listening and/or dancing at these events for greatly extended periods
of time—sometimes to the point of ecstatic trance and exhaustion.
Use of psychedelics or other mind-altering substances is not uncommon, though far from universal, but certainly can intensify the physical
experience of the symbolic order, and in some cases giving it perceived
substance within the altered mind. Therefore this analysis takes into
account geographic and social aspects, in particular the act of leaving
one's familiar surroundings to engage with the individual and social
practice of Deep Listening. To experience the richness of Deep Listening
practice one must be willing to give one's whole self over to the act—and
often this takes time, practice and discipline. The participants in these
small desert events experience their full benefits by giving themselves
over entirely to the process of listening, but they are also traveling great

---

25 Žižek, *Interrogating the Real*, 45.

distances into (often) extreme natural environments to do so. In other words, these participants are trying to get close enough to the edge of embodiment that they can quite literally listen for the nature of reality itself: very deep listening indeed.

The Wobble in the Dubstep: Sub-bass in the Human Herd

By way of introduction to the performative and mimetic agencies discussed, but not applied, above, I will begin with a discussion of a recent release by producer/DJ Bassnectar. Wikipedia describes Bassnectar's style[26] as an:

> "Eclectic electronic mix, combining mainstream music with underground dubs and the common "wobble" bass"[27] used by many dubstep[28] musicians.[29] Many songs contain multiple techniques of composition, such as: a sudden shift from double to triple meter, a sudden drop into half-timings, multiple layers of synthesized arpeggios, rappers, singers, vocal samples pitch-shifted and time stretched.[30] The most utilized

---

26 Wikipedia contributors, "Style" in "Bassnectar," *Wikipedia, The free encyclopedia,* accessed November 30, 2011, http://en.wikipedia.org/w/index.php?title=Bassnectar&oldid=463021994.

27 Wikipedia contributors, "Dubstep – *Wikipedia, the free encyclopedia,*" accessed July 12, 2011, http://en.wikipedia.org/wiki/Dubstep#Wobble_bass.

28 Wikipedia contributors, "Dubstep – *Wikipedia, the free encyclopedia,*" accessed July 12, 2011, http://en.wikipedia.org/wiki/Dubstep.

29 Michael Wilson, "Bubble and Squeak: Michael Wilson on Dubstep," *Artforum International.* (November 1, 2006), accessed March 31, 2011, http://www.thefreelibrary.com/Bubble+and+squeak%3a+Michael+Wilson+on+dubstep.-a0165312289.

30 "Bassnectar Discography," Cozza Frenzy Album Review, Songs, Ratings, accessed July 12, 2011, http://www.starpulse.com/Music/Bassnectar/Discography/album/P585652/R1656381/.

characteristic is focus on various tempos.[31] He uses the broad spectrum of speeds in electronic genres to create what he calls, "omni-tempo maximalism," and describes it as, "an amalgamation of every sound I've ever heard, mixed with ultra-wicked basslines."[32]

The release, *The 808 Track,*[33] for those of us who have been around EDM for a while, is a nostalgic reiteration and refocusing on sounds from the Roland TR-808 machine, one of the first programmable drum machines introduced in 1980, which was quite well known at the time both for its unique drum timbres, and for its ability to produce extremely low bass frequencies—something that Dubstep[34] relies on heavily as a genre today. The TR-808 machine has played a long and illustrious role in myriad releases in Hip-hop and EDM, and particularly Acid House, which is essentially organized around the capabilities of the machine. Since its introduction, the 808 can be heard on countless albums and mixes and verbal references to the 808 pepper tracks from Beck to The Beastie Boys to Beyoncé. The definition of "performative agency" I cite is that which originates in computer programming—virtual "musicians" present in interactive computer music that are written to have various levels of autonomy to act in performance.[35] I have extended this definition to include the host of other DJ technologies and tools including

---

31 "[Bassnectar Interview] An in-depth Talk with Electronic Nomad Lorin Ashton | The Music Ninja," accessed July 12, 2011, http://www .themusicninja.com/bassnectar-interview-an-in-depth-talk-with-elec-tronic-nomad-lorin-ashton/.

32 "(2) Bassnectar," accessed July 12, 2011, http://www.facebook.com /Bassnectar?sk=info.

33 The whole track is available on YouTube "Bassnectar – The 808 Track (feat. Mighty High Coup) [OFFICIAL]," accessed July 8, 2011, http://www .youtube.com/watch?v=IdnBTJiUVDQ.

34 To hear a diverse sampling of Dubstep, I recommend Pandora and iTunes radio channels that feature Dubstep. There are also many examples from individual DJs on Soundcloud–just type in Dubstep into the search engine.

35 George Lewis' *Voyager Computer Music Improviser* would constitute a well-known example of live computer performative agency.

turntables, vinyl, CDDJs, and software such as Ableton Live, because all of these technologies and tools influence the DJ set with their capabilities and design. It must be said, however, that I am using the term "performative agency" more broadly than it is defined by the authors from whom I borrow the term. Thus *The 808 Track* is an ode to the performative agency of the machine within musical culture, sounding a host of sonic relationships across genres, geography and time. It is also an example of its mimetic agency: densely layered with stylistic, technologic, social and sonic memes that constitute not incidental aspects of the EDM to be explored here, but central inspirational, organizational and structural aspects. Further, it references the unique form of nostalgia that seems omnipresent within the EDM scene, as each new track or mix "listens backwards" in time attempting to sound its own cultural context from within.

The ability to create ultra-low frequencies, present in the 808 back in 1980, was only one precursor to Dubstep, a genre that has roots in South London in the early and mid-2000s, but has since spread far and wide. It borrows both from Jamaican Dub (in the sparse style of the MC, or vocals component), as well as from garage 2-step (in its use of unusual and irregular rhythmic cycles that challenge the primacy of regular beats and loops in EDM). Dubstep uses almost constant subbass, ensuring that the listening experience is not only sonic but also physical—it vibrates ones entire body. It has made the ultra-high quality amplification systems mentioned at the opening of this essay absolutely necessary for performance, as its sheer range of frequencies and amplitudes require sophisticated systems such as Turbosound or Funktion-One to eliminate distortion at the lowest reaches of the sub-bass. The wobble bass, or an extended bass note that is rhythmically inflected with rapidly changing volume, filtering or other forms of low frequency oscillation effects on synth patches is another distinguishing feature of Dubstep. Influenced strongly by Drum and Bass,[36] which used rhythmic

---

36 For an in-depth look at some of the sonic and cultural complexities of Drum and Bass, see Renée T. Coulombe, "Postmodern Polyamory or Postcolonial Challenge? Cornershop in Dialogue from East to West to East..." in *Postmodern Music/Postmodern Thought*, ed. Judy Lochhead and Joseph Auner (New York: Routledge, 2004), 177–193.

complexity as a central structural feature, beats are often syncopated, with sudden shifts in tempo or meter—particularly from duple to triple and back, sometimes within the same phrase or loop. I liked to call the extended loops of Drum and Bass "lopsided," and Dubstep has exploited this characteristic extensively.

Dubstep incorporates the break, or the suspension of the beat to great effect. Sometimes the break is so complete that it comes to the point of compete silence—before "dropping" back in with renewed intensity, volume, layering or additional elements. While the "break" in the beat structure gave rise to its own genres of EDM (Breaks or Break beats or Broken beats, etc.) the sheer depth of the sub-bass in Dubstep lends an intensity to the drop impossible to achieve without the use of such low frequencies. The irregularity of rhythms in Dubstep also adds a level of uneasiness to the dancing body—in traditional "breaks" it is typical to know when the drop will come because of the regular beat structure, and so the dancing body can easily determine when the beat will return. In Dubstep, however, because of the irregularities of the beat structures, it is frequently impossible to determine how and when the beat will return—the drop might be into a completely different rhythmic structure altogether. All of this has a powerful effect on the listening body: one feels the music, and the sheer variety of musical elements—from the long and often syncopated rhythmic loops to the dissonant harmonies and samples, the use of minor keys, and the occasional vocals or treble melodies—which gives the listener a depth and breadth of frequencies, effects and sonic elements uncommon outside of a few post-techno genres of EDM.

While Dubstep may have its roots in the studios and clubs of South London, it is in the acoustics of the natural environment that its power can be felt most. I began this essay wanting to hear the way elephants hear—to be connected and share information sonically with family and friends through the rumbles beneath my feet, using the very earth itself as resonator and communication system. One reason that such events are held in remote locations is the ability of the bass to travel great distances—subjecting performances to noise ordinances in populated areas. There is even a classic track by DJ Sugartape called

"Summerdaze"[37] whose chorus begins "we're standing in the beat and the sound, the bass flows through the ground. . . ." This has become important aspect of outdoor events that cannot be duplicated in the club environment: the acoustics of the landscape and its effects on the music. As Dubstep is sounded in the desert, the sub-bass frequencies travel the farthest, through the ground, and that "wobble" can be felt sometimes miles away from the actual system. Participants at such events frequently wander away from the dance area in small groups or alone to hear the music and the environment from new vantage points: climbing hills or rock outcroppings to lay on the earth and feel the vibrations of the sub-bass mix with the sounds of the desert and their own bodies. I have often felt that I could hear the stars above me, and the earth turning beneath me in such moments of sonic connection and solitude.

Wandering too far from the tribe is not a worry if one stays within the radius of the sub-bass—the vibrations will always lead you back. Finding an event at a new location is far easier if one arrives after the sound system—using the bass frequencies rising up from the desert floor as a guide or sonic homing beacon. The distance from the system will determine how wide a range of the music's frequencies one hears: farther away you hear just the rumble, the closer you come to the system the more range and detail you hear. If you are close to the camping area, voices and conversations mix with the music and rise to distant listeners as a sonic "whole" of the event. They float above the bass and become one with the track for those listening away from the dance floor. Participants experiment with various vantage points to create their own deep listening experience, exercising a kind of agency most often associated with the DJs themselves. This is an impossible listening practice to duplicate in a concert or club environment where confinement within walls and carefully tuned sound systems try to ensure a uniform listening experience throughout. In this Deep Listening experience, the desert becomes a resonator, a transmitter and a co-creator between the DJ, the system, and the many listening bodies. All participants exercise "listening agency" in deciding where, how, and to what

---

37 Sugartape, *Summerdaze*, Big Star Records, Big Promo CD 150, 2007, compact disc.

they wish to listen or respond. The event becomes a sonic whole under such circumstances, with no particular event more relevant than any other. This reinforces these events as collective and tribal, rather than hierarchized performances, because ultimately all present are responsible for the content and spirit of the event.

The Memes in the Minimal: Combinatoriality Steps Out

Moving from the sheer sonic depth and abundance of Dubstep to Minimal Techno might be interpreted as jumping to opposite ends of the listening spectrum, but there are important similarities for Deep Listeners. Both genres share rhythmic complexity as a foundational structural element, but whereas Dubstep offers a breadth and depth of the frequencies in the listening experience, Minimal Techno takes a quite different approach. As Philip Sherburne has noted:

> As DJ Culture begat an entire cottage industry of recordings intended solely or primarily for mixing, dance tracks came to be understood as representative of a willfully incomplete form; they came into their own only when paired with other tracks. Minimalisms' reliance upon rhythmic and melodic 'building blocks'—imagine isolating any single phrase of an early Reich composition for example—proved the perfect fit for this combinatory form. As Techno produced various offshoots, each one emphasizing a particular stylistic tendency, certain substrains focused on this combinatory approach to an almost exaggerated degree. So while many Detroit Techno producers continued working within the margins of traditional song form, the more Spartan producers in the UK and Sweden, such as Adam Beyer and Surgeon, made an art out of producing microscopic variations on a single rhythmic theme. Records in this tradition were not designed for home listening, but rather as fodder for performance in the hands of the DJ. Indeed, with their strictly codified breakdowns and

buildups, records like these are often rightly described as 'DJ tools,' something like Lego bricks for the selector's toybox.[38]

Because of its emphasis on the "microscopic variations" in rhythm and stripped-down sound, Minimal Techno encourages a very different kind of Deep Listening, and uses the acoustics of the desert landscape for a much different effect. While Minimal Techno, like Dubstep, comes out of club culture, it too comes into its own in the acoustic environment of the desert.

As Sherburne notes above, there is a strong connection between the Minimalist movement in music and art of the 1960s and 1970s, and the emergence of Minimal Techno. I would also posit that both movements emerged for similar musico-historical reasons. While Minimalism in the 1960s and 1970s was a response to the intense complexity and angularities of Modernism, Minimal Techno in many ways has arisen as a response to the increasing density, self-referentiality and complexity of many EDM genres. Minimal Techno strips the genre down to its barest elements: its atomic and sub-atomic "sonic particles." Sub-bass is almost completely absent here, as are breaks and drops into and out of the beat in the traditional sense. Instead, Minimal Techno sets use near constant repetition to structurally morph: adding or subtracting elements, metrically modulating, subdividing, or multiplying rhythmic elements. This means that even the deepest listener can be caught unaware by shifts in meter or tempo—only to realize they have occurred in noticing how differently they move or respond to the music. Vocals are sparse and equally repetitive, and frequently spoken over the musical texture rather than sung. The repetition of spoken words encourages listeners to experience language in many ways: as text carrying a specific meaning, as mantra, as a series of vocal sounds with no signification—as mimetic as the rhythmic themes they sound with. Such play on the supremacy of the spoken word is far from incidental, but rather it is a strategic intervention into the process of signification, allowing text to become

---

38 Philip Sherburne, "Digital Discipline: Minimalism in House and Techno," in *Audio Culture: Readings in Modern Music*, ed. Christoph Cox and Daniel Warner (New York: Continuum, 2004), 320.

part of the "bric-a-brac" that fills the symbolic order without explicit signification (which would mess with our pleasure, after all). Here we find another powerful example of mimetic agency, this time emphasized not in sheer abundance, but careful deployment of individual sonic and cultural memes. Imitation is key here, as the DJ tools in use are not marked by individuality, but rather by imitation and repetition that can bring us to the first order of the Imaginary, or the imitation of that which we see we are "like" and our own personal identification. Minimal Techno, through its structural elements, sets up a powerful mechanism for imitation and thus self-identification—Deep Listening here means negotiating self within the imitative structures of the music. Challenging signification, both in eschewing the creation of the new *ex nihilo* in favor of remixing the old, as well as using texts for purposes other than signification, this process can happen freely and without loss of pleasure; once again the desert landscape which robs the participant of orienting landmarks participates heavily in this preservation of *jouissance*.

Sound samples and rhythmic loops in Minimal Techno are often clipped and dry, an aspect further emphasized in the desert climate. With no club walls to echo the sound back to the system, Minimal Techno is at its sparsest outside. Here, Deep Listening does not consist of listening into the sonic depth of the moment, but rather giving oneself over to the slow, evolutionary processes of the music as the DJ combines and recombines tracks to create ever-evolving variations on rhythmic themes. It is fully embracing the power that sonic repetition over time can have on human consciousness, particularly in this environment that lacks the landmarks by which we orient ourselves. Repetition and variation require a sustained listening attention that engages musical memory quite differently from other genres–particularly the Dubstep discussed above. Minimal Techno gives the listener time to interpret and reinterpret the materials, becoming co-creators with the DJ in the set. The sparseness also allows listeners the time and space to hear into the history of individual rhythmic loops and samples, recognizing the same or similar "DJ Tools" used in new and varied contexts. Once again sounding history in the present, and for those willing to listen deeply enough, challenging "the illusion of the self as the autonomous agent which is present from the very beginning as the origin of its acts."[39]

Outro

The final aspect of these small desert events in which Deep Listening is an integral embodied practice is not musical at all. While I have already discussed participants listening to the sounds of the environment and their own bodies mixed with the music, there is still more listening that the environment encourages. Part of the experience of traveling to remote locations and participating in a tribal setting is the freedom it gives participants to express themselves fully. Out in the desert, one is free from the need for situational competence required in what is called by many participants the "default world." By creating a space of symbolic order, we reject the "libidinal order"[40] which includes the whole chain of the Imaginary, and therefore the illusion of separation between self and other. Further, this empty space is not incidental but absolutely necessary for any symbolic order—as it is the emptiness that makes room for the sacred.[41] Our increasingly split consciousness in the digital age makes it rare for many to listen fully and deeply to what our fellow humans have to say. Here, no one has to "make sense" or demonstrate a coherent and cohesive "self" to those gathered—we have all embraced the Void, and have listened far past the self and other to the point that such distinction becomes irrelevant. The remoteness of these events encourages a stripping away of the protective layers of behavior and the isolation of contemporary culture. We can feel identification with the other, as well as resistance to that identification at the same time—the perfect recipe for eliminating the illusion of the autonomous self, and embracing all that is both internally and externally as the same. One can almost feel the distinctions fall away when one leaves the paved roads and strikes out onto the dirt. Listening deeply to one another is not an incidental effect of gathering in the same

---

39 Žižek, *Sublime Object of Ideology, 104.*
40 Žižek, *Interrogating the Real,* 33.
41 Ibid., 45.

place at the same time—it is a central, honored and beloved part of these events. It is not uncommon to spend hours listening to someone you've just met speak about what is most important to them, and for them in turn to listen to you. It is not a process of signification, however, but of connection—language is not the mode of communication, and here is seen often as feeble, weak or impotent. This is a particularly important point about language laid out in Žižek's recent work, Living in the End Times. He notes that conversations become steeped in ideology when political or social concepts are discussed in so general a manner as to remove their meaning. "'[I]deology' is precisely such a reduction to the simplified 'essence' that conveniently forgets the 'background noise' which provides the density of its actual meaning. Such an erasure of the 'background noise' is the very core of utopian dreaming."42 While I am not saying that these events lack elements of utopian dreaming, communication is an embodied practice, encompassing all aspects of a being within its environment, "provides the density" necessary for actual meaning. In addition, the lack of a distinct "other" means that all can embrace the connection to all that is, all that was and all that shall be, and recognize these as being one in the same.

This type of intense sharing should not be misconstrued with casual conversations at camp, but instead constitutes embodied Deep Listening that connects participants as closely as their shared love of the landscape and the music. Under such circumstances Deep Listening is a profoundly connective practice, bringing in perspectives and experiences that better us as people, as kindred spirits, as seekers of an ultimate reality that we can never fully constitute but for which we will nonetheless keep striving. In this place that becomes the symbolic order for a time, the practice of Deep Listening to each other constitutes "Real" communication as essential to the process of symbolization as the music, the art, the altars or temples of sound. It brings the shared experience to a whole new level and has arisen in this context spontaneously, as most who participate have never heard the term "Deep Listening" but practice it nonetheless, both in the desert and in everyday life. With continued participation in these desert events, Deep Listening becomes a natural

---

42 Slavoj Žižek, *Living in the End Times* (New York: Verso, 2011), 5-6.

part of the subculture, and a way of life for most participants who carry it back with them into their everyday lives.

The kind of communal bonding and catharsis experienced after desert events (or Deep Listening Retreats) often changes participants' lives at fundamental levels. Relationships formed on the desert floor have founded performance troupes, inspired filmmakers, musicians and visual artists to collaborate in striking new ways. Despite vast age and class differences in participants, most are early adopters of new technologies, new art forms, new modes of expression—and the desire to foster these outside of festival season means that at almost any time of the day or night, somewhere in the world, a metal sculptor and fire performers are welding together giant installations to delight attendees at their next gathering. At any moment in time there are countless producers, musicians and DJs creating performances, discovering new venues, bringing together emergent kinds of performance for this burgeoning and ecstatic culture to consume. Each participant becomes a model for the broader culture of the benefits of routinely communing with the Real, the Void, and those we used to think as "others." No wonder the number of global participants at such events is skyrocketing year after year.[43]

My own participation in these events over many years has led me to a striking new understanding of Deep Listening, the potential functions of musical compositions or performances, and the interdisciplinary necessities of the Symbolic. It has led me to new modes of collaboration with fellow artists, new forms of interactive art-making, and given me new ways to connect the sacred and secular without relying on pre-existing concepts of either. As Deep Listening does not rely on signification for its process, I have come to understand that in the end all Deep Listening is listening into the Void[44]—when there is no separation between self

---

43 See even more evidence of Electronica's growing audience in: Ray Waddell, "Electronica: The New King of the Road? Even Music City will be Spin City this New Year's Eve," *Billboard*, December 10, 2011: 14.
44 Freud, Žižek, Lacan and others are not the first to point out the sacredness of the Void in the illusion of the autonomous self. For more on this concept see Lao Tzu, *The Tao Te Ching of Lao Tzu,* trans. Brian Browne Walker (New York: St. Martin's Press, 1995). While there are many translations of the *Tao,* I offer this one as my personal favorite.

and other, the listener and the listened, the individual and the environment, the embodied and the disembodied, the silent and the sounded. It is then that we are finally in deep enough, listening.

Deep Listening
in the Body

Listening With the Feet

Viv Corringham

VIV CORRINGHAM is a British vocalist and sound artist, currently based in Minneapolis, who has worked internationally since the early 1980s. Her work includes music performances and audio installations. She is interested in exploring people's special relationship with familiar places and how that links to an interior landscape of personal history, memory and association. Her ongoing project "Shadow-walks" has been presented in gallery shows from New York to Istanbul to Portugal. Current musical collaborators include Charles Hayward (ex-*This Heat*) in London, Milo Fine in Minneapolis, Mike Cooper in Rome and Avatar Orchestra Metaverse in Second Life. She received a McKnight Composer Fellowship in 2006, has an MA Sonic Art with Distinction from Middlesex University, London, and earned the Certificate in Deep Listening. http://www.vivcorringham.org/

"TAKE A WALK AT NIGHT. Walk so silently that the bottoms of your feet become ears."[1] This is the instruction for *Meditation V*, "Native," a sonic meditation by Pauline Oliveros. On reading it for the first time, I was very engaged by this idea of allowing the feet to listen.

Throughout my life I have walked: as a mode of transport, as exercise and the fastest way I know to feel connected with a new place on my frequent travels. I have also listened, yet I did not fully make the connection between these two activities until the year 2000, when I began a project in which I let my feet lead me through London. I called this activity Vocal Strolls and it combined drifting through the streets, listening while walking and singing in response to what I heard. Since then, almost all my work has been concerned with walking and "listening with the feet."

---

1 Pauline Oliveros, *Sonic Meditations,* (Baltimore: Smith Publications, 1974).

143

PHOTO: KRIS DOUGLAS

I have long been fascinated by other artists who use walking and listening as their mode of expression, described as "soundwalk artists"[2] by teacher and researcher Andra McCartney. McCartney herself is an example of such an artist, who creates electroacoustic soundwalk art that incorporates audience responses into her walks and installations.

Another is Janet Cardiff, who creates audio walks that lead through semi-fictionalized landscapes in which her words guide us but also transform the walk into an almost cinematic event. The soundscape on the CD she prepares to accompany each walker was recorded on the same site as where it is being heard but at a different time, simultaneously reinforcing and calling into question the sounds around us as we take the walk. In a sense, our feet are listening to the past and the present at the same time.

Christina Kubisch's electrical walks take us another step further away from what the ears can actually hear in the moment to sounds that

2   Andra McCartney, "Soundwalking: Creating Moving Environmental Sound Narratives," accessed November 11, 2010, http://soundwalkinginteractions.wordpress.com/2010/09/27 /soundwalking-creating-moving-environmental-sound-narratives/.

are outside the range of human hearing. The walker is provided with magnetic headphones that respond to electrical fields in the environment and transform them into sounds that are audible. In this way, the characteristic sounds of familiar objects such as a neon light or an ATM machine can be heard while walking the route.

Hildegard Westerkamp is a composer, a pioneering figure within the field of soundscape studies and an integral member of the World Soundscape Project. Her compositions draw on her experience of walking and listening and she regularly leads soundwalks. Soundwalking is a term used by R. Murray Schafer in the 1970s and it is still a central activity of acoustic ecology groups throughout the world. It usually refers to walking quietly, often in a group, while listening to the environment. Westerkamp gives these instructions:

> "Start by listening to the sounds of your body while moving. They are closest to you and establish the first dialogue between you and the environment. If you can hear even the quietest of these sounds you are moving through an environment which is scaled on human proportions. In other words, with your voice or your footsteps for instance, you are "talking" to your environment which then in turn responds by giving your sounds a specific acoustic quality."[3]

The intention to listen encourages a focus of attention and allows the everyday sounds of a place to resonate. "It's not just going on a walk; it's deciding to listen to everything that meets your ears."[4]

When I decide to "listen with my feet," my attention shifts to the place in my body furthest away from my busy mind where it usually dwells. In certain aspects soundwalking resembles the Buddhist practice of *kinhin* or walking meditation, in which we are "walking not in order to arrive, but just to walk,"[5] aware of the contact between our feet and the earth. The physical act of walking encourages sensory awareness: the

---

3 Hildegard Westerkamp, in *Autumn Leaves, Sound and the Environment in Artistic Practice* (Paris: Double Entendre, 2007), 49.

4 Hildegard Westerkamp, "Hildegard Westerkamp," in *Sonic Mosaics* (Edmonton: University of Alberta Press, 2009), 240–248.

5 Thich Nhat Hahn, *Peace is Every Step* (London: Rider, 1991), 27.

transfer of weight from one leg to the other, the experience of balance and falling, the texture of the ground beneath the foot, the feeling of sock on skin, plus all the other sensations, smells and sounds.

With a focus on listening, I can hear the sound of my feet walking. I can also explore the way a sound shifts as I turn towards or away from it and sense the subtle ways in which environmental sounds change due to small fluctuations in temperature and air pressure.

At a Deep Listening retreat that I attended, Pauline Oliveros introduced the practice of listening to music "through the feet" as we took a very slow meandering walk indoors. For the first time I fully experienced the element of music that is not only heard through the ears but also felt physically, with different pitches and timbres resonating different parts of the body. Now, when I listen to a piece of music for the first time, I frequently do so while walking slowly around my room.

Another aspect of "listening with the feet" is my impression that when I walk I am listening not only to sounds but also to unseen traces that exist in a place. This is explored in my current ongoing project Shadow-walks in which people show me their special walks and together we tread both the "real" environment and also their internal landscape of memory and personal history. Later I retrace our steps, my feet listening for echoes of our previous walk to which I give voice through improvised singing.

I am interested in the choices made by people who lead me on their special walks: to go down this side not that side of the road, to cross the street here not there, etc. We forge strong relationships with familiar places and repeat walks whose route has often been arrived at through unconscious decisions, perhaps based on subliminal emotional and sensory responses.

Psychogeography may be relevant here, a term associated with the Situationists and defined in Francesco Careri's fascinating book *Walkscapes* as "the study of the specific effects of the geographical environment, consciously organized or not, on the emotions and behavior of individuals."[6] The Situationists viewed their urban "drifts" as an art activity. Through random (often chance-based) walks, they

---

6   Francesco Careri, *Walkscapes* (Barcelona: Gustavo Gili, 2002), 97.

discovered zones of aversion and attraction in the city, areas that seem to repel or draw a person in to them. This may be interpreted as an intuitive response that occurs when we cease to direct our movements consciously but allow ourselves to fully sense the world through our walking feet.

The notion of a "sense of place" is recognized, but how is place actually sensed? It seems to me that sound is an important factor. Particular sounds become "soundmarks" in a familiar place and can cause a sense of loss or dislocation if they disappear. While walking we can place ourselves by listening out for known sounds and through our sensitivity to the acoustics of a space, a skill that is often well developed in those without sight. Francisco López uses this acoustic orientation in his blind walks, in which participants are blindfolded and walk with an unsighted guide.

In my Shadow-walks project, people have frequently made a connection between sound and place. One person, whose regular walk led through the port of Porto in Portugal, said that hearing the layers of shifting sounds made him want to do the walk with his eyes closed. Another, who had previously told me that her walk in Kingston, New York, was not a personal one, realized that it followed the sound of the train that resonated through her earlier life in other places.

There exist walks without walking that nonetheless connect sound and place and link the feet with listening. Anthropologist Steven Feld describes the song paths of the Kaluli people of Papua New Guinea, in which a person singing a sequence of local place-names takes listeners on a journey of imagination. Feld describes the flow of the song paths as "emotionally and physically linked to the sensual flow of the singing voice" to create a "sense of place resounding."[7] In this instance, listening to the song of the journey connects with the feet walking the well-known route in imagination and memory.

Song paths differ from songlines, which are interwoven path-stories of the Australian aborigines, each path connected to a song and each

7   Steven Feld, "Waterfalls of Song: An Acoustemology of Place Resounding in Bosavi, Papua New Guinea" in Steven Feld and Keith H. Basso, *Senses of Place* (Santa Fe: School of American Research Press, 1996), 91–92.

song connected to one or more mythological stories telling of the origins of mankind. "It is as if time and history were updated again and again by walking them."[8] These stories, singing the world into existence, are drawn up out of the earth by the feet, which listen for them as they walk.

It seems that our walking feet can listen to the sounds of a place, to music vibrating the floor, to traces of previous walks, to past sounds that no longer exist, to walks in the imagination, to sounds inaudible to the ears, to subtle qualities of the environment we travel through, to the echo of our ancient origins, and to our own memories and associations.

The essence of a place is revealed to the feet that move through it and listen. As art writer Lucy Lippard has stated, a place can "be felt as an extension of the body, especially the walking body, passing through and becoming part of the landscape."[9] In a sense a location is embodied in us and we are placed in it through our walking, listening feet.

---

8   Careri, *Walkscapes,* 44.
9   Lucy Lippard, *The Lure of the Local: Senses of Place in a Multicentered Society* (New York: The New Press, 1997), 34.

Deep Listening Through Movement: A Personal History

HELOISE GOLD lives in Austin Texas. She is a dancer, performance artist, choreographer, T'ai Chi/ Qi Gong instructor, co-founding director of Art From the Streets (a project for homeless artists) and director of a movement/arts studio in Austin. She has co-led twenty years of Deep Listening Retreats with Pauline Oliveros and Ione. Heloise is the recipient of numerous grants for performance from the City of Austin, the Texas Commission on the Arts and the NEA, and has been creating original works with many interdisciplinary artists for over thirty-five years. Her love of experimentation and innovation and her commitment to collaboration and community are present in all of her creations. http://www.deeplistening.org/heloise

Heloise Gold

DEEP LISTENING is a way of life and a way of being. As a practice for art-making, it gives us the tools and the permission to slow down with ourselves and others, to become present, and to respond spontaneously and creatively from a deep source of wakefulness. As a focus for living our lives fully, it supports us in the very same way.

Deep Listening involves a committed community of practitioners who have had the great fortune to come together in a variety of settings and configurations, under the strong and gentle guidance of Pauline Oliveros, who lives and breathes her practice.

I came into contact with Pauline in New York in the mid-1970s. Before even meeting her, I somehow miraculously obtained a copy of her *Sonic Meditations*.[1]

---

1 Pauline Oliveros, *Sonic Meditations* (Baltimore: Smith Publications, 1974).

149

I co-founded a Sonic Meditation Study Group which met weekly in the apartment I was living in on the Upper West Side. Invitees were asked to arrive in silence, and to then form a circle and practice/perform these sonic/listening recipes. This was my formative immersion into a method that has now become integrated into my entire life.

Shortly after our study group got under way, I attended one of Pauline's solo performances with accordion. We trudged up the narrow stairway of the loft where she was performing, and as soon as I saw her sitting there like a female Buddha, waiting to begin, I felt that something life-changing was about to occur. Sure enough, the presence of Pauline, the slow steady breathing and undulation of the accordion's bellows and the exhilarating sounds that filled the space caused a shift in my entire being. My cells knew that something thrilling and important was taking place. After the performance, I introduced myself to Pauline and told her how I was already studying and experiencing her work; I mentioned my career as a dancer/performance artist/T'ai Chi practitioner. We clicked!

The next time I saw Pauline was in a spacious, sunny kitchen in Austin, Texas, in 1981. She was commissioned to compose a piece for the Deborah Hay Dance Company and I was a member of that company. We greeted each other enthusiastically and then began a sparring match, martial arts style, in a comic sort of way. We clicked again!

In 1991, I invited Pauline to co-lead a retreat with me at Rose Mountain Retreat Center in New Mexico. What ensued was a twenty-year teaching partnership with Pauline, and also IONE, of Deep Listening Retreats. It was during this time of continual deep immersion into the practices of Deep Listening that the concept of a "listening body" began to emerge for me. What I began to experience and articulate is a sense that we have ears sending and receiving signals all over and through the body. Every cell, every bone, every organ is alive and listening. And as a result of that practice, we can feel ourselves more easily, sense more profoundly, and respond more sensitively and immediately.

When we invite ourselves to listen with ears all over the body, this image and experience of ourselves activates our proprioceptive sense and our nervous systems become more completely engaged. We can all take pride in our bodies as instruments of creative expression. And we can literally utilize our bodies as a resource for listening. This becomes whole body listening.

As we went deeper into the work and play of Deep Listening I went deeper into the process of developing exercises, meditations and improvisations to help us experience this concept of a listening body. I invited people to treat their bodies as their best friends. To learn how to listen to it rather than marginalize and ignore it. To become more trusting of the signals and impulses that our bodies emit. To sensitize and quiet ourselves enough to notice how and where sounds from the environment land and reverberate in the body. And notice what the effects of these sounds are. We can also cultivate our own vocalizing and direct it into the body for healing. Sound in the body creates vibration, and vibration encourages blood flow that in turn, helps the body tissues to be more vibrant and healthy. And so, we continue to emerge into whole body listeners.

One of the great gifts for me as an instructor on the retreats is that I have been able to interact with so many wonderful musicians and sound artists through the years. It has been a joy to emphasize the body with folks who have had their primary training in sound and music. I have been inspired by the particular sensitivity that comes from that music focus which is different than that of artists in other disciplines or people from other backgrounds. And at the same time, I have so loved helping and encouraging folks to become more sensitive to their bodies as an instrument in and of itself. As a result of a gentle nudge from Pauline I wrote *Deeply Listening Body,*[2] a book of exercises, meditations and improvisations that have been presented on the Deep Listening retreats.

Through the years, I have had the great fortune to collaborate with Pauline on a number of performance projects as well. This fun, creative work, using our listening as the primary resource is always inspiring.

As both avid performer and audience member, I notice that I have become highly sensitized and alert to the way sound, silence and music are utilized. In my work, how I use sound/or not is as important as any

---

2 Heloise Gold, *Deeply Listening Body* (Kingston, NY: Deep Listening Publications, 2008).

other aspect of the piece. Lately, I have become curious about the notion of movement and sound happening simultaneously so that there is no hierarchy. If I am vocalizing and moving, I give this challenge to myself and further explore this concept when collaborating with others.

The ongoing practice of Deep Listening is just that, ongoing. The concept itself is an open and elegant system, allowing for a continual change of perception. This happens sometimes quite subtly and sometimes more obviously. The exchange between listening and receiving and expressing and responding makes for a beautiful, often surprising, and always wonderful sense that our lives are open to abounding possibilities.

Deep Listening and Touch:
Unwinding the Body of My Voice

LESLEY GRECO lives in Toronto, Canada. She has participated in Deep Listening retreats in New York and Ireland as well as spending two years involved in the certificate program. The practice of Deep Listening lies at the heart of her voice, movement and bodywork explorations. http://www.lesleygreco.com

Lesley Greco

Inclusiveness is essential to the process of unlocking layer after layer of imagination, meaning and memory down to the cellular level of human experience.[1]

Harmony in the Outer World

Athens, Greece 2001: *I leave Epidaurus and a few days later have arrived in Athens. The Pláka is alive. Layers of history and myth woven like a fine and sturdy gauze around the slopes of the Acropolis. It is night, just after the rainfall. Steam is rising and the air is full, damp.*

I am sitting against a stone wall on a stool in the street, my wrist freshly tattooed and now this woman, a new immigrant from Russia is busy at work tattooing Heather. Something about her has touched me, I can't say what but I am moved to stillness.

---

1 Pauline Oliveros, *Deep Listening; A Workshop Manual with Pauline Oliveros* (Kingston, NY: Deep Listening Publications, 1998), 4.

153

LESLEY GRECO

It begins to rain again; the sound of wet cobblestone touches my ear. The click click click of heeled shoes, an accordion breathing somewhere up the alleyway and soft sounds of speaking, the cry of a baby. I am full, still and listening.

Suddenly I am hearing everything, everysound and every sound has a place in the Great Rhythm.

Nothing is excluded. The light and the dark of all things moving together.

This music of life.

Harmony.

This was the first time I'd consciously experienced listening inclusively, something I would years later hear Pauline Oliveros speak about in the context of her compositional sound practice of Deep Listening. This experience in Greece changed everything for me. I knew deeply in that moment that there is a place for everything whether or not I understand or experience on an ongoing basis this inherent rhythm or harmony of life. Like the tuning of a radio dial I can choose to turn my attention toward it.

On the more micro level of the body the same is true. There are underlying rhythms that, while not audible to me, are palpable. These rhythms are inclusive of everything we are, there is no way to manipulate or control them but we can tune in and come into harmony with them. They support us, organizing and regulating our physical body and being. To experience this is to remember that we are already whole. To experience this is to know harmony on a cellular level. We can listen for this.

Listening can happen through hearing and listening can happen through seeing, through tasting. Any of the senses can be the doorway into listening; it is a state of being occurring within a person.

We are not hearing out there, sound waves are entering our ears, light waves enter our eyes. These are processed internally and so to listen is to become receptive.

I am both a practitioner and a recipient of craniosacral bodywork. Listening for me happens most deeply in this work through touch. Craniosacral touch facilitates a listening state of being and an inclusive listening relationship to our body facilitates the natural ease of our voices.

Harmony in the Inner World

Your deepest presence is in every small contracting and expanding, the two as beautifully balanced and coordinated as birds wings.[2]

Toronto, July 6, 2011: *I lay down on the table, we chat. I try to relax.*

Hands soft on my feet—breathe. Nadine[3] moves to my side.

Sacrum and belly the boundaries of her hands contain me.

My body feels tense, held and irritated. I am trapped in the cage of my head.

I am thinking a lot about listening and touch and voice. Busy. She waits, breathes, listens for me.

I'm drawn and my breath moves down into her hands—my hips. I feel volume, substance, space.

My breath moves out from my body in all directions. 360. I am here.

We spend a long time with my diaphragm; it is a clenched fist today. Slowly slowly like a whale sinking below stormy waters I am moving into stillness.

My heart sits upon the central tendon of my diaphragm, my tongue has grown out of the embryological tissue of my heart. I feel each of them beginning to unfurl.

Soon all the bowls and domes of my body are singing together, moving in the rhythm of my breath.

I want to move now and sit on the edge of the table, Nadine is standing beside me, a hand on my forehead, one on the base of my neck.

Listening for sensation, for vibration in the spaces of my body.

I feel the tissues of my pelvic bowl relax heavy and soft, air flows in like cool water.

My attention is between her hands, listening outwardly to the sounds of the street, the hum of the room. Listening inwardly to these stories of folding and unfolding.

---

2 from "Birdwings" in *The Essential Rumi: New Expanded Edition*, trans. Coleman Barks with Reynold Nicholson, A.J. Arberry, and John Moyne (New York: HarperCollins, 2004), 174.

3 "Craniosacral Therapist, Registered Somatic Movement Therapist," accessed November 30, 2011, http://www.nadinesaxton.com.

She follows the subtle movements of my spine as a feeling of grace descends on both of us.

Deeply into stillness now, feeling all the cells of my body, breath moving through them as the swell in the ocean.

The song of my body.

Listening for Health

> It is in the ability to be still and listen that the truth of the human system unfolds its mysteries.[4]

Early in his career as a medical student Dr. William Sutherland noticed that the bones of the head looked like they were designed for movement. In his exploration he had a profound realization that the cranium is designed to express small degrees of motion. During many years of groundbreaking research he demonstrated the existence of this motion and concluded that it is produced by the body's inherent life force which he called "The Breath of Life" or Primary Respiration.[5] Primary respiration produces a palpable series of rhythms which make up and maintain our physiological form, balance and order. In other words our bodies are self-organizing and self-regulating systems.

In *Craniosacral Biodynamics* Franklyn Sills speaks eloquently about the role of listening in craniosacral therapy:

> Truth is found in the depths of our listening. The purpose of this work is not to release resistance or to process issues, but to liberate the health inherent within the resistance or disturbance. Listen for expressions of health. . . . This is your challenge.[6]

In my approach to craniosacral bodywork, blockages or disturbances are seen as healthy responses from an intelligent body that has been

4 Franklyn Sills, *Foundations in Craniosacral Biodynamics: Vol. 1 The Breath of Life and Fundamental Skills*, 2nd Ed. (Berkeley, CA: North Atlantic Books, 2011), 10.

5 Huge Milne, *The Heart of Listening: A Visionary Approach to Craniosacral Work*, Vol. 1 and 2 (Berkeley, CA: North Atlantic Books, 1995).

6 Franklyn Sills, *Craniosacral Biodynamics: The Breath of Life, Biodynamics, and Fundamental Skills* (Berkeley, CA: North Atlantic Books, 2001), 431–434.

stressed beyond its capacity. Rather than aiming to eliminate limitations, craniosacral touch includes them in the dialogue, respecting that limitations have the ability to draw out something that is known inwardly by the person about the state that they are in. Listening touch is concerned with cultivating an awareness that draws us into relationship with our animal bodies. It does not discriminate against what is happening in the body by attempting to challenge or change it. Instead, through listening attention, it offers relationship and a reference point around which consciousness can organize. Stillness often occurs naturally in a body that is listened to in this way. In a state of deep listening or "stillpoint" as it is called in craniosacral work, impulse begins to arise. We begin to hear the natural voice of our body and its underlying rhythms of support, organization and regulation. We begin to witness the intelligence of nature.

Weaving the Worlds Together

> I started training myself to listen with a very simple meditation when my mother gave me a tape recorder for my birthday in 1953. . . I immediately began to record from my apartment window whatever was happening. I noticed that the microphone was picking up sounds that I had not heard while recording was in progress. I said to myself then and there: Listen to everything all the time and remind yourself when you are not listening.[7]

On the level of our body the parasympathetic or craniosacral branch of our nervous system is our recording system. It continually records new experience. During a craniosacral session our nervous system is recording, storing and processing our bodily experience.

Although craniosacral unwinding is a term which often refers to the process of releasing physical and emotional blocks, I use it here to describe a reorientation, or tuning, to the natural intelligence of the body. According to co-creative science researcher Machaelle Wright,[8] nature intelligence doesn't just know order organization and balance; it *is* order

---

7   Pauline Oliveros, *Deep Listening; A Workshop Manual with Pauline Oliveros* (Kingston, NY: Deep Listening Publications, 1998), 2.

8   Perelandra Center for Nature Research, "Center for Nature Research @ Perelandra, Ltd.," accessed May 20, 2011, http://www.perelandra-ltd.com.

organization and balance. This bodily intelligence knows exactly how to organize in order to best support the voice; we see this most clearly in babies. Craniosacral listening attunes us to this wisdom unwinding the body of the voice.

When I want to give expression to the voice of my body, I have the recorded experience of deep orientation and relationship to my nature intelligence to draw on in order to give body to my voice. I feel body in my voice when I can feel all of my parts, when I feel breath vibrate the resonant spaces in and around me. I feel body in my voice when from an *eye of the storm* or *center of the tornado* type of stillness I can listen to the emotional and feeling-based impulses arise, interacting with the space outside of me and returning in a flow of relationship, inner to outer, outer to inner. Impulses carried by the sounds and silences of my breath resonating within my body.

I have struggled with my voice throughout my life. I'd adopted patterns of breathing that restricted and restrained it. When I sang I often pushed, pulled and manipulated my voice until finally it seemed to give up altogether. By the time I found expert voice teacher Fides Krucker[9] I no longer felt I had access to the feeling of vocal freedom. With great respect for the way my body had adapted, Fides gently and masterfully guided me through the process of remembering on a cellular level how my body knows to breathe when it is at ease; naturally and fully. We began by listening to the patterns of breath in our bodies through touch: my hands on her recording the thirty-plus years of vocal experience she has in her body, her hands on me in order to facilitate listening to areas of my body that I had forgotten how to hear.

As breathing occurs, the nervous system records the experience. . . integrating each breath within the context of our historical behaviour and present environment."[10]

The nervous system unlearns old habits and integrates new patterns slowly. The body is faithful to the whole of its experience just like a tape

9 "Fides Krucker," accessed November 30, 2011, http://www.fideskrucker .com.
10 Bonnie Bainbridge Cohen, *Sensing, Feeling, and Action: The Experiential Anatomy of Body-Mind Centering* (Northhampton, MA: Contact Editions, 2008), 178.

recorder is faithful. When we can listen to the body without bias we have access to a more inclusive relationship with, and can give voice to, the fullness of our human experience: the body of our voice.

I work patiently[11] and continue to unwind the depths of release and emotion as well as rebuild the architecture of vocal technique through the foundation of my body.[12] Through Deep Listening practice, craniosacral bodywork, and diligent vocal training, small but lasting changes are happening over time. As my body and breath unwinds and becomes more natural so does my voice, so does my life.

---

11 most days

12 Fides Krucker, "*Chiaroscuro: the Bodhisattva in the Voice*," accessed December 27, 2011, http://www.fideskrucker.com/blog/wp-content/uploads/2011/10 /Article-11-10-Chiaroscoro-BoddhisattvaVoice.pdf (also published in *POIESIS: A Journal of the Arts & Communication*, XIII, (2011): 40-51).

Corporeal Listening: The Hands of a Builder

Lara Davis

LARA DAVIS is an architect, shell-builder, and doctoral research assistant at the Department of Architecture, ETH Zürich. She holds an MArch from the Massachusetts Institute of Technology, a BFA from the NYS College of Ceramics, School of Art & Design at Alfred University (New York), and has pursued research at the Institute for Lightweight Structures and Conceptual Design at the University of Stuttgart (Germany). She has worked extensively in the field as a mason, foreman, project manager and designer for non-structural masonry and thin-shell compression structures, most recently supervising the construction of a low-cost housing prototype in Addis Ababa, Ethiopia. She has led workshops on vault construction in Addis Ababa and Deri Dawa (Ethiopia), Zurich (Switzerland), Cambridge (UK), Boston and New York (USA). Her research focuses on constructibility in thin-shell masonry vaulting, addressing appropriate building technology, capacity-building, pedagogy of building craft and applied structural theory in the developing context. http://sudu1construction .wordpress.com/

AS A YOUNG VISUAL ARTIST—eighteen years old at the time of my first experience with Deep Listening—I often wondered exactly how it could influence material-based art investigations. I recognized how Deep Listening methods could alter an art practice in general, along with the story by which an artist comes to know their work out of the well of their personal experience. It was clear to me also how it would profoundly influence, in a much more medium-specific manner, a creative practice in music, composition and sonic arts. My work, however, was quite evidently outside of this terrain.

I was, in fact, at the time, an artist without a medium. I was searching for my work without a vehicle, and had only a vague intuition that my future work would involve a kind of material-intensive, corporeal practice. Every art medium I experimented with in this period seemed somehow inadequate, as though my engagement with it was only at a conceptual level, and not sufficiently visceral

161

or materialized. I felt a disconnect, alienated from art mediums which were necessarily produced within a kind of perceptual black-box (e.g. sterile studios or dark editing suites) that caged the perceptual faculties of the body. I wasn't satisfied with visual art as a metaphor; I wanted my work to express a corporeal experience of space.

The months I spent working as an intern for Pauline in the late 1990s radically altered my theoretical understanding of space. Exercises such as the arbitrary arrangement of chairs for a concert in a performance space underscored for me the visual, spatial and corporeal aspects of an expanded listening practice. I recognized how listening could impact a spatial sensibility, how a spatial context or mobility altered listening, and how attention could transform both. I was fascinated with the corporeal, sonic spaces—evoked in the articulation of sound and language—which emerged from Pauline's work. I remember listening to *Dream Horse Spiel* (1989)[1] over and over, its effect a sensation of spatial and cognitive unfolding. I noticed that the reciprocally-linked listening and sounding triggered a perception of hyperembodiment. That summer, I learned to play the didjeridu and experimented with the acoustic impact of spatial resonances. I wasn't particularly interested in the *sound* of the didjeridu, as a musical effect, but I was fascinated with the resonances one could achieve within spaces of the body (e.g. within the chest cavity) as one changes tone, pitch and vocalizes while playing. I became aware of the potential to train the body as an intuitive sensory tool.

In subsequent years, these experiences quickened an ongoing change in dimension in my art practice, literally, from a two-dimensional manipulation of space in the form of printmaking to a kind of spatialized sounding, a material practice which manipulated both visual and sensory information. I combined material-intensive and spatial art forms into site-specific installations, inserting small hand-built models or projecting light and video into abandoned architectural spaces and industrial sites. These first proto-architectural experiments were no doubt inspired by the Deep Listening Band's recordings in unique

---

1   Pauline Oliveros, "Dream Horse Spiel" excerpted on CD accompanying *The Roots of the Moment: Collected Writings 1980-1996* (New York: Drogue Press, 1998).

acoustical spaces, spaces which immersively shaped both sound and image. I felt that there was an affinity between installation art and the practice of musicians; both had the capacity to manipulate resonant sound at the architectural scale (within space) and at the corporeal or material scale (through the body or material). While I was already then engaging myself in space production, it would be the latter that would capture my attention in the craft of construction.

Years later, my material practice has become clearly manifested—I am an architect, a structural mason, a shell-builder. I work with architects, structural engineers, urban planners, and builders—a professional medley of often highly compartmentalized fields, which requires still other types of listening practices for the translation of professional languages. I specialize in the construction of thin-shell masonry vaults, a six-hundred-year-old Mediterranean construction technique called thin-tile or "timbrel" (drum) vaulting, named for the audible acoustic response when one taps on a very thin masonry shell. Most vaults vibrate in response to an impact, though this is particularly the case with thin shells. The response is acoustically perceptible if they are struck hard enough with respect to their thickness; however, below this threshold, the hands are one's ears, so to speak. They may sense an infinitely subtle vibration in a structural shell.

As a vault builder, a teacher, I train crew members to build, many of whom don't speak English. One cannot only be a specialist or technician when teaching without shared language; one must be rather a generalist *par excellance*, paying attention to every little cue in order to glean understanding, or exaggerating important lessons so that their value stands out. When I instruct young builders, I will sometimes put my hands or ear to the vault for emphasis, intently tapping a masonry shell with the thickness ratio of an eggshell, capable of spanning many meters. When students inquisitively respond, I explain that I am listening. It is an uncanny concept, which quite often captures their attention and encourages them to more carefully register the vibration they feel with their hands on the shell.

A mason sharpens his or her skill and instinct through years of experience and attention handling the course materials of building—bricks, mortar, tools, or the masonry surface itself. In building, one must develop a sensitivity to the behavior of materials and structural phenomena, and become adept at sensing these with multiple perceptual faculties. Visual criteria are of course important, but tactile perception (the hands) and an extended proprioceptive awareness (balance and spatial perception) are critical. Occasionally, even taste is employed (e.g. to tell the difference between chalk and lime).

Sound and response to acoustical feedback, however, play a special role. The impact of a tool upon a material (e.g. a chisel against brick) produces a sound, and the nature of this sound may be used to ascertain the quality of an intended action. For example, if a well-bonded brick has been set poorly and needs to be removed, a very blunt impact from a tool (e.g. a rubber hammer) would transmit a great deal of vibration throughout the shell and might compromise its stability. Alternately, a rapid, sharp motion with a pointed tool (e.g. the end of a trowel handle) would strike the target brick and rebound off of the surface. The latter would cause a local failure, breaking only the individual brick bond, without breaking adjacent bonds or causing failure mechanisms in the thin shell. The distinction in pitch between a sharp "ping" and a diffuse "pong" means in this case the difference between an effective and a hazardous action. Such response is critical for identifying mistakes and modifying techniques in construction, providing feedback about the stability of a shell, indicating whether the masonry course is closed or in cantilever, whether or not the structural form has integrity, and ultimately if the crew is exposed to risk.

The hands may be trained to simultaneously perform a task and receive sensory information. Tapping one's fingers, for example, creates audible feedback on the shell when a brick is setting. One may observe how the properties of a gypsum mortar are affected by this induced vibration: it is more evenly distributed to make full contact within a joint, course particles are consolidated, and then water content is brought to the surface of the mortar, before it sets at speed to establish a stronger bond. The frequency of sound from tapping is in turn altered by the changing properties of the mortar. When the bond is sufficiently set, the vibration is transmitted across mortar joints into a shell surface. The change in sound is barely audible, but the transmitted vibration can be easily felt. This is the craft of construction through corporeal listening.

For the engineer, these phenomena are entirely scientifically quantifiable. Natural frequencies occur in masonry vaults as a function of the shell's geometry and the material properties. For example, when one jumps in the middle of a footbridge, its structural behavior, essentially a deflection, has a natural frequency and resonance. A frequency from 4 to 8 Hz (cycles per second) may elicit a discomforting experience, for it is only within this range that frequencies are perceived by the standing body.[2][3] The range is increased, however, for the body lying down on this same surface, as the greater bodily contact increases the proprioceptive ability. The human hand, amazingly, is most sensitive to vibration energy from 8 to 16 Hz.[4] Yet, while natural frequencies may be accurately measured with instrumentation (e.g. accelerometers), the human hand rarely develops a facility to measure them with great sensitivity—perhaps with exception to those of the musician or the master craftsman.

And in this capacity, the musician and the master builder have a great deal in common. I often think of my musician friends while visiting the extraordinary vaults built by master masons, such as King's College Chapel in Cambridge, England, which displays the largest fan-vaulting in the world. For the musician, the greatest appeal is the sublime acoustic environment created from reflected sound within the resonant space of the chapel. For the architect, the master builder or the engineer, however, the sublime experience is to jump on the ridgeline of

---

2   International Organization for Standards, *Evaluation of human exposure to whole-body vibration - Part 1: General requirements* (Geneva, Switzerland: International Organization for Standards, 1985), International Standard ISO-2631/1-1985(E).

3   International Organization for Standards, *Evaluation of human exposure to whole-body vibration - Part 2: Continuous and shock-induced vibration in buildings* (1 to 80 Hz) (Geneva, Switzerland: International Organization for Standards, 1989), International Standard ISO-2631/2-1989(E).

4   Canadian Center for Occupational Health and Safety, "OSH Answers: Vibration – Measurement, Control and Standards," last modified October 21, 2008, accessed November 30, 2011, http://www.ccohs.ca/oshanswers /phys_agents/vibration/vibration_measure.html.

the 12.66 meter span—with a shell thickness in some places only of 10 cm—and experience the resonance of the vault itself as it is transmitted to the body.

The old master masons trained these physical, intuitive sensibilities with an empirical practice; the builders' hands translated course imputs into a fine intuition. They refined at once systems of measurement and proportion for the design of structures, and their own sensory feedback tools measuring the quality of their craft in space. While the hands may be a crude tool for the purpose of pure measurement, they are a corporeal construction tool with an immeasurable intuitive capacity—and the most trusted tool for the craft and creativity of the builder.

Deep Listening
in Pedagogy
and Music Theory

Cognitive Consonance: Deep Listening in Today's Schools

SUSAN KEY is Special Projects Director at the San Francisco Symphony, where she works on a variety of public and media-based initiatives. After eleven years of high school teaching, she earned a PhD in musicology and taught at the College of William and Mary and Stanford University. She has spoken and published on a broad range of topics in American music, including Stephen Foster, Aaron Copland, and early radio. She has served on the boards of the Society for American Music and the Los Angeles Public Library and has developed educational programs for the San Francisco Symphony, the Los Angeles Philharmonic, and the J. Paul Getty Museum. Her current passion is playing old-time fiddle.

Susan Key

I never really understood classical music before, but more than that, I think I never realized how to listen, I mean I'm always listening in the car, doing the dishes, you know, but not *listening*. . . if I can do it, my kindergarteners can.[1]

PROPONENTS OF DEEP LISTENING are aware of the profound impact the practice has on both individual and collective perception, experience, and relationships. For an individual, cultivating the practice enhances not only musical skills but many aspects of overall mental and physical health. Any such individual impact, in turn, spills over to the contexts in which we interact with each other, enhancing empathy and

---

1 Anonymous interview response by *Keeping Score* Education participant, 2007. Information provided by David Reider, Education Design, LLC Inc.

collaboration. The commentary about Deep Listening generally reflects an adult perspective, but it is striking that much of the same vocabulary is also at the center of the active and often rancorous debate about how to improve the effectiveness of public schools in developing literacy, information processing, problem solving, creativity, collaboration, and communication—those key elements of the new "twenty-first century learning skills" that are often cited as crucial to success in a rapidly evolving world. Although there is no simple way for Deep Listening to reach the millions of children in America's classrooms, my own experience has convinced me that even small amounts of the practice could yield great benefits in the cognitive development of children.

I was familiar with the work of Pauline Oliveros for many years before my experiential introduction, which came at a 2005 conference of the Society for American Music. Oliveros accepted honorary membership in the Society and offered a group workshop that included a simple exercise: we each sang a song of our choice as slowly as possible while walking around and listening to the group. I was struck by the combination of discipline and freedom in the practice as well as the integration of individual and collective voices. At the time I was beginning to develop a teacher professional development program for the San Francisco Symphony—part of its *Keeping Score*™ media project. My charge was to provide training and resources to K-12 teachers to support the development and implementation of music-integrated teaching and learning.[2] The training involved a week-long Summer Institute, followed by four full-day school-year professional development training sessions. Teachers then developed music-integrated lesson plans and contributed them to an online lesson plan library. I was intrigued by the idea of incorporating Deep Listening into the process but wasn't certain exactly how a group of teachers, many of whom had no formal musical training, would react.

I used the Deep Listening exercise as the last session of our pilot year program with twenty teachers from Fresno, California. While it did not produce an instant "aha!" moment for everyone, it did give me

---

2   The program completed its sixth and final year in 2011 and has reached over 350 teachers and 47,000 students.

confidence to continue working along those lines. Over the six years of the program, my curriculum team and I gradually adapted both specific tools and general orientation of Deep Listening into the *Keeping Score* Education workshops. As we went along, I realized how closely the principles of Deep Listening were aligned with the principles of effective teaching and the ways in which they shared a deeper approach to the processes of perception and engagement that are central to educational success. In this paper I will describe some examples of listening practices for both children and adults (some of which are directly based on Deep Listening, some of which are indirectly inspired by the practice). These examples are mostly drawn from Western classical tradition but, like Deep Listening itself, would not have to be limited to any single style or genre. While a specific, large-scale Deep Listening program for public schools is unfortunately unrealistic for a single organization to implement, the results from *Keeping Score* Education suggest that there are potentially fruitful avenues to explore.[3]

The Context

Today's schools are in a precarious moment. Most Americans are aware of funding cuts, arguments about teacher quality, and the extent to which standardized testing has become the driver of content, accountability and resources. This scenario has eroded the arts, and is especially frustrating since research in the field strongly suggests that there are powerful connections between the arts and gains in both affective development (student engagement, attendance, community involvement, and social development) and cognitive skills (literacy, spatial reasoning, and scientific problem-solving). As one study put it:

> The researchers found that young people in "high-arts" groups performed better than those in "low-arts" groups on measures

---

3　The material described in this essay represents the collective wisdom and collaborative practice of hundreds of *Keeping Score Education* teachers who participated in the program. Although only a few are mentioned by name, their impact will continue to resonate in the experience of thousands of students. This essay is an attempt to disseminate their work to a larger audience.

of creativity, fluency, originality, elaboration and resistance to closure—capacities central to arts learning. Pupils in arts-intensive settings were also strong in their abilities to express thoughts and ideas, exercise their imaginations and take risks in learning. In addition, they were described by their teachers as more cooperative and willing to display their learning publicly.[4]

These reports confirm what many of us know intuitively: the arts are central to optimal development, and their neglect is eroding the quality of education today, as teachers around the country feel an unrelenting pressure to focus on the short-term accountability of tests in math and language arts. Ironically, this "teaching to the test" parallels the weakness of traditional approaches to music teaching that Oliveros and others have identified: emphasis on uniformity and short-term correctness at the expense of long-term musicality.

Exacerbating the problem of "teaching to the test" is the steady decline in arts as part of both teacher preparation and ongoing professional development. A study of arts education in California public schools found that participation of classroom teachers in the available arts-related professional development has been limited by a lack of sufficient funding and competing demands in other core subjects. Combined with the minimal pre-service training classroom teachers receive in the arts, this limited participation in professional development is highly problematic given reports by principals that the lack of arts expertise among classroom teachers is a major barrier to the delivery of arts instruction at the elementary level.[5] California's problems are not unique. Across the country, the decline of arts instruction in

---

4 Judith Burton, Robert Horowitz, and Hal Abeles, "Learning in and Through the Arts: Curriculum Implications," in *Champions of Change: The Impact of the Arts on Learning* (Washington, DC: Arts Education Partnership, 1999), 36. Subsequent research has reinforced findings about the efficacy of the arts in developing a broad range of cognitive and emotional skills. For information on current research, see "Arts Education Partnership," accessed November 30, 2011, http://www.aep-arts.org.
5 Katrina R. Woodworth, H. Alix Gallagher, Roneeta Guha, Ashley Z. Campbell, Alejandra M. Lopez-Torkos, and Debbie Kim. *An Unfinished*

K-12 education and the decline or complete dismantling of arts education requirements in teacher credentialing programs have resulted in an entire generation of teachers and administrators who bring a minimal arts background into their roles as educators.

While there is no easy fix to this problem, current research underscores the importance of professional development as the most effective vehicle for making fundamental change in classrooms. The effect holds true for all subjects, but because of the changes in teacher preparation this is especially magnified in the case of the arts. Teachers are often intimidated by their own perceived lack of talent and ability in the arts, and classical music is especially intimidating because of the time and resources needed to build skills. A 2004 study put it this way: "The most frequently mentioned issue [by teachers]. . . was the need for more training to gain skills and build self-efficacy in using the arts.[6]

Many organizations are attempting to support what little capacity schools have for the arts through professional development programs such as *Keeping Score* Education. The goal is to offer teachers a basic comfort level in music as well as support in finding ways to slip the arts in among the myriad obligations of curriculum.[7]

Adult Education

Most teachers who entered *Keeping Score* Education expected to gain some knowledge about classical music and some lesson plans using

---

Canvas. Arts Education in California: Taking Stock of Policies and Practices. Summary Report. (Menlo Park, CA: SRI International, 2007), 53.

6 Barry Oreck, "The artistic and professional development of teachers: a study of teachers' attitudes toward and use of the arts in teaching," *Journal of Teacher Education* 55, no. 1 (January/February 2004): 55–69.

7 Even when educators are committed to music listening as a core element in the classroom, there is no general agreement about how to do it best. The topic of music listening has been subject of debate for many years. See Magne Espeland, "A century of music listening in schools: toward practices resonating with cultural psychology?" in Margaret S. Barrett, ed., *A Cultural Psychology of Music Education* (Oxford and New York: Oxford University Press, 2010), 143–78.

classical music. They were motivated to give their students exposure to the arts. But given the lack of even superficial exposure that teachers experience in their education and school environments, it is not surprising that many teachers came to *Keeping Score* Education with great anxiety about both their musical skills and their ability to integrate this challenging art form into their teaching.

Overcoming these obstacles required challenging the typical professional development model of giving teachers a specific set of instructions which they are then expected to implement exactly as outlined. *Keeping Score* Education, in contrast, built on the principles of Deep Listening and used an open-ended, experiential, discovery process. We stressed:

- *The multi-dimensional nature of listening*: listening with ears, eyes, bodies, minds, and emotions.
- *The effectiveness of focus and filters*: exercises to hone aural sensitivity in multiple environments.
- *The importance of active music making*: active engagement and improvisation on musical elements.

Using these principles was radical, but we knew that true change would only happen when teachers internalized the content through engagement. Similar to Deep Listening, we provided an entry point to a powerful experience but left specific classroom applications and modes of implementation up to the teachers. Because their musical immersion extended into active music making, teachers internalized an approach to the material that transferred into their entire pedagogical practice. As one teacher reflected:

> I expected we would learn a lot about music integration, but I didn't expect to have such enriching musical experiences ourselves. It makes the impact of the workshop so much greater, because we were able to experience what our students will be going through as they engage these concepts for the first time. I had many "aha!" moments as a learner, and this encourages me to create those for my own students.[8]

---

8 Anonymous survey response from *Keeping Score* Education participant, 2008. Information provided by David Reider, Education Design, LLC Inc.

The *Keeping Score* professional development process began with listening, frequently a Deep Listening exercise: "Sit and note all the sounds you hear for five minutes."[9] For teachers, this activity served two purposes: the experience of quiet, focused listening and an appreciation for the myriad sounds that make up our soundscape—natural, human, and mechanical. The concept of soundscape translates especially well to school curricula in science and social studies, as it asks students to perceive, to distinguish, and to analyze the meaning of both individual sounds and their combinations. As Pauline Oliveros reminds us: "sound pressure patterns assist hearing but cultural history and experience influences listening."[10]

Teachers were also introduced to the idea that the listening experience is multi-dimensional. Figure 1 (see page 188) shows an introductory handout. The initial emphasis was not so much on the music as an object but on the subjective listening experience. Technical vocabulary was introduced gradually, beginning with terms that were easiest to grasp from everyday experience: loud/soft; fast/slow. In this way, teachers were in a position to approach music of the Western classical canon with openness to their own listening experience. Preparation for the musical immersion of the Summer Institute involved listening exercises and journal responses based on a custom audio CD that included both the summer's focus work and additional music drawn from its cultural and historical context. For example, when preparing for Dvořák's *New World* Symphony, teachers listened to selections that created a multi-ethnic "soundscape" of 1880s New York City, including the African American spirituals and "Indianist movement" music from the period when Dvořák was composing and teaching at the National Conservatory of Music. For the *New World* Symphony itself, teachers were asked to listen to the work from a variety of perspectives and sensory filters: the journal page for the first movement of Dvořák's symphony asked: "Dvořák has just dropped you into an unfamiliar

---

9   This is a variant on "The Poetics of Environmental Sound," in Pauline Oliveros, *Software for People* (Baltimore: Smith Publications, 1984), 28.

10   Pauline Oliveros, *Deep Listening: A Composer's Sound Practice* (New York: iUniverse, 2005), xxiii.

landscape. Look around: what do you see? Explore your new landscape and make notes about how and where it changes."

Once at the Summer Institute, teachers continued to hone their listening skills and begin to consider how to transfer those skills into the classroom context in grade-level sessions that introduced the idea of using listening filters to help students listen most deeply to classical music. Figure 2 (see page 189) demonstrates a "Listening Toolkit" exercise developed for primary grade teachers, appropriate to adult learners but also usable at the grade level these participants taught. The exercise moves from open listening, to filtered listening, to a creative process that integrates visual and/or kinesthetic work. The active participation in the creative process throughout the Institute involved singing, dancing, and visual work. One teacher at that year's Summer Institute answered the survey question: "What single music integration skill or knowledge morsel did you take away from today's work?" with a simple yet profound affirmation: "I can sing. Everyone CAN sing."[11]

After the Summer Institute, teachers continued their listening activities in preparation for the follow-up school-year workshops. Figure 3 (see pages 190–192) illustrates the listening exercise based on the first movement of Beethoven's Fifth Symphony. The idea of a journey then framed all the activities throughout the day-long workshop. One teacher reacted this way:

> I have come to understand that Beethoven is expressing emotion with his music. That makes all the difference to me. It used to seem disjointed to me—hard to listen to. Now, I love all of the variation. I was very moved yesterday while listening to the music.[12]

It may seem incomprehensible to many of us that a listener could have been unaware of the emotion in Beethoven's music. Yet this teacher's conditioning had so eroded her ability to connect with the music that it

---

11 Anonymous survey response by *Keeping Score* Education participant, 2008. Information provided by David Reider, Education Design, LLC Inc.

12 Anonymous survey response by *Keeping Score* Education participant, 2007. Information provided by David Reider, Education Design, LLC Inc.

took a re-training process to strip away the artificial barriers and allow her to *listen*, not just *hear*.

In the Classroom

Ultimately, of course, the goal of *Keeping Score* Education was to make an impact on students in the classroom. As the program developed, we became increasingly convinced that the same principles and practices that we used in working with teachers could be transferred to the classroom, where listening skills are increasingly challenged by the nature of contemporary life. As Oliveros notes, "urban living causes narrow focus and disconnection,"[13] and no group has been more impacted than children. Although children begin as natural listeners, the amount of "sonic clutter" in students' lives has eroded this ability and created a disconnect between mind and body. Oliveros also notes the need for a balance of focal and global attention—a crucial element of success for a child in a classroom.

There is often an initial concern from teachers that the students will resist music. To address this, the curriculum team developed a "5 x 5" activity that teachers implemented before beginning their own training. (See Figure 4, pages 193–197.) The activity begins by focusing children's attention on the music, then engaging with the music through different modalities. The simple 5 x 5 activity helped address teachers' anxiety about the reactions of their students to unfamiliar music and laid a foundation for their own engagement in a learning process that was both personal and professional. Both adult learning and student learning include elements of awareness, mindfulness, multi-dimensional understanding, attention, and articulation. Rather than a directive about what they needed to hear, teachers learned to allow both themselves and their students the experience of listening.[14]

---

13 Oliveros, *Deep Listening*, xxv.

14 Also important is that the practice of listening, even to classical music, is not isolated to "music class" and that even performance-based assessment is not rated by traditional measures of "correctness." Often music teachers were initially the most resistant to an approach to music that lacked the comforting objectivity of these traditional measures.

The results of engaged listening in the classroom are remarkable even in children as young as kindergarten age. Researcher and independent program evaluator David Reider describes one manifestation:

> The teacher played a recording of Chopin's well-known "Rain-drop" Prelude,[15] a slow piece with very clear delineations between sections and tonal episodes. The composition contains several easily identifiable musical elements such as repeating bass notes, and "sing-able" themes that repeat, making it useful for musical discussion, vocabulary building, and listening skill development, even for kindergarten students.
>
> Eighteen students sat on the floor around the stereo and listened quietly to the five minute performance without interruption. After completion, the teacher led a discussion on what they heard. Comments included mood shifts with the student identifying where the tonality changed from major to minor, ". . . the storm part," the raindrops (the insistent bass line setting the rhythmic pattern), the motivic return, "the sun came back," and the conclusion with the barely breathing ritardando pulse, "I think he fell asleep." The conversation included students saying words such as major, minor, "sad-but happy" (a particularly astute observation since the compositional mood is altogether melancholy though in a major key) fast, slow, beat, changes, more notes, and the like. In the kindergarten context, this awareness seemed especially keen.
>
> Then, the students were told to close their eyes and think about what the composition might look like as a picture. Finally, they were sent to desks to draw the composition on a four-segmented page, guiding them to drawing different episodes from the listening. The piece was played again during the drawing session. Many of the drawings showed dark rain, clouds moving in, sun coming up, some contrast between happiness and sad, and at least a few connections to the textural differences Chopin penned. Pictures were quite different from child to child.
>
> The teacher commented on how the piece consisted of different sections, just like a story they were reading at the time; how

15 Frederic Chopin, *Prelude in D-flat Major*, Op. 28, No. 15 (1839).

music and literature shared fundamental structural connections.

This process allowed students to translate their own aural perceptions into words while respecting the contributions of others; then into a visual medium, then into an understanding of fundamental structural connections across disciplines.[16]

This listening experience was focused, but also functioned as a conduit to levels of understanding beyond the musical object. To achieve this does not happen without careful planning; a listening exercise is as dependent on good design as any other lesson. As Reider goes on to describe:

> In another kindergarten class, the teacher played a recording of the same Chopin Prelude, only this time the children were at their desks, drawing pens in hand. They did not experience the pure listening part of the activity, only went straight to drawing. The results were quite different. Most pictures depicted a dark rainstorm, presumably because the teacher told them the piece was about rain. There were no contrasts with sun, light, or any nuance; most seemed very similar. There was no conversation about what they had heard. Though the music was pleasant, it made little impression upon the students since it was presented as background to another event rather than as central unto itself.
>
> The first teacher explained later that the presentation of classical music at the Summer Institute and workshops helped her understand exactly what music was: seeing and hearing the instruments up close, listening to musicians talk about their lives and those of the composers. Without those experiences, classical music would have remained the wallpaper she had previously considered it to be. Because of that transformation, she now listens to classical music with focus and tries to hear connections to the knowledge gained in the professional development.[17]

---

16 David Reider, Education Design, LLC Inc. Report from classroom observation, 2009.
17 Ibid.

An effective exercise is built on elements that promote receptivity and that allow students to be drawn *into* the music rather than distracted *from* it.

The kindergarteners in the example above articulated their listening experience through words and visual arts, but this process of translation can take many forms. A third grade teacher wove together listening to Beethoven's music with reading from his emotionally powerful Heiligenstadt Testament and then videotaped the results.[18] Students then chose passages from the Testament to read aloud. Students answered the question about why they chose a particular passage. Responses included:

- "It felt like I knew how you were feeling."
- "He's not lying to people."

These student comments are a clear example of the process of aesthetic perception noted by John Dewey:

> "to perceive, a beholder must create his own experience. And his creation must include relations comparable to those which the original producer underwent. They are not the same in any literal sense. But. . . without an act of recreation, the object is not perceived as a work of art."[19]

Of particular importance here is the use of emotional vocabulary. Teachers today are often distressed by the extent to which students have difficulty identifying and articulating their own feelings. Listening helps them do this in a safe environment. It can also offer students an entry point into those "intellectual" aspects of music, as demonstrated in a "portfolio conference," structured interviews in which students described their learning process. In the following excerpt, the researcher (LS) is speaking with third grade students Caitlin, Marcus, Sidney, and Lindsey.[20]

---

18 Footage of this exercise at http://www.deeplistening.org/essays, created for the San Francisco Symphony's *Keeping Score* Education program by Bonnie Raines in 2010.

19 John Dewey, *Art as Experience* (New York: Perigee Books, 1934), 54.

20 David Reider, Education Design, LLC Inc. With contributions by Larry Scripp and Fred Sienkiewicz, New England Conservatory Center for

LS: Let's listen to Beethoven's Fifth Symphony together. What was that?

Caitlin: He was expressing his feeling. . . . Beethoven, the one that makes music and he has expression because he is losing his hearing. . . .

Marcus: We can experience like. . .

Sidney: . . . feeling the music, it sounds like somebody is getting into a fight or an argument.

(LS sings the first four notes)

Sidney: It's like when me and my brother have an argument about a toy. . .

LS: What is the story here?

Sidney: It's about Beethoven and he is losing his hearing, it's a piece of music that is about how he feels.

LS: What is the dialog?

Marcus: [It's] like something is going wrong between two people. . .

LS: Does it get resolved?

Marcus: Yes, it gets resolved.

LS: Where in the music does it get resolved?

Marcus: At the end.

LS: How is it resolved?

Marcus: They're angry.

LS: How does this conversation proceed?

Caitlin: They are arguing about something.

Lindsey: It stopped and they got mad again.

On first reading, this conversation might not suggest a profound understanding of Beethoven's symphony. Unlike traditional "music appreciation" exercises, there is no emphasis on technical vocabulary, identification of instruments, or the like. Yet the student responses include recognition of internal tension, form, and emotional vocabulary that connected the student's individual experience to music—and, arguably, closer to the words with which Beethoven himself would have described his music. Even the perception that the music resolved but in an angry

---

Music-in-Education. *Keeping Score* Education Evaluation Report Year 4 (2008), 25.

way represents close listening, as the movement ends with emphatic minor chords.

A technique for creating the safe environment often involves asking students to listen with eyes closed. As one teacher explains:

> Kids are extremely social and if their eyes are open, they look at others for attention or approval or agreement. . . With their eyes closed, it's a safe place for every kid to have his/her own unique experience and to really listen. I encourage kids to move in place if they want to. Sometimes I have kids sit (as in the Beethoven shots) and other times to lie down. I always turn the lights off too. Even if kids open their eyes occasionally, they go back to the closed eyed place when I remind them and also because there really is more happening inside their head than outside. It seems easier to get into an imaginative state with music with closed eyes.[21]

The same teacher allows the imaginative state to cross disciplines into poetry. Examples of student work (a slide show of the entire class's poetry plus their interpretation of the iconic image of Beethoven) are available online[22] to demonstrate the way the same exercise can stimulate a range of creative responses:

> Beethoven
>
> A Music genius
> his music light as a feather
> his life hard as a rock
> his feeling
> joyful and sorrowful
> his pieces colorful as a rainbow
> Some are gray as smoke
> This is Ludwig van Beethoven
> The one and only
> His massive music warms the hearts
> Of even depressed people
> What a man![23]

---

21 Bonnie Raines, email correspondence with author, June 11, 2011.
22 See http://www.deeplistening.org/essays.
23 Ibid.

This example clearly begins around a biographical entry point and moves outward to the music and its impact. A different student's composition plays with second-person references; we as readers do not know whether the poem is addressed to Beethoven, or to us, or to both, creating rich layers of meaning.

> Beethoven's Music
>
> Beethoven
> Sad as the night sky
> Glide
> Through the music
> Dance
> With the one you love
> Seek the moon
> You will find the music
> Slide through
> The smooth music notes[24]

The quality of these poetic responses reflects a carefully designed listening process that allows for multi-layered responses, including kinesthetic. As the teacher explained:

> When we move [from listening] to movement, I of course want their eyes open but rules for this are: move to the music, don't make eye contact, and avoid body contact with others. After a few trials, they really get this and it's pretty effortless.

Scientific concepts can also be taught through engaged listening. A second grade teacher began with a listening to Francis Poulenc's *Sonata for Two Pianos*. Students described the music. One student noted "it's like a pattern." Patterns pervade every subject area: math, science, language as well as the arts, and the ability to recognize patterns through aural and kinesthetic means is a fundamental cognitive skill. The class then described the texture of different rocks, then integrated the two both verbally and with a creative movement exercise.[25] This teacher, like many others, noted that often those students most responsive to the listening activities were those with cognitive or emotional disabilities:

---

24 Ibid.
25 Janet Greene, Oak Grove Elementary School, Sonoma County, California.

Several of the students who have either learning and/or emotional challenges are often the ones who respond most strongly and creatively to the musical selections, through their movements or verbal responses. Other students who are usually reticent or English Language Learners are excited to voice their opinions about the music.[26]

Elementary school teachers have some definite advantages in making Deep Listening a core element in the classroom: more flexible curriculum and time management. *Keeping Score* Education teachers at upper grade levels, however, also found ways to integrate music in a meaningful way. The following learning sequence[27] was developed for sixth grade but could easily be adapted for older students:

DAY 1: Listen to Fugue 1. Ask students: If a movie was set to this music, Toccata and Fugue in D Minor, and you were the director, what would be on the screen? (Note: This composition is nine minutes long; a two-minute excerpt can be created using Audacity for PC or GarageBand for Mac.) 2. Tell students that they are about to listen to Toccata and Fugue in D Minor by Johann Sebastian Bach. While listening they should draw or write about what they imagine when they hear this music. It can be a series of scenes or a story. 3. When the music is over, allow a minute or so of silence, then have students share in small groups or pair-share the imagery or stories which they imagined.

DAY 2: Listen to Fugue 4. Tell students that they will add details about setting and mood to their imagery while they listen to the music again. Teacher asks questions—before, during, or after student listening—to help students evoke additional imagery. Suggested guiding questions: What do you see in the landscape? In the cityscape? In the skyscape? If you are in a room or a building, what furniture do you see? Do you see people? What is the weather? 5. Play the musical selection.

26 Janet Greene, correspondence with author, June 2011.

27 Anita Ullner, created for the San Francisco Symphony's *Keeping Score* Education program in 2010.

6. Students pair-share new details of imagery or story line. 7. Teacher asks students about general mood and settings they have imagined. Students share their imagery. 8. Teacher asks students to think about: "What is it in the music that elicits that imagery?" Inform students that they will listen to *Toccata* one more time on the next day and they will annotate music elements and share responses to this question: What is it in the music that elicits imagery?

DAY 3: Listen to Fugue 9. Remind students of previous day's question: What is in the music that elicits imagery? Allow students to share if they have opinions or ideas before listening again. 10. Direct them to listen for a specific music element as they listen to Toccata (this can be teacher assigned or free choice): dynamics (loud/soft), tempo (speed), timbre (instruments), or articulation (translation of the notes). 11. Play music and have students annotate listening guide according to the tracked element. Listening guide is divided into timed columns. Teacher keeps track of time. 12. After listening to this musical selection: students discuss in small groups, followed up by whole class discussion: What is it in the music that caused you to imagine what you did? Chart student responses. 13. Teacher states that composers often choose musical elements to achieve or communicate a mood. (NOTE: Most students have identified the "high point" in both of these pieces of music, if students are familiar with story elements, like exposition, rising action, high point, falling action, and resolution.)

OPTIONAL ACTIVITY: Repeat the steps from Day 1 through 3 using a different Bach composition. In this lesson, I used the Prelude from J.S. Bach's first Cello Suite.

What is it about this lesson that involves good listening practices? Part of the answer is what occurs before the lesson starts: the teacher has created an environment in which students expect to listen with receptivity. Within the lesson itself, at each step of the way, the teacher returns the students' attention to the music, which stimulates a level of deeper and longer-term engagement that transcends the short-term emphasis of so much educational practice today. As one teacher summed up the "key take-away:":

> "Anything is possible." Listening to music and learning about it opens the mind to experience so many great things on a higher level, it allows individuals to make connections to the world around them that cannot be explained in words. It provides a vehicle for the mind to manifest creative expressions that can only be facilitated by sound.[28]

The process begins with the teacher, moves to the classroom, and loops back to the teacher. As one survey respondent described: "Just being allowed to do this kind of thinking with music lets me think about the other ways my teaching can be expanded."[29]

Reflections

What conclusions can be drawn from a single program that wove Deep Listening principles into a professional development program for public school teachers? Independent formative and summative evaluations of the program give ample evidence of significant gains in teacher and student learning in the arts. As researcher Larry Scripp observed:

> [*Keeping Score* Education] represents one of the most impressive displays of depth and reach of music listening program in schools I have ever seen. . . In my opinion, this program's evolution reflects an extremely significant contribution to growth in the field of music in education, and bodes well for the direction of music listening as a prominent focus in the future school and arts organization partnerships.[30]

Although the formal *Keeping Score* Education program has ended, these results suggest that Deep Listening can prove transformative for both

---

28 Anonymous survey response by *Keeping Score* Education participant, 2008. Information provided by external evaluator David Reider, Education Design, LLC Inc.

29 David Reider, Education Design, LLC Inc., with contributions by Larry Scripp, Fred Sienkiewicz, Larry Scripp and Fred Sienkiewicz, Helen Liu, Michael Glicksman, New England Conservatory's Center for Music-in-Education. *Keeping Score* Education Year 3 Evaluation Report (2007), 19.

30 Letter to Grawemeyer Foundation in support of *Keeping Score* June 26, 2009.

teachers and students. Precisely because this approach is appropriate for both adults and children, Deep Listening exercises represent a potentially powerful tool for professional development. The training creates a positive loop from teacher, to student, back to teacher, promoting enthusiasm and engagement in the learning process for all parties.

The gulf between Deep Listening and public school bureaucracy is wide. But both objective and anecdotal evidence suggest that it is an element with great potential for students—and one that teachers at all levels can successfully adapt to their needs. I encourage Deep Listening practitioners to reach out to educators in their communities on three levels:

- Public policy advocacy efforts at both local and national levels on behalf of arts education[31]
- Formal contacts with local educators through professional organizations of music educators and PTAs: e.g., proposing sessions at educator conferences; disseminating information about Deep Listening opportunities to educator listservs.
- Informal contacts with local educators: e.g. offering to lead a Deep Listening exercise in a local classroom or professional development session; talking to local parents and teachers about Deep Listening opportunities.

Making a difference in today's educational context will require both persistence and resourcefulness. But as I found in *Keeping Score Education*, the rewards for teachers and students who adopt Deep Listening-inspired practices in their classrooms are both extensive and profound.

---

31 Information about how to get involved in advocacy efforts can be found on the website of the Arts Education Partnership (http://www.aep-arts.org) as well as those of state arts agencies.

Figure 1: Introductory handout

SAN FRANCISCO SYMPHONY
MICHAEL TILSON THOMAS MUSIC DIRECTOR

Keeping Score Education: Pre-Institute Listening Journal

Listening skills are at the heart of Keeping Score! While we hear a lot of music, often we don't really listen. You will get the most out of your listening experience with a few simple guidelines.

First, consider the many dimensions that go into our listening experience:

<u>We listen with our *ears*.</u> Hearing sounds: loud and soft, tinny and woody, fast and slow, smooth and choppy. . .

<u>We listen with our *eyes*.</u> Watching the musicians, the audience, and creating images in the "mind's eye" of our imagination. . .

<u>We listen with our *bodies*.</u> Sensing our heartbeat, temperature, goose bumps, toes tapping, skin tingling, tasting sweet and bitter. . .

<u>We listen with our *memories*.</u> Remembering this music, music it reminds us of, times we have been in similar spaces, environments . . .

<u>We listen with our *emotions*.</u> Feeling joy, pain, nostalgia, triumph. . .

<u>We listen with our *minds*.</u> Analyzing relationships, form, pattern, design. . .

<u>We listen with our *"sixth sense"*.</u> Connecting to our spirit, transcending the everyday. . .

<u>We listen with *each other*.</u> Feeling the "vibe" of the group, feeling intimate even with strangers. . .

Second, consider the elements of an effective listening exercise
(The good news: there are only two!):

1. FOCUS

There's a simple device here: always give yourself something to focus on. It could be a musical element: tempo (how fast or slow the music is), dynamics (how loud or soft the music is), timbre (what instruments are playing), etc. You'll discover that this narrow focus on one element actually results in better listening to all aspects of the music! Plus it's a great way to help when the mind is wandering.

Beyond the musical elements, don't be afraid to take advantage of music's many connections to all facets of our experience *while keeping a clear focus*. Give yourself freedom to think about the music as a movie score, or to explore your emotions, or to let your body create a physical gesture.

2. REPETITION

The great quality of classical music is its combination of breadth and depth: its ability to express the grandest and the subtlest ideas and emotions. Because of this, it isn't always something you can grasp the first time, the way you might with a popular song. Classical music may at first seem forbiddingly complex or esoteric but you'll be surprised how much you begin to appreciate after listening several times with focus.

Figure 2: Listening exercise for primary grades

"Listen To the Birds" in Dvorak's New World Symphony

1. Listen to the section inspired by Dvorak's interpretation of the song of the Robin and the Bluebird.

2. Listen to selection a second time using the theme of "Nature" as a filter; discuss how that filter affects what is heard in the music.

3. Listen to recorded bird calls:
Robin	"Cheerio! Cheerily!"
Bluebird	"Deary! Deary!"
Ovenbird	"Teacher, teacher, teacher!"
Doves	"Ooooh! Woooooh!"

4. Create a Bird Symphony. Divide into four groups. Each group has one of the four birdcalls listed above. All groups sing together to make a "bird symphony."

5. Teachers conduct/lead Bird Symphony. Signs with the bird names and calls are placed on the floor in the middle of the circle. When the conductor taps his or her foot on the corresponding sign, that group begins to sing their part. Gestures can also be used to bring volume up or down, cut offs, etc.

6. Variation: The whole group mixes up. Players close their eyes and sing their "bird call." They try to find the rest of their group by listening around them.

7. Listen to the New World Symphony again and have students conduct the song of the Robin and the Bluebird.

Developed and presented by Kim Morin (California State University, Fresno) and Cindy Scarberry (Oklahoma A+ Schools).

Figure 3: Beethoven Exercise

Ludwig van Beethoven, Allegro con brio from Symphony No. 5 in C minor
"I shall seize fate by the throat; it shall not crush me completely."

First Listening(s): Immediate Reactions

Find someplace quiet and listen to this familiar piece and jot down your immediate reactions: What are the things you notice? These could be musical characteristics – even if you aren't sure how to describe them with technical vocabulary. Or they could be something about your personal listening experience: how the music affects you, what associations it brings up, etc. Don't worry about being "correct" -- just pay attention to your listening experience. Use the timing bar at the top to help keep track of where you are within the piece.

ext Listening(s): Guided Reflections

Now use a specific filter in your listening: the way Beethoven creates a kind of musical journey from the beginning to the end of the music. Below are some words associated with journeys to get you started. Note: not all will apply, nor will they necessarily apply in this order. Feel free to substitute your own words.

Journey Descriptions...Emotional Connotations

Preparation	Crossroads	Uphill	Anticipation	Confidence
Setting Off	Detour	Downhill	Determination	Trepidation
First Step	Off track	Meandering	Excitement	Relaxation
Steady progress	Temporary halt		Hesitancy	Tension
Uneven progress	False turn		Fear	Triumph
Rushing forward	Retracing steps		Relief	Surprise
Slowing down	Milestone		Awe	Despair
Climax	Last push		Confusion	Hope
Stride	Goal		Stumbling	

Figure 3: Beethoven Exercise (Continued)

Ludwig van Beethoven, Allegro con brio from Symphony No. 5 in C minor
"I shall seize fate by the throat; it shall not crush me completely."

Putting it all together: How did Beethoven do that?

Then identify what you feel are the words that describe the way the music creates a journey. Pay special attention to the important structural points identified on your sheet. Don't worry about the vocabulary you don't know; use the vocabulary you do know. Don't overlook the most obvious (fast/slow; loud/soft), and don't worry if you don't know a particular technical term. Just make sure that what you are describing is a *musical* characteristic:

Tempo (fast or slow or in-between)	Tone color (choice of instruments)	Accents (on or offbeat)
Acceleration vs. deceleration	Rhythm (patterns of short and long notes)	Getting louder vs. getting softer
Dynamics (loud or soft or in-between)	Smooth (legato)	Choppy (staccato)
Melody: simple or complex		

Figure 3: Beethoven Exercise (Continued)

Ludwig van Beethoven, Allegro con brio from Symphony No. 5 in C minor, 2

timing	0:00	1:00	1:30	2:00	2:30	3:00	3:30	4:00	4:30	5:00	5:30	6:00	6:30	7:00 7:10
N O T E S	The Journey *1:24* *2:49* *4:11* *5:42*													
	Stage 1	Stage 2			Stage 3			Stage 4			Stage 5			

Figure 4: *"5 x 5"*

One of the most valuable qualities of classical music is that the more you listen to it, the more you hear. These short (5 – 10 minute) activities will give you and your students the opportunity to discover some of the many ways music makes us hear, see, and feel.

A Note About the Music: **We have selected two pieces for the activities; however, if you wish to choose two different selections, we recommend that you limit the time for each selection to 1-2 minutes.**

Keeping Score 2010-11: Two Music Selections --- Five Days --- Five Minutes a Day	
DAY 1 Selection #1: Tchaikovsky, "Waltz of the Flowers"	
"JUST LISTEN"	Students "open their ears and minds" and "just listen" (without identifying the name of the piece) to Selection #1 (*"Waltz of the Flowers,"* from Tchaikovsky's *Nutcracker* ballet)
DISCUSS	In partners or as a whole group, briefly discuss **"What did you notice about the music?"** Additional guiding questions (choose the ones that best fit your students): *What movie does this music remind you of? What images or pictures come to mind? What colors? What emotions? Did you notice any patterns in the music? When do you think this music was written? Where? What was it for?*
"SKETCH TO STRETCH"	Give students paper and pencils, markers, or crayons. Students then listen to Selection #1 again. This time students "sketch" as they listen. They can draw pictures or images that come to mind from their first listening, or draw free-form lines that match what they hear. **For Upper Grades:** *"As you listen to the selection, draw free form lines that show character or emotion that matches the music. The marks may be vertical, horizontal, diagonal, straight, curvy, thick, thin, zigzag, spiral, rough, or broken, depending upon what you hear.* **Hint: If you have time, practice just drawing lines on paper before you listen:**
IDENTIFY	Tell the students the name of the piece and the composer. Refer to the background information as time allows.

Keeping Score 2010-11: Two Music Selections — Five Days — Five Minutes a Day

	DAY 2 Selection #1: Tchaikovsky, "Waltz of the Flowers"
"MOVE TO THE MUSIC"	Students listen to Selection #1 ("*Waltz of the Flowers*," from Tchaikovsky's *Nutcracker* ballet) and move as they listen. **Note: As an alternative you can repeat the "Just Listen" activity from the day before with an additional guiding question drawn from what stood out for students the first time around.)** **Suggestions for ways students can move:** a. "Be the Conductor" -Sitting in their desks, they can use their arms to "be a conductor," and follow the music. b. "Eyes Closed" – Students sit at their desks or on the floor with eyes closed and move their arms and upper bodies. c "Freestyle" -Students move around the room keeping within their own space or "bubble" as they listen. d. "Mirrors" - Partners face each other. Partner "A" leads as Partner "B" follows, as if looking in a mirror.
"ONE WORD RESPONSE"	Each student responds with one word that describes the music.
"QUICK-WRITE"	Students are given paper and pencils. They listen again to Selection #1 and write all of the words or phrases that come to mind as they are listening.
IDENTIFY	Remind the students of the name of the piece and the composer. Discuss additional background information as time allows.

Figure 4: "5 x 5" (Continued)

Keeping Score 2010–11: Two Music Selections — Five Days — Five Minutes a Day

	DAY 3 Selection #2: Tchaikovsky, "Trepak"
"JUST LISTEN"	Students "open their ears and minds" and "just listen" (without identifying the name of the piece) to Selection #2 ("Trepak" from Tchaikovsky's *Nutcracker* ballet).
DISCUSS	In partners or as a whole group, briefly discuss **"What did you notice about the music?"** Additional guiding questions (choose the ones that best fit your students): *What movie does this music remind you of? What images or pictures come to mind? What colors? emotions? Did you notice any patterns in the music? When do you think this music was written? Where? What was it for?*
"SKETCH TO STRETCH"	Give students paper and pencils, markers, or crayons. Students then listen to Selection #2 again. This time students "sketch" as they listen. They can draw pictures or images that come to mind from their first listening, or draw free-form lines that match what they hear. **For Upper Grades:** *"As you listen to the selection, draw free form lines that show character or emotion that matches the music. The marks may be vertical, horizontal, diagonal, straight, curvy, thick, thin, zigzag, spiral, rough, or broken, depending upon what you hear. **Hint: If you have time, practice just drawing lines on paper before you listen:***
IDENTIFY	Tell the students the name of the piece and the composer. Refer to the background information as time allows.

Figure 4: "5 x 5" (Continued)

Keeping Score 2010-11: Two Music Selections --- Five Days --- Five Minutes a Day	
DAY 4 Selection #2: Tchaikovsky, "Trepak"	
"MOVE TO THE MUSIC"	Students listen to Selection #2 ("Trepak" from Tchaikovsky's *Nutcracker* ballet) –and move as they listen. (*As an alternative you can repeat the "Just Listen" activity with Selection 2*) (**See Day 2 for suggestions for ways students can move**)
"ONE WORD RESPONSE"	Each student responds with one word that describes the music.
"QUICK-WRITE"	Students are given paper and pencils. They listen again to Selection 2 – *Nutcracker "Trepak,"* and write all of the words or phrases that come to mind as they are listening.
IDENTIFY	Remind the students of the name of the piece and the composer. Discuss additional background information as time allows.
DAY 5 Selections #1 and #2: "Waltz of the Flowers" and "Trepak"	
COMPARE	Give students their sketches and quick-writes from Days 1-4.
"JUST LISTEN #1"	Students listen to Selection 1, "Waltz of the Flowers," as they review their sketches and quick-writes of the piece.
"JUST LISTEN #2"	Students listen to Selection 2, "Trepak," as they review their sketches and quick-writes of the piece.
VENN DIAGRAM	Students complete a Venn Diagram comparing and contrasting the two music selections.
DISCUSS	Students discuss the similarities and differences.

Figure 4: "5 x 5" (Conclusion)

	Keeping Score 2010-11: Two Music Selections --- Five Days --- Five Minutes a Day
	OPTIONAL FOLLOW-UP WRITING ACTIVITY
DIAMANTE POEM	Write a Diamante (diamond) poem (See Guidelines) 1. Students look at the VENN Diagram and identify which words are nouns, adjectives, or verbs. 2. They use these words to write a Diamante poem that exemplifies the contrasts between the two selections of music.

Deep Listening: A Method Towards Focusing Consciousness in a Multi-Mediated Student Body

Suzanne Thorpe

SUZANNE THORPE is a performer, composer, educator and arts-activist who strives for breakthroughs in understanding via sound. Thorpe composes site-specific works that employ psychoacoustic phenomena, tuned filtering systems, and social practice. From 1989 to 2001, she was a founding member of Mercury Rev, an internationally acclaimed band with whom she earned critical praise, and a gold record for 1998's *Deserters' Songs*. Over twenty recordings of her work appear on the labels Sony, V2, Beggars Banquet, Geffen, Specific Recordings, and Tape Drift. Currently she is an Adjunct Professor at Marymount Manhattan College, teaching Sound Design and Sense and Medium, and co-founder of Techne, a program that provides workshops in electronic music techniques for young women.
http://suzannethorpe.com/

AT MARYMOUNT MANHATTAN COLLEGE (New York, NY) I co-teach *Sense & Medium: Introduction to Creative Media*. The course is designed to orient incoming Communication Arts students with various media including sound, video, and graphic design through experiential practice. The component of the class I focus on is sound, addressing issues of critical theory, practice and design. Before my class engages with any of the aforementioned topics, however, my students must learn how to listen.

One might assume that students enrolled in a sound design class would be predisposed to listening, but this is often not the case. Instead students often come to class visually oriented. They are typically saturated by media, frequently lacking critical filters that allow for the construction of personal choice, voice, and action. In order to focus students towards an aural orientation, the practice known as Deep Listening, which builds a sensitivity towards the sonic as information source, is incorporated. Through Deep Listening students learn to craft internal filters to engage with their surroundings. They begin to recognize their bodies as the final medium and develop increasingly dynamic sensory orientations. With newly focused senses, students expand their creative potential and become more discerning, critical participants in the world around them.

The Experiential as a Learning Tool for Digital Media

Sense & Medium: Introduction to Creative Media is an experiential learning course that introduces students to media practice and theory through guided exercises. Students learn how to apply perceptual awareness to the creation of digital, sound and video projects. A main goal for the students is to develop their observational and listening skills. Proficiencies in these areas support coexisting goals, such as the development of compositional strategy, expressivity with digital media, and critical choice as to which medum best suits an idea. The Sound Design block concentrates on listening as the experiential learning tool for creative work using sound. Along with soundwalks and field record-ing exercises, Deep Listening is one of the methods employed to focus students towards an aural modality.

From Generation Eye to Generation Ear

New students arrive in *Sense & Medium* with an unprecedented level of experience with digital media. Levels of proficiency vary, but most students have engaged with an iSomething that has enabled them to begin creative projects with digital tools. They also enter class with the ability to rapidly transition between virtual and actual realms (perhaps they don't perceive the distinctions as older generations do?). They arrive with a new understanding of networks, and practice unparalleled acts of acceptance of a culture that hyper-stimulates the senses with media input (but is it hyper to them?). Although most students listen to music as a pastime, and some create music, many, if not all, default to the visual as their primary source of sensory information. This default is a common position in today's visually oriented society, and supported in part by basic critical theorists like John Berger, with statements such as "it is seeing which establishes our place in the surrounding world,"[1] or Michel Foucault's observation in his *Le corps utopique*, "My head, for example, my head: what a strange cavern that opens onto the external world with two windows. Two openings—I am sure of because I see them in the mirror..."[2] These statements establish consciousness in the visual realm, but what of the aural? What about the ears? My goal is to focus the mind towards the aural as an information source, a challenge for the visually dependent, media saturated, multi-tasking student body.

As a first step towards this goal I lead an experiential activity inspired by the Deep Listening exercise, *Environmental Dialog*.[3] Students are asked to listen to their surroundings and radiate their aural focus from themselves, to their neighbors, to their immediate environment and beyond. They identify a sound of their choosing to emulate, and, when a bell sounds, imitate their sound with their voices, interacting with the group and their surroundings until the end. As Giovanna Chesler, Assistant Professor of Communication Arts and video instructor for *Sense & Medium* has observed, the exercise "allows for waves of understanding to emerge, which emanate from the listener's position and reveals how students listen to those around them, the architecture of the room, and the city space beyond the walls and windows. What they hear and how they understand it is revealed as the students perform the sounds back in the second half of the exercise." Quickly the group has a new awareness of the aural as information source. From this simple exercise participants develop a new relationship with sound, employing it to forge connections between themselves, their neighbors, and

---

1 John Berger, *Ways of Seeing* (Great Britain: British Broadcasting Corporation and Penguin, 1972), 1.

2 Caroline A. Jones, "Introduction," in *Sensorium: Embodied Experience, Technology, and Art,* ed. Caroline Jones (Cambridge, MA: MIT Press, 2006), 230.

3 Pauline Oliveros, *Deep Listening: A Composer's Sound Practice* (New York: Deep Listening Publications, 2005), 35.

environment. With this activity students also link the experiential with their creative output in a direct manner.

To foster this burgeoning consciousness, Deep Listening has been incorporated further into the *Sense & Medium* curriculum. When students arrive in the sound block, they spend the first day discussing the difference between hearing and listening, which their reading from Oliveros' *Deep Listening: A Composer's Sound Practice*[4] so clearly outlines. Students are guided through Oliveros' *Ear Piece*[5] to tune their ears and minds, and then taken on a soundwalk. Soundwalks are mapped to lead students through three aural environments with strikingly different acoustic characteristics. This mapping enables students to clearly identify distinct sonic attributes of each environment. Post-walk dialog reveals awakened attentiveness to sound as information. Students are freshly aware of the physical characteristics of the soundscape around them. They perceive how the architecture, or lack thereof, contributes to what they are hearing, and begin to recognize the cultural information embedded in the sounds they hear. Of the walks, Andrew Warshaw, Associate Professor of Music and Dance at Marymount Manhattan College, and co-instructor of *Sense & Medium*, has observed, "what is most gratifying is how appreciative students can be when listening is the lesson. In the first class of the Audio module, after walking through a noisy cityscape, not speaking until the time comes to collect comments, their faces are almost always calm but excited, their comments animated and thoughtful. It's as though they've always wanted permission to listen, and listen more closely, and then even more closely, but had rarely been offered it."

The group is then asked to gather field recordings of sounds that stand out to them. Subsequent listening sessions reveal newly alert minds and ears. It is at this stage, as Warshaw has observed, that students "engaged in the act of recording sounds, of isolating them and trying to capture them, taking note of their characteristics and transforming them during compositional work. . . effectively link the power of listening to the production of powerful art."

---

4 Ibid., xxii–xxiii.

5 Ibid., 34.

Continuing Ed

At this point students are asked to employ their new skill sets to develop a sound project. Projects can be narrative, abstract or of a *musique concrète* nature, but must include found-sound that they themselves have recorded. As hoped for, their final projects reveal a more highly developed sensibility towards the aural landscape. Using field recordings, students compose works that evoke specific environments and/or create spaces of abstraction that are open to interpretation. They use sound to articulate specific concepts, and employ it to alter or challenge preconceived notions. Often they layer *musique concrète* techniques over more derivative counterpoint, displaying an ability to dislocate an assigned meaning from a sound. Also, through Deep Listening exercises and on their soundwalks, students interacted with the world through the more spherical sense of hearing, allowing them to experience simultaneity through sound. With Oliveros' *Ear Piece*, they were asked to recall a sound while listening to a current sound, or listen to an existing sound while imagining a future sound. Awakened to a wider radius of sensory input, and the possibility of layering the experiences of past, present and future, students' final projects began to flirt with fluctuating temporal relationships as, with Deep Listening, they had arrived at the idea that experience isn't always linear. In their final pieces, students began to experiment with vertical in addition to horizontal composition, challenging elements of narrative to occur in a non-linear fashion.

Students also begin to redefine their concepts of noise. What they had previously observed as harsh or dissonant later became material representing comfort or beauty. In confronting the cacophony of New York City students became aware of noise as politic. Clamor typically represents industry, which in turn symbolically represents success in Western culture. As students attempted to focus their attention on the aural, identifying and capturing sounds, they awakened to the idea of a new currency: quiet. They began to realize that spaces of sensory calm are often a privilege to which many don't have easy access. All of these results exhibit thoughtfulness toward sound that is surprisingly sophisticated for students new to the concept of interacting with the world through an acoustic modality. This understanding did not exist prior to their engagement with Deep Listening, or if it did, the method served to heighten their sensibilities.

It can also be noted that Deep Listening practices heighten awareness to the fact that our senses are constantly being bombarded by outside stimuli in an increasingly prolific fashion. As students begin to listen to their surroundings, the blast of information they hear can be over-whelming. Students begin to realize that sensory data is being projected at them at a brisk pace, and that they must develop skills to support a state of active agency. As these skills are honed, students begin to posi-tion themselves differently in relationship to their media. They are able to locate how their bodies are interacting with their environments. They realize that regardless of the media with which they engage, it is the individual that proves to be the final medium. When students move on to learn other media their freshly-tuned ears and minds serve to deepen their engagement with their new tools. As Chesler has observed, "the exercises continue when they produce an experimental documentary video that explores the city through a sense. Many choose sound, and in creating a silent film they connect the visual to their auditory experi-ence, honed through the Deep Listening exercise and its extension in the Sound Design block."

Deep Listening: An Express to Understanding

Deep Listening has proven to be an incredibly effective experiential learning tool for *Sense & Medium*. Students come to class with a desire to be heard, and want to voice their ideas in a unique and creative manner using new media. However, media can confuse and confound commu-nication, an ironic symptom of instruments developed to increase the transmission of ideas and inspire the imagination. With Deep Listening students learn to focus their attention. Through the practice of Deep Listening, they gain a greater understanding of themselves, achieve enhanced relationships with their surroundings, and develop more dynamic interactions with the world. From this stance they can create. From this platform they can find a true voice that will sustain their actions and interactions with their environment and creative tools, whatever they might be.

Virtuosic Listening:
Context in Soundscapes and Music

SCOTT SMALLWOOD is a sound artist, composer, and sound performer who creates works inspired by discovered textures and forms, through a practice of listening, field recording, and improvisation. He also designs experimental electronic instruments and software, as well as sound installations and site-specific performance scenarios. He performs as one-half of the laptop/electronic duo Evidence (with Stephan Moore) and has performed with Seth Cluett, Curtis Bahn, Mark Dresser, Cor Fuhler, John Butcher, Pauline Oliveros, and many others. He has written acoustic and electroacoustic works for a variety of ensembles, most recently for the New York Virtuoso Singers, the Nash Ensemble of London, and the Princeton Laptop Orchestra. His work has been released on a variety of imprints, including Deep Listening, Wowcool, winds measure, and others. Smallwood currently lives in Edmonton, Alberta, where he teaches composition, improvisation, and electroacoustic music at the University of Alberta. http://www.scott-smallwood.com/

Scott Smallwood

Shuffle Play

ONE OF MY FAVORITE things to do when I'm working mindlessly at home or in the studio is to listen to my iTunes library on shuffle play. I'm not the only person that I know who does this, and as anyone who does knows, it's a fascinating channel of discovery and aesthetic pleasure. My library is fairly broad, containing a lifetime of interests, and some of it, of course, is not familiar to me, since I probably haven't listened to every audio file in my collection. So, as my brain allots more attention to the music and I notice things like "oh, this tune. . ." or "yeah, this is nice," or "no please. . . don't do this now. . . Ack!," it is always nice when the music-information retrieval system my particular brain uses says, "hey, what is this?"

This happened to me recently, and it was quite an eye-opener. I heard music that sounded like. . . nothing I could quite put my finger on. I sat back and gave it my full attention. I didn't recognize a "musical style," or a particular instrumental combination, although for a moment, I felt that it could be acoustic. But it had a fuzzy quality—almost a lo-fi texture, yet seemed very aesthetically considered. There were pitches present, and even pitched "flutters" and structures, pianistic even, but nothing particularly melodic or theme-like. It had a mechanical-sounding rhythm, at times, which shifted and seemed to change direction in haphazard ways. There were times when I could identify mechanical sounds, sort of, but was never able to make out the sources clearly. It was very warm and colorful, but still fuzzy, in ways that reminded me of the bands My Bloody Valentine or Boards of Canada. But then, the overall timbre and texture of this music began to suggest that it was an early electronic work. It really had me going for a while, and I experienced listening to it in that truly abstract space where I was unable to conjure up instruments, sources, style, nostalgic references, anything. I was able, then, to listen in a purely aesthetic space that was admittedly analytical but not held to any ground rules.

Finally I had to look. It turned out to be Pierre Schaeffer, and not just any Pierre Schaeffer, but one of the original five etudes from *Cinq études de bruits*; specifically, the *Étude noire*. Pow! And then it all came into focus. I heard the piano sounds, the clumsy turntable cycling, the hissing and distorted mechanical recordings, and all of the associations: *musique concrète*, *musique acousmatique*, and his seminal theoretical writing, the *Traité des Objets Musicaux*,[1] and accompanying recording *Solfège de l'Objet Sonore*,[2] in which he theorizes on the "sound object" and on the classification of sounds.

So, this perhaps says more about how long it's been since I have actually listened to the *Cinq études de bruits* then anything else, but I was a bit surprised nonetheless. This experience got me to thinking about Schaeffer's whole idea of *acousmatic* listening, which was largely abandoned by many of Schaeffer's own colleagues, but which still affects

---

1 Pierre Schaeffer, *Traité des objets musicaux* (Paris: Le Seuil, 1966).
2 Pierre Schaeffer, *Solfège de l'objet sonore*, ORTF, SR 2, lp, 1967 (also issed on CD as INA-GRM, ina c 2010/11/12, 475 602, CD, 2005).

the values many electroacoustic artists hold about the receptivity of their work. A conflict remains between those who espouse a possible non-referential, receptive state of listening, and those who claim that the reference cannot be erased and that extra-musical associations will always exist, albeit in different ways with different people. But what was it about that searching that I did before I knew the source? That inquiry? My aesthetic regard for the music included the process of searching for signifiers, of something to relate the sounds to, while simultaneously enjoying the mystery and elusiveness of the non-identifiable sounds. How quickly this process of listening changed when I sought and received the information! I was instantly thrown into a very different listening state, like finding the trail, or turning on the light. It started to make a different kind of sense to me, but not one that I would say is inherently better or worse, just different.

Turning on the Light

In 2001 I attended a conference at Dartington College of the Arts in England entitled *Sound Practice: On Sound, Culture and Environments*. Giving one of the keynote lectures was a blind theologian by the name of John Hull. Hull lost his eyesight over thirty years ago, and thus, happened to be an excellent listener who also excelled at articulating what it means to live in a world of sound without sight. I'll never forget him relating the following:

> When I enter a hotel room—whether it's night or day makes no difference to me because I can't tell the difference except by observing my stomach—the first thing I do is get out my little portable radio set, which I carry with me almost always. And the first object I come to, which might be a bed, it might be a cupboard, it might be the place where you put your cases, I lay my little radio down and I turn it on. That is my way of turning on the light.[3]

Hull is describing his way of revealing space, which for the blind is a void until sound can reveal boundaries through acoustical reflection

---

3 John Hull, "Sound: An Enrichment or State," *Soundscape* 2:1 (2001): 10.

and resonance. This is a very different, much more fundamental listening concept than the one I describe above, but it's a nice metaphor for what the kind of "sea change" that happens in any listening environment when a collection of information arrives, reframing and contextualizing the listening situation. Hull's talk contained many powerful metaphors and lessons about listening. He described his love of thunder, and how it places a ceiling over what is otherwise a world of infinite vertical space. He described how the sounds of trees reveal seasons, and how he learned to listen to the rain and its ability to describe space.

> I would press my nose hard against the window. And gradually it was as if the glass disappeared, because now my consciousness extended out from my nose pressed upon a panel of glass until it became unconscious, and I became aware that the sounds of the rain on the surrounding panels—it was one of those windows made up of those little panels with beading between them—that the sound on the different panels of glass was different. Each tiny panel gave a different sound. And as I concentrated now on this sound—I don't mean to say I tried to concentrate, I was too depressed for that—as the sounds of these panels of glass became noticeable, became impossible not to notice, then it was as if my consciousness gradually spread out: first, the differentiation between the little panels of glass around my face, and then the wider sound of the panels of glass where the rain hit them on the edges of the windows, and beyond that, I realised I could I hear the rain hitting the wall. It was different, where it hit the wall from where it hit the window. Where it hit the window it reverberated with little echoes. Where it hit the wall it was dull. But then I realised I could hear the water running down the wall. And now I became aware of a distant rushing sound—a spout from the corner of the house, and the water was gushing down it. Beyond that something else. . . yes. . . the rain was falling upon a large bush, I could detect it. And what was this between the bush and the spout?. . . Yes. . . there was a different sound where the rain was hitting the lawn, from where the rain was hitting the

path. I listened more acutely. . . 'swish,' 'swish'. . . I could hear
cars going past in the road. The rain had turned the light on.[4]

I quote this passage because it illustrates this idea of searching in such
a beautiful and powerful way, this idea of expanding one's awareness outwards, revealing more and more of the space. This mirrors
one of Pauline Oliveros' Deep Listening exercises, known as "Global
Listening,"[5] in which she encourages listeners to hear their bodies, their
own breathing, and to expand the listening awareness outwards in a
circle, first to those nearby, then to the outer reaches of the room, then
into the hallway or into adjacent rooms, outside of the building, out to
the street, to the outer reaches of the region, to the next town or city.
Can you hear the sounds happening on the other side of the world?

This searching, straining to hear, to listen to what is being revealed,
is perhaps not explicitly exercised by the sighted at all times, except in
situations where it is necessary to do so for the sake of survival. Oliveros'
life-long work has been to encourage a practice of such listening awareness at all times; to achieve what Hull described in his talk as "organic,"
where the "the ability to hear becomes organic in the body as a whole."[6]
So, what does this mean in terms of listening to music? What are we
searching for when we listen to music? In the case of the Schaeffer
excerpt I encountered in my shuffle play listening experience, there were
many different kinds of listening happening. I listened for sources, style,
genre, timbre, and probably many other things. I anticipated what might
happen next. I was ready for the thing that would cause me to say, "ah,
OK I know what this is." This very particular kind of searching put the
experience into a very different frame that would have existed if I were,
for example, listening to this piece on the radio in France in 1948, or
in an electroacoustic music concert of historic works. I don't claim that

---

4 Hull, "Sound: An Enrichment or State," 11–12.
5 Pauline Oliveros, "Quantum Listening: From Practice to Theory (To
   Practice Practice)," *Deepplanet Magazine*, accessed January 25,
   2011, http://deepplanetcom.yourwebhosting.com/magazine/articles
   .asp?ArticleID=7&SectionID=6.
6 Hull, "Sound: An Enrichment or State," 12.

this experience was inherently better or worse than any other, but in the context of shuffle play listening, it created an interesting aesthetic experience that was pleasurable and interesting for me personally. It has become a way of listening that I indulge in quite often, and that often results in such experiences. Brian Eno has described this way of listening as it relates to the aesthetics of recording technologies: "You become acutely aware of the different sort of recording aesthetics when you hear things next to each other. When you hear a contemporary recording followed immediately, as often happens when you have shuffling forms like Spotify and the iPod, by something from 1958, you think, 'My God, he was so close to the microphone then. Or, listen to those strings. they've [*sic*] got a whole orchestra there, but it's about at the level of a very quiet high-hat.' The differences become so apparent when things are next to each other, and I think that makes you much more acutely aware of the medium of recording than we've ever been. . ."[7]

Acousmatic Listening

Acousmatic, the Larousse dictionary tells us, is the "Name given to the disciples of Pythagoras who, for five years, listened to his teachings while he was hidden behind a curtain, without seeing him, while observing a strict silence." Hidden from their eyes, only the voice of their master reached the disciples.[8]

This introduction to the concept of *acousmatic* listening by the father of *musique concrète*, Pierre Schaeffer, describes a way of listening that stems from the phenomenological philosophy of Edmund Husserl, in which an experience can be described without reference to its source. Schaeffer's use of this ancient word allows him to link the ancient

---

7 Randall Roberts, "A conversation with Brian Eno: 'We are all singing. We call it speech, but we're singing to each other,'" *Pop and Hiss* (blog), *Los Angeles Times*, July 5, 2011, accessed November 30, 2011, http://latimesblogs.latimes.com/music_blog/2011/07/a-conversation-with-brian-eno-we-are-all-singing-we-call-it-speech-but-were-singing-to-each-other.html.

8 Schaeffer, *Traité des objets musicaux*, 1.

Pythagorean curtain to the new set of tools he is so famous for having exploited for artistic means: the radio studio and its tools for reproduction. Schaeffer, whose art revolved around materials that are abstracted from their source, the *objets sonores*, understood that in the world he lived in, and the musical culture with which most of his fellow humans were familiar, the visual symbol of the sound source was as important as the sound itself, whether or not the instrument or object of sonic delivery is seen or hidden. For Schaeffer, it was important to create a new culture of listening in which the instrument is no longer seen as the sole articulator of musical civilization, and in fact, no element or means is necessary at all in order to hear music. Schaeffer was asking us to deliberately forget "every reference to instrumental causes or preexisting musical significations," and to "then seek to devote ourselves entirely and exclusively to *listening*, to discover the instinctive paths that lead from the purely 'sonorous' to the purely 'musical.'"[9]

I can recall being very excited by this revelation as a student, when I learned about this concept, as well as by the writings of Cage, Feldman, and so many others who seemed to suggest that there was more to music than the virtuosic performer on a concert hall stage. This somehow justified what I already had experienced intuitively throughout my childhood musical explorations, having grown up well into the age of recorded media. I can recall, for instance, the pleasure of listening to American and British popular music in the 1970s on my father's stereo using headphones, and being transported into that imaginary acoustical space that is the result of modern recording and production techniques. I recall being disillusioned and somewhat disappointed upon hearing some of these tunes performed live by actual musicians in real-time, without the production and stereophonic sound world I had come to know and love. Though this listening experience may not be correctly categorized as *acousmatic*, since it is mostly clear that many of the instruments could be identified, I couldn't *see* these instruments being performed, particularly the electronic ones that I couldn't even picture in my mind. Even those instruments that I understood—the electric

---

9 Schaeffer, *Traité des objets musicaux,* 1.

guitar, piano, drums, bass—these were not visually experienced. I didn't imagine the players playing these instruments so much as I imagined a kind of abstracted world of sound, color, and time. I felt them in my body. I often didn't even parse the content of the lyrics so much as I did the sound of the voice. In fact, while this is certainly not always true, I still to this day hear songs that I know inside and out while not actually knowing or caring what is being sung about. In fact, I have been embarrassed by this fact more than once upon sharing a song with someone and suddenly realizing how offensive or ridiculous the lyrics are. My listening experience, indeed, changes drastically when I'm in "sharing" mode, an interesting fact in and of itself.

The acousmatic tradition has been written about extensively, and for the past ten years has been the subject of much questioning and criticism, both for the idea and against. Joanna Demers, in her discussion of post-Schaefferian electroacoustic music,[10] points out that while *musique concrète* was founded on the idea of acousmatic listening, the *Traité des Objets Musicaux* being Schaeffer's culminated research on the subject, most other composers and artists who developed work at Radiodiffusion-Télévision Française largely abandoned the idea that one could really expect an audience to achieve a true state of "blind listening," since our nature is to search, identify, and try to make some kind of sense out of what we are hearing. Schaeffer himself famously abandoned his life's work, claiming in the end that he had "wasted his life."[11] Others, such as Francisco López, have worked to revive the concept, not only in written form,[12] but in López's case by literally blindfolding his audiences during his live performances in order to coerce them into a state of acousmatic listening. While this certainly removes the impetus some audience members have for locating the performer

---

10 Joanna Demers, *Listening Through the Noise: The Aesthetics of Experimental Electronic Music* (Oxford: Oxford University Press, 2010).

11 Tim Hodgkinson, "Pierre Schaeffer: An interview with the pioneer of musique concrète." *RēR Quarterly* 2:1 (1987): 2.

12 Francisco López, "Profound Listening and Environmental Sound Matter" in *Audio Culture: Readings in Modern Music*, ed. Christoph Cox and Daniel Warner (New York: Continuum, 2004).

in the space and trying to track what they are doing, it doesn't really remove attempts one might have to identify what the sound sources are, to speculate about how they were made, etc. What is interesting about experiencing these concerts is that López quite often succeeds in masking his sources, which are largely field recordings, often layered, processed, and obscured through various means until they really do seem to emit a kind of sonic purity. And yet there are other ways in which my searching can spotlight an idea or event in these sounds that reveal something about them, even to the extent of comparing López to other noise artists. "This sounds a bit like the Zbigniew Karkowski performance I heard last year," or "This sounds a bit like that Yellow Swans track."

And yet, there are times when I truly enter into that state where, for a moment, I'm not searching for sources or analyzing styles; rather, I am simply in a state of pure sensation. Maybe not for long, for eventually I may find myself "snapping out of it" and going back on the hunt, trying to identify, contextualize, categorize. But for a moment I'm in that blissful state of pure sensation, which can be a powerful and profound experience. And as I alluded to above in my shuffle-play experience of rediscovering Schaeffer's *Étude noire*, I think this often occurs when we are not necessarily giving the music our full attention.

While perhaps too often quoted in writings like these, it seems apt to revisit Brian Eno's ambient music. When Eno coined the term ambient music in the 1970s, he was describing a kind of music that represented a particular type of listening: one in which the music becomes part of a larger tapestry of sound in space, one that allows for the ambient noise of our environment to enhance and be enhanced by a more idealized sonic accompaniment to the moment. He states:

> This became clear to me when I was confined to bed, immobilized by an accident in early 1975. My friend Judy Nylon had visited, and brought with her a record of seventeenth century harp music. I asked her to put it on as she left, which she did, but it wasn't until she'd gone that I realized that the hi-fi was much too quiet and one of the speakers had given up anyway. It was raining hard outside, and I could hardly hear the music

above the rain—just the loudest notes, like little crystals, sonic icebergs rising out of the storm. I couldn't get up and change it, so I just lay there waiting for my next visitor to sort it out, and gradually I was seduced by this listening experience. I realized that this was what I wanted music to be—a place, a feeling, an all-around tint to my sonic environment.[13]

Through this experience, Eno discovered a way of designing music for a situation many people find themselves in, that of listening to a prerecorded piece of music, the reception of which is compromised by the other sounds that exist in that listening space. In the properly designed concert hall, these sounds are minimized and the performers are able to monopolize the sound space. But elsewhere—in the car, at the airport, in the grocery store—other sounds get in the way. Eno is suggesting that these are legitimate listening spaces, and it is clear today that a culture of this kind of listening in such spaces already exists. Eno's *Music for Airports* (1978), as well as other pieces of his from this period have often been background accompaniment for me as I work on mindless tasks. Is this a "bad" way of listening to music? I don't think so. I think, in fact, that this kind of listening can actually bring us closer to a possible state of acousmatic listening, much more so than the experience of listening to this music in the concert hall, with or without live performers.

Bull Dozing

Pauline Oliveros' Deep Listening practice encourages an engaged, aware, and sustained listening state at all times, not only when listening to music, but to the soundscape as well. One of my favorite quotes from her sound journals is:

The bulldozer starts again moving the air like an audible crooked staircase before reaching its full power. As I lean on my wooden table, my arm receives sympathetic vibrations from the low frequencies of the bulldozer, but hearing seems to take place in my stomach. A jet passes over. Some of its

---

13 Brian Eno, *A Year With Swollen Appendices* (London: Faber and Faber, 1996), 294–95.

sound moves through my jawbone and out the back of my neck. It is dragging the earth with it. I would like to amplify my bowl of crackling, shaking jello. (Once in 1959 a bulldozer came through the side of my house while I was eating lunch. The driver looked at me, backed out, and continued to operate the bulldozer.) I would like to amplify the sound of a bull dozing.[14]

What I love about this passage is the way she combines a whimsical and bodily listening experience of the environment with a kind of mind-wandering about her own work as an artist, about how she might "play" with these sounds, and how they serve as potential inspirations, as well as evoking memories. She listens deeply, and allows the sounds to guide her into a thinking space.

When I was young, growing up in Colorado, we used to travel to Texas several times during the year to visit family. My maternal grand-parents lived in Dallas, and I can recall being soothed to sleep by the sound of their air conditioner. More importantly, however, was the day that I really became consciously aware of this. I was probably eight or nine, and as I lay in bed trying to sleep, the air conditioning kicked in, and the particular airy sound of the air vent in that room blew its familiar song. I remember thinking about how I had come to remember this sound, and that I liked it, and that it felt soothing to me. It made me think of the kindness of my grandmother, and her peculiar airy whistling as she worked around the house. To this day I often find comfort in such sounds, and those kinds of sounds have even become important voices in much of my music.

The American composer George Crumb once wrote about his belief that composers are naturally attuned to certain sounds from their childhood:

> Although technical discussions are interesting to composers, I suspect that the truly magical and spiritual powers of music arise from deeper levels of our psyche. I am certain that every

---

14 Pauline Oliveros, "Some Sound Observations," in *Software for People* (Baltimore: Smith Publications, 1984), 18.

composer, from his formative years as a child, has acquired a "natural acoustic" which remains in his ear for life. The fact that I was born and grew up in an Appalachian river valley meant that my ear was attuned to a peculiar echoing acoustic; I feel that this acoustic was "structured into" my hearing, so to speak, and thus became the basic acoustic of my music. I should imagine that the ocean shore or endless plains would produce an altogether different "inherited" acoustic. In a broader sense, the rhythms of nature, large and small—the sounds of wind and water, the sounds of birds and insects—must inevitably find their analogues in music. After all, the singing of the humpback whale is already a highly developed "artistic" product: one hears phrase-structure, climax and anticlimax, and even a sense of large-scale musical form![15]

This is undoubtedly true not only in terms of the sounds of our environment, but to the music of our lives as well, which is really just another variety of soundscape. When I hear Boston's "Hitch a Ride"[16] I am transported to my childhood and long family road trips in our Volkswagon van, driving through the American Southwest with my father at the helm. He would pop in one eight-track after another, from a collection of mix-tapes he made for our journey. This song represents to me the wide landscape of the panhandle of Texas, memories of childhood ambitions and dreams as I gazed across the landscape, feelings of love for my father and his love of this music as he sang along, and my mother and her banana pudding that she packed for our lunches. It's a song that will always mean so much to me, and yet I can never represent this information through any kind of musical analysis or aesthetic discussion of the music itself. Music so often is connected to us in these subjective, emotional, nostalgic ways that ultimately find their way into our own musical values.

15 George Crumb, "Does Music Have a Future?" in *Profile of Composer George Crumb*, ed. Don Gillespie (New York, London, Frankfurt: Peters Corp, 1986), 19.
16 Boston, "Hitch a Ride," from *Boston*, Epic/Legacy 69699 86322 2, CD, 1976/2005.

I particularly like Ola Stockfelt's idea of *adequate listening*: "To listen adequately hence does not mean any particular, better, or 'more musical,' 'more intellectual,' or 'culturally superior' way of listening. It means that one masters and develops the ability to listen for what is relevant to the genre in the music, for what is adequate to understanding according to the specific genre's comprehensible context."[17] Therefore, in order to listen to any piece of music adequately, one must develop an understanding of the cultural context of that music. It is, therefore, not possible for an expert in Western classical music to adequately respond to music by a hip-hop artist from Philadelphia without at least attempting to learn and understand all of the attributes that contribute to the culture of that music. To attempt to make authoritative value judgments on this music without adequate listening is to claim cultural superiority.

But is there any value in non-adequate listening? While it may be true that non-adequate listening modes can lead one to make questionable aesthetic judgments, perhaps it can still lead to interesting observations. This is where an interesting conflict lies, similar to the question of acousmatic and non-acousmatic modes of listening discussed above. For example, I have had many interesting discussions about music with other artists who are non-musicians, and who may not have the background to understand some of the technical and cultural things going on in a particular piece of music. And yet, so often these listeners are able to discuss the music with uncanny insight, pointing out features in the music and making references to ideas and concepts that I never would have thought of. In fact, I can compare two different kinds of analytical sessions I have been involved with: the "composition seminar" and an integrated arts "crit." In the former, very common in larger composition programs at music schools, a group of student and faculty composers gather to discuss work in progress. This usually involves a composer presenting his or her piece, followed by a critical discussion of the work. These sessions tend to be heavy on technical critique and

---

17 Ola Stockfelt, "Adequate Listening" in *Audio Culture: Readings in Modern Music*, ed. Christoph Cox and Daniel Warner (New York: Continuum, 2004), 90.

nuance, and generally are excellent forums for receiving and giving feedback. In art schools, this same kind of forum is accomplished through the group crit, where students and faculty make visitations to student art studios, where work in progress is discussed. When I worked in the integrated electronic arts program (iEAR) at Rensselaer Polytechnic Institute, I experienced crits that were truly interdisciplinary, because of the integrated nature of the department. Here, students were working in multiple disciplines: painting, installation, sculpture, sound, video, tactical media, usually with a technological component. I found these sessions to be quite incredible, listening to faculty from different disciplines comment on sound work and music was such a different experience. Obviously the nature of the music was quite different than what might be produced in a traditional composition program, but not always. Regardless, the discussions that emerged during these sessions were a unique mixture between an adequate reading of the work by artists from the same discipline, and a kind of naïve non-adequate reading that often revealed truly insightful commentary. It also frequently resulted in arguments and confusion, but in the end, I feel as if all parties left these sessions having really learned something new about their own discipline.

In some ways, I think the whole experimental music tradition is a kind of reaching out, an attempt to seek out non-adequate listeners. Experimental artists look both inside their own genres for inspiration, connections, commentary, understanding; and outside of it for new perspectives. I can certainly say that in my own work, I do want to be able to connect with listeners inside of whatever genre may exist in the space, but I also want to be able to speak to those outside of it, who may not necessarily connect with the values of the genre but somehow are moved by the music anyway. Ideally, a diversification of the listening public and their experiences can result in truly meaningful and groundbreaking dialogue. This is becoming more common as genres continue to fracture and branch, and we lose our ability to snap things into the traditional three or four streams of musical thought. What is particularly exciting to me is how the mixing of media and artistic disciplines enhance this situation, which is why I'm so passionate about the idea of inter-arts collaboration. There is so much more to say about any genre of music if we can connect it to the other arts.

Virtuosic Listening

So what does all of this say about listening, and what does it mean to be a deep listener, to be a virtuosic listener of music? As an educator, I have a vested interest in promoting the idea of virtuosic listening: that is, to being a listener who can engage with music on multiple levels, and to be able to contextualize the meaning of the music in a way that makes it clear what the musical values are in any particular example, but to also be able to listen intuitively with pure sensation. As well, I want to be able to discuss the idea of aesthetics and value without being too wishy-washy. And yet, I find myself constantly coming up against this real and interesting shift that happens when certain lights are turned on or off, when information reveals something that drastically changes the scope of listening. I think it's good to be able to turn on and off those lights, but it obviously makes aesthetic judgment more difficult to posit.

Going back to shuffle-play: what I find intriguing and exciting about my experiences listening to my music collection this way is that it reminds me of the sheer volume of different styles, aesthetics, languages, and practices that have emerged over the past one hundred years. So much music, so many different kinds of musical values; it just confirms yet again that the ways in which we are often taught to analyze and appreciate music in the traditional Western conservatory is simply inadequate to the task of helping us learn to listen. Obviously there is great value in understanding the technical systems of music, whatever kind it might be, and virtuosic listeners must be able to engage with those systems. Virtuosic listeners should be prepared to deal with the complex historical traditions and cultural values of whatever kinds of music they are engaged with. Virtuosic listeners should have a grounding in acoustics and psychoacoustics, understanding how our ears and brain work on the sounds that we hear. Virtuosic listeners should understand that music doesn't exist in a vacuum, and that perhaps the other art disciplines may have real insights and connections to the music in question. Virtuosic listeners need to hear all sounds at all times, and be able to connect with our soundscape, and to have opinions about it! [18]

Virtuosic listeners should also be able and willing to occasionally turn off the lights, to listen for pure sensation, and so allow for surprises, serendipity, emotions, confusion, and self-reflection. I think we should embrace the elephants in the room, whether they be those nostalgic biographical connections we have to music, the music in our dreams and fantasies, what music does to us when we've had too much to drink, what our extreme dislikes and prejudices are. Why do I hate Top 40 country music? The reasons must be complicated and multifaceted, but it probably has very little to do with the inherent value of that music.

Our music, as well as our soundscape, is as diversified as ever, thanks to the global exchange of the mediascape. It is becoming more and more challenging to pigeonhole what music is or isn't. In order to function in this environment, we must try harder than ever to understand what we are hearing, not only in terms of each piece of music and its subcultural context, but also in terms of our own histories, biases, emotions, and ambitions. It is not easy to do this, and we all must come up with ways of keeping our ears fresh, of changing perspectives, of hearing what is and how is this thing called music. For me, shuffle play helps me keep some perspective. I consider this one of my own Deep Listening practices, as well as many others that include intense observations of my soundscape and of my own inner voices, my "natural acoustic." My rediscovery of Schaeffer's *Étude noire* through shuffle play surprised and delighted me through a truly, albeit short-lived, acousmatic lens. It served as a reminder that ignorance, or at least mystery, can be blissful, if it can be kept within a healthy perspective. Pure sound sensation, non-referential and full of surprises, is worth experiencing, even if just for a moment.

---

18 e.g. Is our daily soundscape healthy to our ears?

Emphasizing the Aural: Deep Listening as Engagement with Acoustic Space

GAYLE YOUNG began in the late 1970s to present concerts as a composer/performer, playing microtonal music on two acoustic instruments of her own design. She composes for these as well as orchestral and electronic instruments, often using text as a structural element to enable a performer to be guided by the inner hearing of the text. She has often included pre-recorded environmental sound in her music, and her interest in soundscape led her to create site-specific installations which invite participation by the public. She leads workshops on listening, and has participated in several Deep Listening Retreats, receiving a Deep Listening Certificate. She has written articles on her own music and that of other artists, addressing issues related to contemporary sound arts, often addressing challenges associated with the perception of unfamiliar music. Young wrote the biography of Hugh Le Caine (1914–1977), an early inventor of electronic music instruments, and is the publisher of Musicworks Magazine. http://www.gayleyoung.net/

Gayle Young

A SOUND is a resonant sphere suspended briefly in the atmosphere. Each sound vibrates with its own energy, filling space with its unique ebb and flow of pulsation. Sound is air in motion, vibration extending outward from its source until we can no longer hear it. Our experience of sound in space is subtly different from our experience of vision. Sound is transient and transparent; visible objects appear solid and permanent.[1]

Acoustic Space

In the summer of 1966, while Pauline Oliveros was composing her pivotal electronic composition *I of IV* at the University

---

1   In this essay I will demonstrate that Marshall McLuhan's concept of acoustic space provides a broad cultural context within which Deep Listening can be understood to have contributed tools needed to enhance listening within changing cultural contexts.

221

of Toronto Electronic Music Studio, Marshall McLuhan, nearby at the Centre for Culture and Technology, was introducing the idea of acoustic space to the world. His 1962 book *The Gutenberg Galaxy*, in which he first described acoustic space in contrast with visual space, was followed in 1964 by *Understanding Media: The Extensions of Man* in which he coined the phrase "the medium is the message" which would bring international attention to his work. As Oliveros worked nearby in the electronic music studio, he was preparing to publish the 1967 "hit," *The Medium is the Massage: An Inventory of Effects* which extended his acclaim into popular culture with its comic-book format. Recalling this rapid succession of books by McLuhan provides some insight into the excitement that was in the air during that summer of 1966. It was a time of great imagination—ferment, even. Glenn Gould had already abandoned the concert hall, and his first voice-collage radio documentary, the hour-long *Solitude Trilogy*, would be broadcast a year later, in 1967. The World Soundscape Project in Vancouver had been researching environmental sound since 1965, led by R. Murray Schafer. The year 1968 would see intense youth revolt across two continents. In the midst of this, McLuhan's books described changing experiences of "space" which he believed were causing transformations in human cognition, and leading to major cultural shifts.

In *The Gutenberg Galaxy* McLuhan described visual space as a byproduct of the phonetic alphabet, a medium of communication in the form of a one-dimensional sequence of graphic symbols representing sounds—a medium that depends solely on the eye for comprehension.[2] The cultural effect of the alphabet was later intensified by typography and the printing press, increasingly dominating European culture as printing became mechanized, and the industrial revolution took shape. Up to the time of the printing press, reading remained primarily an aural and oral experience.[3] In scribal culture—as McLuhan dubbed preliterate Europe—texts were written by hand, using the alphabet,

---

2   Marshall McLuhan and Quentin Fiore, *The Medium is the Massage: An Inventory of Effects* (New York: Bantam, 1967), 44.

3   Marshall McLuhan, *The Gutenberg Galaxy: The Making of Typographic Man* (Toronto: University of Toronto Press, 1962), 82.

but they were intended to be read aloud, and the voice remained primary. By the seventeenth century the printed phonetic alphabet in the form of mass-produced books was firmly established.[4] Silent reading became commonplace, and language was stripped of its acoustic component, except to the degree that we imagine the sounds of words as we read. McLuhan identified the acoustic component as the emotional dimension of language, perhaps because of the interpersonal acoustic exchange inherent in speech. Print led toward visual space, a mechanistic culture that was metaphorically related to the experience of the visual, but extended to include cultural experience as a whole. In visual space everything was assumed to be part of a linear sequence that had a beginning, a middle, and an end.

John Cage and James Tenney, both composers associated with the American experimental music tradition, have noted changes in the cultural context for music that took place in the seventeenth century, although neither connects these changes with the development of the printing press and the increasing dominance of a visual experience of space as did McLuhan. Austin Clarkson discusses Cage's references to Thomas Mace, a seventeenth-century English composer who observed, and disapproved of, changing roles of music, specifically a reduced emphasis on music as a means of opening listeners to "Heavenly, and Divine Influences."[5] Clarkson links Mace's negative opinions on "modern" music with the response of the Cambridge Platonists to the apparent materialism of Hobbes and Descartes, which implies that these changes in the roles of music were related to broad cultural shifts. For Tenney, the cultural turning point was the Camerata and the development of dramatic music, exemplified by opera: "It seems to me that at

---

4 In 1620 Francis Bacon wrote that typographical printing had "changed the whole face and state of things throughout the world." Francis Bacon, *Novum Organum, Liber I, CXXIX*. By that time an estimated 150 to 200 million books had been produced. See http://en.wikipedia.org/wiki/Printing_press.

5 Austin Clarkson, "The Intent of the Musical Moment: Cage and the Transpersonal," in *Writings through John Cage's Music, Poetry, and Art*, ed. David W. Bernstein and Christopher Hatch (Chicago and London: University of Chicago Press, 2002), 79.

about this time we first see a new paradigm in effect, a new idea about what music could do. And that was to express and describe the human condition. At its most extreme this paradigm holds that the psychological state of the composer is expressed directly into the music: agitation or serenity, for example. . . before [this] if music was 'about' anything, it was about the cosmos, about religious conceptions. . . . It was looking out rather than looking in."[6] This musical redefinition developed as the printing press came into the cultural foreground. The parallel development of introspective music and silent reading supports McLuhan's contention that this was a broad cultural change toward the dominance of visual space in European culture—a context which he described as looking inward and accepting containment.

Cultural conditions shifted again towards the acoustic when the telegraph was invented. This was the first technology to release communications from the constraints of time and space. McLuhan comments: "The telegraph translated writing into sound. . . . The electrification of writing was almost as big a step into the nonvisual and auditory space as the later steps soon taken by telephone, radio and TV."[7] McLuhan describes two periods dominated by acoustic space: the period before the printing press, and the electronic era begun in the twentieth century. The mere presence of the new communication technologies affects the way we experience space and sense the universe. Acoustic space emphasizes the ear, and "The ear favors no particular 'point of view.' We are enveloped by sound. It forms a seamless web around us. We say, 'Music shall fill the air.' We never say, 'Music shall fill a particular segment of the air.'"[8] The sphere of sound surrounding its source has no distinct boundaries, and spreads out in every direction until it fades to inaudibility. It cannot easily be divided into segments, and is experienced as a whole. Even though many electronic communications technologies use the alphabet, as the telegraph did,

6 James Tenney, "Transparent to the Sounds of the Environment: in conversation with Gayle Young," *Musicworks* 64 (1996): 9.
7 Marshall McLuhan, *Understanding Media: The Extensions of Man* (New York: McGraw-Hill, 1964), 248.
8 McLuhan and Fiore, *Medium is the Massage*, 111.

they function within a context dominated by acoustic perception, in a world focused metaphorically on the experience of sound, decentralized, engaging multiple senses simultaneously. In the chapter entitled "The Phonograph" in *Understanding Media*, McLuhan comments: "That the world of sound is essentially a unified field of instant relationships lends it a near resemblance to the world of electromagnetic waves."[9]

Listening through Sound Recording

Pauline Oliveros has engaged creatively with new technologies whenever possible, integrating sound recording with her creative processes and in the presentation of her music. When her mother gave her a reel-to-reel tape recorder for her twenty-first birthday in 1953, soon after such recorders became available, she decided to record the soundscape outside her window. Upon playing it back, she noticed that the microphone had heard things that her ears had missed: "Although I thought that I was listening while recording, I was surprised to find sounds on the tape that I had not heard consciously."[10] McLuhan points out repeatedly that each new technology is an enhancement of human abilities, something many of us have experienced, and a theme that has consistently been pursued through Deep Listening initiatives.[11] Oliveros describes her use of the tape recorder as an instrument that intensified her hearing: "My understanding of listening was changed by my experience even though my ears were physically the same. The microphone and tape recorder became extensions of my body and amplified my hearing."[12]

---

9 McLuhan, *Understanding Media*, 241.

10 Pauline Oliveros, *Sounding the Margins: Collected Writings 1992–2009* (Kingston, NY: Deep Listening Publications, 2010), 28.

11 Oliveros continued using technology to enhance performance with the Expanded Instrument System developed by the Deep Listening Band and later, through the Deep Listening Institute, the Adaptive Use Musical Instrument applied electronic technology to empower those who could otherwise not make music.

12 Oliveros, *Sounding the Margins*, 123.

My own attempt to record bird calls ended when I realized that the equipment had found the distant highway and the not-so-distant mosquitoes much louder than the flickers' calls I had set out to record, which to me were the dominant sounds of the forest. I let the matter drop. Oliveros, in contrast, responded actively. She created a guideline for herself that she has maintained ever since: "Listen to everything all the time and remind yourself when you are not listening."[13] The crucial element here was her identification of the reason she did not hear those sounds: incomplete attention. She followed this insight with the decision to consciously direct attention to listening, and to learn to control that attention. She often listens to recordings of her own playing to gain awareness of details that she did not notice during a performance, further developing her practice of conscious listening as it became a key element of her compositional practice and her performances with the Deep Listening Band. Implicit in this practice is an inclusive, multidimensional field of perception. Oliveros was listening to the soundscape as acoustic space. My own response stands as an example of visual thinking brought into the acoustic realm, without questioning the biases and habits of visual space: the goal-directed focus that characterizes a visual bias can influence the experience of the audible and the visible. My objective was to record a specific sound, and my listening was linear, forming a straight line from where I stood to the birds in the treetops, largely excluding other sounds. When it didn't work I gave up the attempt.

Oliveros' formative experience with the tape recorder brought her attention to the importance of listening as a skill that can be learned, and to the broad cultural neglect of those skills: "Noticing the intermittent nature of listening through my own practice, I was increasingly drawn to encourage and promote listening for performers and students through my composing and teaching. Listening is rarely explored or taught even in music schools."[14] Oliveros' response marked the beginning of her Deep Listening practice, its foundations laid by her regular personal

---

13 Ibid., 28.
14 Ibid.

listening, which she developed further as a composer/performer, and then through group participation in sonic meditations and training exercises. Participants are led to develop an open approach to listening that enables them to deal effectively with the challenges of controlling attention in the often-changing cultural contexts that have located the experience of music in the concert hall, in the home stereo, and in mobile playback systems. This transition in the ways we listen locates our experience progressively further from single-minded focused listening, and increasingly closer to the experience of a multidimensional acoustic space as music becomes ever more integrated with the everyday world of sound.

Awareness

McLuhan draws a subtle distinction between perception and experience, parallel in some ways to the distinction between hearing and listening. Just because something can be perceived does not guarantee that it will be experienced. When he speaks of acoustic space he does not mean to imply that the visual is not as clearly perceived as the auditory, only that it is experienced within a perceptual framework that is structurally parallel to the nature of sound. For example, preliterate people could perceive visual information as clearly as we can, but their experience of the world was primarily acoustic.

Though it might be tempting for those involved in sound to understand McLuhan's concept of a transition into acoustic space as an opportunity to achieve greater balance between the auditory and visual domains, our experience of acoustic space is, rather, one of increasing information overload of all media, not only of sound, in a cultural context that often appears to lack opportunity for contemplative attention. As McLuhan points out, ". . . the effect of technology since the telegraph has been to recreate the conditions of simultaneity which characterize preliterate cultures."[15] Information comes to us, like sound, from all directions, sometimes overwhelming us. Even before electronic

---

15 Marshall McLuhan, *Counterblast* (Toronto: McClelland & Stewart, 1969), 78.

communications, humans were unable to assimilate the full complexity of the sensory world. We notice only a small fraction of what is going on around us, usually filtering the information according to our biological needs, unaware that the goal-directed attention we all need to survive influences our cultural perceptions, that our imaginations are habitually self-censored.

This poses a challenge for those who want to free the imagination from perceptual habit. Oliveros responded specifically to this challenge in listening, highlighted by her experience with the tape recorder, and began to study the nature of awareness itself. She describes graduated levels of perception: "My interests turned to the study of consciousness and the study of intention. Listening involves the direction of attention. There are two modes of attention: 1) focal attention, which corresponds to an all or nothing state—attention to one point and nothing else, and 2) global attention, which corresponds to an open receptive state—attention expanded to a field. Focal attention is sharp and clear. Global attention is warm and fuzzy. The two modes work together as expansion and contraction."[16]

The two types of listening posed by Oliveros can loosely be matched with McLuhan's two competing experiences of space, visual and acoustic. Focal attention is roughly equivalent to visual space with its linear goal-direction; global attention shares the multidimensional and undifferentiated nature of acoustic space. The challenge in sustaining global attention is to remain open to all sound, to resist the habitual filters, while remaining exposed to a huge and confusing array of possibilities. Focal and global listening work together as expansion and contraction, but the two are seldom experienced simultaneously. A listener loses perspective on one as he or she directs attention to the other. It is challenging to assimilate the complexity of global listening because it lacks a unifying focal thread.

Oliveros began in the early 1970s to lead sonic meditations, guiding groups of participants as they explored listening and sounding, and publishing descriptive directions so that these pieces could be

---

16 Ibid., 29.

performed by others during workshops or in concert settings. David Gamper describes his own responses during a concert in which one performer was "doing his best to break the boundaries of our (later termed) Deep Listening. At first I was terribly annoyed at what he was doing, but then I realized I could bring it into my own soundings so that his outbursts became part of the piece rather than a confrontation with it. It was the power of sonic meditation that led me to include rather than exclude."[17] Since 1991 Oliveros and her associates have offered Deep Listening retreats that provide an opportunity for participants to withdraw from the world of obligations for up to a week to fully listen to the entire range of sonic possibility. It is an extremely valuable process of discovery because it frees the imagination, and provides an environment in which to share a wide range of experience: dream, movement, poetry, theatre, intuition, emotion, all with an emphasis on creativity and on sound. The role of teaching in the retreats is subtle, sometimes disguised by the safety of the inclusive and accepting environment, but participants are nonetheless learning the skill of listening.

The guidelines for Deep Listening reflect the assimilation of an oral history that is part of the American experimental tradition in composition, as well as of non-idiomatic free improvisation. For example, it is not possible to create an authentic performance of Christian Wolff's *Exercises*, Earle Brown's graphic scores, or many of Morton Feldman's works through reliance on the written scores alone. The underlying assumptions that guide both listening and playing in these works are crucial to a complete understanding of the music, yet have never been verbalized within the scores. Clarkson discusses elements of this oral history when he addresses the difficulties experienced by John Cage, caused largely by the unfamiliarity of musicians and listeners with what Clarkson refers to as presentational states.[18] There may be a mismatch between language and experience at work here that renders verbal

---

17 David Gamper, "Years of Listening: Recollections of Sonic Meditations with Pauline Oliveros," *Musicworks* 78 (2000): 38.

18 Clarkson, "The Intent of the Musical Moment," 91. Clarkson continues this discussion by outlining educational experiences during which his students were able to experience presentational states.

description ineffectual: the sharing of the experience of listening itself is possibly the most effective method of learning.

Deep Listening retreats provide a certification program through which participants learn over the course of several retreats to teach listening skills and lead sonic meditations. The learning process is based primarily on experience and creative exploration rather than on absorbing written explanations. The fact that this training is necessary is a testament to the difficulty of listening, particularly as we increasingly retreat to the familiar in an attempt to defend ourselves against an overwhelming quantity of information.

Community

McLuhan's term 'the global village' is often assumed to have been a prediction of a world unified by the internet, but he himself often described it as a state of discontinuity, maximal disagreement, social fragmentation and factionalization. As we retreat from information overload, as we all must do, we align ourselves with one or more of the countless global villages in which each villager remains out of contact with, and unable to listen to, anyone who does not share habitual assumptions, that is, anyone who does not live in the same village. In apparent contrast is McLuhan's description of the single global village unified by electronic technology: "The speed of information movement in the global village means that every human action or event involves everybody in the village in the consequences of every event. . . . In the global village of continuous learning and of total participation in the human dialogue, the problem. . . is to extend consciousness itself and to maximize the opportunities of learning. Ours is the age of implosion, of inclusive consciousness and deep personal involvement."[19]

Deep Listening training facilitates communication beyond the borders of habitual perception, and beyond the borders of factionalized villages. Nowhere is this more apparent than in the Adaptive Use Musical Instrument (AUMI), a recent project of the Deep Listening Institute, in which computer software enables people with little voluntary mobility

---

19 Marshall McLuhan, *Counterblast*, 41.

to create and perform music using electronic sounds and sequences. Online video footage shows the delight of participants, many of them denied social interaction due to their limited verbal ability. In playing the AUMI they overcome their often-intense social isolation and find their creative voices.[20]

The AUMI has been used to improve physical co-ordination and functionality for people with brain and spinal cord injuries, but the primary focus of the project is on increasing access to participation in creative music to unlock communication and creative expression. It is highly innovative, applying the most recent digital technologies, yet it remains accessible to the widest possible range of participants, with free software available at the Deep Listening Institute website. Essentially, a camera tracks head (or other) movement, and translates such movements into a graphic pallet of sound from which the participant can select to create their music.

Because the AUMI offers an opportunity for artistic expression through improvisation and composition, it builds confidence and maximizes potential creativity in a population often assumed to be inadequate due to physical or mental limitations, providing a channel for communication even for those who cannot speak, or who have reduced language ability. In doing so it underlines the importance of creative expression, reminding us that freedom of expression is a basic human right for the verbally-enabled, and raising the question whether this right should also be extended to those who cannot speak for themselves: a lack of mobility and/or verbal ability is not linked with reduced cognitive function. In allowing participants to communicate with one another in sound alone, the project provides a further example of the importance and experiential validity of the non-verbal communication inherent in music, bringing to the foreground a means of expression that takes place beyond the limits of language, where listening and response form their own realities. In doing so it exemplifies the second of McLuhan's two

---

20 See Deep Listening Institute, "Adaptive Use About," accessed January 29, 2012, http://deeplistening.org/site/adaptiveuse and "Adaptive Use In Action," accessed January 29, 2012, http://deeplistening.org/site/content /adaptiveuseinaction.

descriptions of the global village, providing opportunities for learning and emphasizing the inherent value of inclusive consciousness and deep personal involvement characteristic of global communications.

Imagination and Language

McLuhan pointed out that language, as a medium of communication, plays a key role in shaping consciousness, and framing an individual's worldview: "All media are active metaphors in their power to translate experience into new form. The spoken word was the first technology by which man was able to let go of his environment in order to grasp it in a new way. Words are a kind of information retrieval that can range over the total environment and experience at high speed. . . . By means of translation of immediate sense experience into vocal symbols the entire world can be evoked and retrieved at any instant."[21]

Decades before McLuhan, Benjamin Lee Whorf speculated on the roles of language in shaping collective cultural understanding, pointing out that language organizes key elements of our experience: "We are inclined to think of language simply as a technique of expression and not to realize that language first of all is a classification and arrangement of the stream of sensory experience which results in a certain world order. . . ."[22] Language includes formal elements that simplify our experience, usually by categorizing it in familiar terms, but in doing so it also influences our awareness, and reduces our ability to observe details that are not in the verbal foreground. Whorf described several aspects of European languages that distort our images of reality in one way or another, commenting on the one-dimensional sequence of verb tenses, the separation of noun and verb, and the dominance of visual imagery.[23] In this article I want to focus on one example: music as a mass noun.

---

21 McLuhan, *Understanding Media*, 64.
22 Benjamin Lee Whorf, *Language, Thought and Reality* (Cambridge, MA: MIT Press. 1939), 55.
23 Ibid., 55.

In English the word "music" is, like "air," a mass noun, continuous without implied boundaries.[24] We do not speak of "a music," but instead provide an imaginary container for it, always preceding the mass noun with an "of," as in "a piece of music," not unlike "a piece of cloth." Mass nouns thus become descriptive within their imaginary containers, telling us about the types of piece, but unable to be part of a sentence as active or passive nouns. The container-plus-substance formula for mass nouns is an example of non-spatial entities imaginatively spatialized by grammatical structures.[25] How does this quirk of language influence the ways we think about music, the ways we imagine it? In some respects this spatialization brings our perspectives closer to McLuhan's visual experience paradigm with its acceptance of containment. The word music is indeed "contained" within the descriptive phrase, unable to function directly in relation to a verb. It is only "a piece" of music that can actually do anything. Music on its own may therefore be thought of as inherently inactive, something in the background, easily overlooked, taken for granted. Paradoxically, the spatialization of music as a mass noun also leads to a surprisingly contemporary understanding of music as surround soundscape, closely aligned with the continuity, inclusiveness, and multidimensionality of acoustic space. In this context music is a pervasive uncontained presence—like air, like water to a fish. Do we enter an imaginal world here—and according to Whorf it is an ancient one—where music is everywhere, you just reach out and grab a piece of it, cut it out of its surroundings? Maybe you download it. Listen, if you like—it all depends on your attention. The practice of Deep Listening addresses both of these aspects of the word "music," moving it to the foreground of attention, but at the same time addressing the pervasive simultaneity of the experience.

Playing in Acoustic Space

Perhaps the most important challenge is to overcome habits of listening, many of which are embedded in the words we use to describe

24 Ibid.,140.
25 Ibid.,147.

an experience. One option is to develop conscious awareness of the patterns implicit in language and the ways that such patterns guide our perception. Music, for instance, can be understood as a language-like narrative translating vocal intonation and emphasis into instrumental melody and rhythm. Experimental music often bypasses those elements of traditional music, and limits narrative and representation by avoiding such associations, building music with little reference to language.[26] Tenney outlines an evolutionary process that involves new ways of hearing and in which learning plays a crucial role: "What I'm learning is to hear in different ways, and I'm teaching that to other people. And that's producing a different kind of musical experience for audiences."[27]

In her pivotal 1966 composition *I of IV*,[28] Oliveros conducted an orchestra of tones, working primarily with difference tones and delay processing, navigating a musical world with no predetermined notes, using only her ability to listen and respond, combined with her comprehensive understanding of the electronic equipment and the nature of sound. To do this she had to think of sound in a different way.[29] The composition is not notated other than as descriptive text, and in this it is similar to many of the *Sonic Meditations*.[30] Oliveros points out that through her listening practice she "began to rely on listening in order to make music rather than on reading and writing. I gradually released

---

26 Clarkson, "The Intent of the Musical Moment," 67.

27 Tenney, "Transparent to the Sounds of the Environment," 16.

28 Pauline Oliveros, *I of IV*, in *New Sounds in Electronic Music*, CBS Odyssey 32 16 0160, lp, 1967 (also available on Pauline Oliveros, *Electronic Works 1965 +1966*, PD 04 PARADIGM, CD,1997).

29 In this respect *I of IV* reminds me of Hugh Le Caine's recordings of his solos played on the 1954 Sackbut synthesizer, in which he was able to simultaneously control six continuous parameters of the sound, a complex act of simultaneous listening and response that I described as intuitive psychoacoustics in my biography *The Sackbut Blues: Hugh Le Caine, Pioneer in Electronic Music* (Ottawa: National Museum of Science and Technology, 1989), 79.

30 Pauline Oliveros, *Sonic Meditations* (Baltimore: Smith Publications, 1974).

the need to control pitch and rhythm through conventional notation in favor of the freedom to sculpt sound in time."[31]

Difference tones, the material of the sculpture in this case, are an arithmetical artifact of acoustics where two sounds combine to create a third perceptible sound. For example, two high pitches played together, separated by 200 vibrations per second, will produce a difference tone of 200 vibrations per second, which will be audible even if the first two pitches lie outside the range of human perception. Oliveros had first become familiar with difference tones when she played them on her accordion: "If I played an interval in the high register of my instrument and pulled hard on the bellows I could hear the difference tones. I had always wondered how it would be to just hear the difference tones without the generating tones."[32] In *I of IV* she succeeded in doing that. The sounds fill the space, freed from the audible arithmetic that might result if the generating tones were heard. The hypnotic droning effects and the sometimes-massive floating clusters of sound were created by amplifying the difference tones from oscillators set high above the range of human hearing and layering them over one another with tape-delay, with one oscillator set at a sub-audio frequency to shape intermittent amplitude modulations.[33] In *I of IV*, all the generating pitches are either too high or too low to be perceived: it is only their differences that create quite-audible shimmering washes of tone.

As the title implies, *I of IV* is part of a series of pieces, all of which were related to a technique Oliveros had developed in 1965 at the San Francisco Tape Music Center. *I of IV* illustrates many of the practices of Deep Listening, demonstrating that these were an established element of Oliveros' creative processes well before she articulated the term Deep Listening. She describes the creation of the piece as a continual journey

---

31 Oliveros, *Sounding the Margins*, 28.

32 Pauline Oliveros, "From Outside the Window: Electronic Sound Performance," in *The Oxford Computer Music Handbook*, Roger T. Dean, ed. (Oxford: Oxford University Press, 2009), 468.

33 Pauline Oliveros, personal correspondence with the author, November 1, 2011.

of discovery, involving plenty of listening and responding.[34] It demanded balanced listening and nuanced response, resonating with the multiple attentions of acoustic space. In bringing such previously unheard sonic phenomena to the listener, this composition opened the world of the ear to new possibilities. Because this was the first of her electronic music pieces to be released as an LP,[35] this piece established her reputation as an innovative and highly original musician and composer.

I of IV is a twenty-minute recording of a real-time performance in the electronic music studio—and in 1966 such studios were not well suited to real-time composition. This performance could have taken place on stage if the equipment had been portable. Oliveros describes the instrument—the orchestra she conducted: "I had created a very unstable non-linear music making system: Difference [*sic*] tones from tones set above the range of hearing manipulated by the bias frequency of the electromagnetic tape recording, feedback from a second tape machine in parallel with newly generated difference tones as I responded instantaneously with my hands on those dials to what I was hearing from the delays and as the sounds were all being recorded on magnetic tape."[36] It was not by accident or convenience that the piece was performed in real time. Oliveros has consistently sought an intense physical engagement with sound, which she contrasts with the disembodied music that she heard on the radio and phonograph as she grew up.[37] In this piece, she observes: "I found a way that allowed me to perform my music in real time in the so-called classical electronic music studio. I needed to map my '*human motoric input*' onto the machine and '*feel my corporeal fallibility and virtuosity*' in the process."[38]

In basing the piece on an acoustical phenomenon, difference tones, Oliveros translated her physical engagement with sound to the conceptual level. Tenney shared this interest in the physical basis of sound and perception, often working with tunings based on phenomena of

---

34 Ibid.
35 Pauline Oliveros, *I of IV* (see note 28).
36 Oliveros, "From Outside the Window," 468.
37 Oliveros, *Sounding the Margins*, 122.
38 Oliveros, "From Outside the Window", 467–8.

acoustics. He believed that the biological aspects of sound perception were shared among all people, regardless of cultural context, and he aspired to engage "in the primitive, precognitive and pre-emotive auditory process of hearing. One important reason why I'm interested in this is that this is one thing we have in common with each other. . . those things we have in common are the things that interest me the most: perception and observation—perception as sharp, focused and acute as possible."[39] We function simultaneously in the interconnected world and within distinct communities united by shared interests and beliefs. Music based on shared physical realities can enhance communication beyond the borders of the many self-referential global villages.

To the listener, *I of IV* introduces a context in which a musical experience can take place without traditional markers of expectation, providing a glimpse into the multidimensional world of sound that must have animated the electronic music studio as Oliveros made the recording. Floating and pulsating tones and clusters emerge, seemingly organically, from an electrical-sounding buzz. Heidi Von Gunden points out that while Oliveros was composing in Toronto she spent time listening to a nearby electrical power station. She goes on to describe *I of IV* as "a statement about the nature of electricity, the very medium of electronic music."[40] This is electricity in the very real physical sense, interconnected with an auditory experience that remains open to imagination and metaphor. *I of IV*, like the soundscape outside that window in 1953, does not rely on structures based on pitch or rhythm, and in that detail alone it defies expectations about what a piece of music can be. It demonstrates alternative modes of listening that characterize key elements of acoustic space and highlights the primacy of the physical in the experience of sound that is engaged listening.

---

39 Tenney, "Transparent to the Sounds of the Environment," 16.
40 Heidi Von Gunden, *The Music of Pauline Oliveros* (Metuchen, NJ: Scarecrow Press 1983), 59.

The Listener

Tenney describes a pivotal point in music history that he refers to as the Cage revolution, beginning in 1951 with Cage's definition of music simply as sounds we hear, and leading to a radical reconsideration of the basic nature of music which "shifts the focus of the musical enterprise from the feelings and thoughts and so forth of the composers to the experience of the listener: this becomes the central point of the whole exercise."[41] This definition was demonstrated a year later in Cage's (in) famous 4'33"[42] for unplayed piano, in which the experience revolves solely around creative participation through listening: without the listener's attention the piece cannot exist; indeed in this piece the listener is the sole creator of the experience.[43] That experience consists almost entirely of what Oliveros would describe as global listening, presented in the cultural context of a concert hall that normally encourages focused listening. The Deep Listening practice encourages an interplay among modes of listening, bringing attention to the multidimensional nature of sound. It forms connections among performer, listener and soundscape, developing an inclusive awareness that can integrate and interact with unpredictable environmental sound—a thunderstorm, for example— during an instrumental performance.

McLuhan pointed out that the acoustic experience of space regained dominance in the twentieth century through the introduction of electronic media. Tenney seems to illustrate this observation when he describes effects related to the mid-century Cage revolution: "in a sense, maybe one could say that since 1951 there has been more of a tendency to look outward and not so much of a tendency to look inward."[44] McLuhan points to a similarly outward orientation: "art ceases to be a

---

41 Ibid., 9.

42 John Cage, 4'33" for any instrument or combination of instruments (New York: Henmar, 1960).

43 Clarkson, "The Intent of the Musical Moment," 80.

44 Tenney, "Transparent to the Sounds of the Environment," 9.

form of self-expression in the electric age. Indeed it becomes a necessary kind of research and probing."[45]

In marking a return to acoustic space in the practice of experimental music, the Cage revolution was not a simple cyclic return to the pre-seventeenth-century world, but an example of the cumulative interplay among elements of both visual and acoustic space. The acoustic space of the twentieth century envelops both visual and acoustic experience, leading to what McLuhan called audio-tactile space. McLuhan comments on this expansion of acoustic space: "Today the return to oral conditions of communication is not merely to be noted in the strictly acoustic sphere."[46] Literacy, for example, obviously remains paramount in Western culture and is growing throughout the world as electronic communications expand.

Audio-tactile space is distinct from both visual and acoustic space in that it brings the interplay of the senses to the foreground of experience.[47] The world of electronics is a world of inclusiveness and simultaneity, and whereas separate media tend to isolate one another—the visual and the acoustic, the global and the focused, for example—tactility overcomes this isolation: "Tactility is not a sense, but an interplay of all senses."[48] Significantly, within this sensual interplay, "Tactility is the world of the interval, not of the connection, and that is why it is antithetic to the visual world. For the visual world is above all the world of the continuous and the connected."[49]

---

45 Marshall McLuhan and Harley Parker, *Through the Vanishing Point: Space and Poetry in Painting* (New York: Harper Colophon, 1968), xxiv.

46 Ibid., 83.

47 Richard Cavell "McLuhan, Tactility and the Digital," accessed January 29, 2012, http://mcluhan2011.eu/conference-abstracts/. In the abstract for the keynote address at the McLuhan in Europe 2011 conference. Richard Cavell points out that "'Tactility' was McLuhan's term for the senses in interplay which, he theorized, was definitive of the electronic era. McLuhan deployed tactility to identify the involving qualities of electronic culture, as opposed to the abstract qualities of print culture."

48 McLuhan, *Counterblast*, 22.

49 McLuhan and Parker, *Through the Vanishing Point*, 264.

The experience of tactility resides primarily in the acoustic realm, as McLuhan points out: "The oral is the world of the non-linear. . . . There are no lines or directions in acoustic space, but rather a simultaneous field."[50] That field extends to include touch, in combination with acoustic and visual space, to form audio-tactile space, paradoxically emphasizing the element of touch in a world of electronic communications through which touch is impossible. The experience of extended tactility was overlooked while visual space was dominant, and its rise was for McLuhan the most significant change in sensibility during the twentieth century. He pointed out that: "The social, the political and the artistic implications of tactility could only have been lost to human awareness in a visual or civilized culture which is now dissolving under the impact of electric circuitry."[51] In a note on tactility at the end of *Through the Vanishing Point* McLuhan observes: "tactility is a matter that has hardly been discussed, and yet is crucial in the world of the arts."[52]

Many contemporary composers and musicians have commented on the sculptural nature of sound in space. As we have seen, Oliveros observed that through live electronics she gained the freedom to sculpt sound in time. R. Murray Schafer wrote about the interactions among sound, painting and literature in *The Tuning of the World*.[53] These references imply tactility because they relate an invisible medium, sound, with the physical and spatial presence of sculpture. Composer Herbert Brün recalls that Stefan Wolpe taught his composition students the importance of touch, inviting them "to look more carefully. Touch. Touch with the eyes, touch with the ears, touch with the fingers. Everything's touch."[54]

---

50 Ibid., 83.

51 Ibid., 265.

52 McLuhan and Parker, *Through the Vanishing Point*, 263.

53 R. Murray Schafer, *The Tuning of the World* (Toronto: Random House, 1977).

54 Stefan Wolpe Society, "Recollections of Stefan Wolpe" [by Herbert Brün], accessed January 29, 2012, http://www.wolpe.org/page10/page10 .html#Herbert%20Brün.

Oliveros' *I of IV* is an early demonstration of the sculptural and tactile dimensions of listening. Its creation, and the experience of listening to it, encapsulate the essence of a new world of music, based essentially on the direct experience of acoustic phenomena by both creator and listener. It is this direct experience of the physical realities of sound as material that characterizes experimental music in audio-tactile space. In this piece, as in *4'33,"* and many other works by composers within the experimental tradition, the listener is empowered to make the creative connection independently of inherited cultural or linguistic assumptions. As Clarkson points out, Cage's purpose was to activate the creative process in the individual musician and liberate sounds from the constraints of tradition.[55] When music listens outward it can open the listener to the multidimensionality of our physical experience of the sound, and of the world.

As we have seen, McLuhan described arts practice as research and probing. He also implicitly emphasized the importance of listening skills: "What we call art would seem to be specialist artifacts for enhancing human perception."[56] This comment raises a question that is often awkward for artists to answer: why is it so important to enhance perception, to research and probe? McLuhan implies that we must be seeking some kind of nourishment: "Man the food-gatherer reappears incongruously as information-gatherer. In this mode, electronic man is no less a nomad than his Paleolithic ancestors."[57]

In his biography of McLuhan, Douglas Coupland comments: "An artist, according to Marshall, is someone on the frontiers of perception, who looks at information overload with the goal of pattern recognition, to see things before anyone else does."[58] One might modify this somewhat in light of this discussion: *to see or hear.* Deep Listening shows us the way to the frontiers of perception.

---

55 Clarkson, "The Intent of the Musical Moment," 80.
56 McLuhan, *Counterblast*, 32.
57 McLuhan, *Understanding Media*, 248.
58 Douglas Coupland, *Marshall McLuhan* (Toronto: Penguin Canada, 2009), 143.

Meditations on Form:
Toward a Theory of Inclusive Music

Lawton Hall distills our sensory environment with delicate precision and clarity of thought and expression. In his musical and multimedia works, disparate stimuli —harmonics of string and wind instruments, irrational vibrations of percussion, oscillating video and audio signals—flow in streams that are natural and otherworldly, existing in unstable harmony with our consciousness and perception of the world. Lawton worked alongside Pauline Oliveros at the Deep Listening Institute, editing her collected writings, *Sounding the Margins*. Other mentors include Mary Ellen Childs, Ben Johnston, Asha Srinivasan, and John Mayrose. He studied horn with Tod Bowermaster and James DeCorsey, Balinese gamelan with I Dewa Ketut Alit Adyana, and intermedia art with Julie Lindemann and John Shimon. His works have been performed at Bard College, SEAMUS, Electronic Music Midwest, the International Electroacoustic Music Festival, Brooklyn College, the CUNY Graduate Center, and the DLI Dream Festival. Lawton is a graduate of Lawrence University.
http://www.lawtonhall.com

Lawton Hall

IN MUCH WESTERN MUSIC, an oral tradition or musical notation is used to describe the sonic characteristics (pitch, loudness, dynamics, articulation, etc.) of a unique series of sounds. The series of sounds which exhibits these particular characteristics is considered a "piece of music"—a discrete aural-temporal form which may contain in itself many other forms, structures, and hierarchies. This music is *prescriptive*—aural-temporal forms of this kind exist apart from and before the experience of sounding or hearing the sounds which they prescribe—and *exclusive*—only those series of sounds which exhibit (within an acceptable margin of error) the prescribed sonic characteristics of a given form can be said to constitute that form in time; all other sounds either exist outside of the form, or undermine the integrity of the form as it is temporally experienced.

243

In recent decades, an expanded consciousness and desire for alternative modes of musical expression have led many musicians to create musical forms without prescribing the specific sonic characteristics of their aural-temporal content. This music is often *generative*—unprescribed sounds are made which comprise larger musical forms—or *reactive*—indeterminate sounds trigger responses in the performer or listener (or both) which lead to the creation of larger musical structures. Often in this music there is a rapid oscillation between generation and reaction, where the creation of each new unprescribed sound triggers reactions in the listener/performer which itself may lead to the generation of new sounds, etc. This music is *inclusive*—since no sonic characteristics of a form are prescribed, any sounds which occur during the experience of listening to or creating one of these forms necessarily constitute the form itself. Inclusive forms do not exist apart from experience.

The desire for inclusivity has manifest itself in many different genres of music. It has had a tremendous impact upon the Western experimental music tradition through the work of composers such as John Cage, David Tudor, and Cornelius Cardew, who often maintained the strictures of composition and ritual of performance in their works but infused them with elements of indeterminacy, resulting in complex, unpredictable musical forms which varied from performance to performance. The field of free improvisation—both jazz and non-jazz—exists as an entirely nonprescriptive, inclusive genre in which performers generate musical forms "on the spot" in performance. Live electronic sound processing allows for reactive and generative musical forms to be created out of any sound sources. Recent advances in digital audio technology and artificial intelligence make it increasingly possible to create nonprescribed forms which reflect the perceptive capabilities of human listeners, allowing for the real-time creation of musical forms which resemble traditional exclusive compositional processes.

The philosophy and practice of Deep Listening is based upon purely inclusive listening. In 1953, after hearing sounds captured by her first reel-to-reel tape recorder, Pauline Oliveros gave herself this succinct

244   ANTHOLOGY OF ESSAYS challenge: "Listen to everything all of the time and remind yourself when you are not listening."[1]

In the early 1970's, before the founding of the Deep Listening Band or Institute, Oliveros undertook a period of intense research and study at the University of California, San Diego. During this period, she focused on the challenge that she set forth for herself in 1953 and explored the integral role that attention, memory, and perception play in the creation of music. With the ♀ Ensemble (an all-female group of musicians and non-musicians from the San Diego area), Oliveros applied and experimented with these ideas through improvisatory, group-participation pieces which were communicated to the ensemble verbally, rather than through the use of any special musical notation. These pieces were eventually collected and published as the *Sonic Meditations* in 1974,[2] and formed the basis for much of the practice of Deep Listening that would follow.

As both a deliberate response to the challenge "listen to everything all of the time" and as the foundation of Deep Listening, the *Sonic Meditations* are the logical jumping-off point in the endeavor to construct a theory of inclusive music.

In her introduction to the *Sonic Meditations*, Oliveros writes that each piece is a procedure for one or more of the following processes:

1. Actually making sounds
2. Actively imagining sounds
3. Listening to present sounds
4. Remembering sounds[3]

As will be seen, these processes (of sounding, imagining, perceiving, and remembering), which are essential in the performance of the *Sonic Meditations*, must also be central to the analysis and formal understanding of inclusive music.

---

1   Pauline Oliveros, "Quantum Listening: From Practice to Theory (to Practice Practice)" in *Sounding the Margins: Collected Writings 1992-2009* (Kingston, NY: Deep Listening Publications, 2010), 70.
2   Pauline Oliveros, *Sonic Meditations* (Baltimore: Smith Publications 1974).
3   Oliveros, "Introduction II," *Sonic Meditations.*

This desire to understand inclusive music in terms of traditional ideas of formal structure is not an attempt to diminish the originality of Oliveros' work or Deep Listening, which does, indeed, represent a thoroughly innovative, egalitarian approach to music-making. Rather, it stems from my belief that if a thorough theory of inclusive music could someday be constructed, we may come to realize that the performance of much "exclusive" music is not as exclusive as we initially thought it to be. After studying and embracing Deep Listening, it becomes difficult to hear musical forms as being entirely separate from the whole sound-environment; pieces of music become vulnerable and can be altered by ambient noises, performances spaces, the eccentricities of recording media, or countless other sounds that can permeate a musical form as it is experienced in time. To understand inclusive music is to understand the myriad connections and structures that result when music is considered in a global context.

It is worth noting that even superficially, inclusivity and exclusivity are not themselves mutually exclusive from one another—musical forms may exist which contain both inclusive and exclusive elements. Pieces modeled on Terry Riley's *In C*[4] are examples of this; rhythms and pitches of melodic fragments are specifically prescribed, and the fragments must be played in a particular order, but players are free to choose exactly when they move from one fragment to the next, so that a nearly infinite combination of concurrent fragments can exist at any point in the piece. As a result, the form of these works is only fully manifest in performance. Every musical form, then, comes into being through processes which exist somewhere on a continuum between pure inclusivity and pure exclusivity.

The analysis or identification of exclusive musical forms can be attempted by studying the scores (or recordings, if no score is available, though recordings may include errors, ambient noises, or other sonic artifacts which exist outside of a prescribed form) that prescribe a form's sonic characteristics. If any analysis of inclusive musical forms

---

4   Robert Carl, "Terry Riley's In C," New Music Box, January 14, 2010, accessed October 27, 2011, http://www.newmusicbox.org/articles /Terry-Rileys-In-C/.

is to be attempted, however, it must necessarily take into account the dynamism of our perception and the integral role that perception must play in the formation of aural-temporal forms.

Here again, the *Sonic Meditations* are an excellent point of departure, since they make listening and perception integral elements of the musical experience. Many Meditations require that the listeners/performers go to a particular location (i.e. a canyon, near the ocean, on Lake Winnepauskee at sundown, etc.), but make no stipulations about the specific sounds that they will make or hear in that location. One's aural-spatial perspective of the sound environment affects the sonic construction of the Meditation, since perspective and proximity affect our perception of the sounds around us, making them essential elements in the creation of musical forms.

Often, in pieces like *Meditation V*, "Native," the aural perspective is the only stipulated dynamic parameter of a piece: "Take a walk at night. Walk so silently that the bottoms of your feet become ears."[5] By prescribing that the listener walk silently, Oliveros ensures that the listener does not contribute to the sound-environment herself, but that the musical form of her listening experience is defined entirely by her shifting proximity to various sound sources during the night-time walk. Dynamic perception (shifting aural perspective) is the central formative parameter of the piece and must be the basis for any kind of formal analysis of this Meditation.

Though myriad methods exist for the analysis of music (some being better suited to particular genres, historical eras, etc., than others), the phenomenological theory of form developed by James Tenney is a method that could, if adapted and developed further, bridge the apparent disparity between the study of inclusive and exclusive form and eventually lead to a understanding of formal integrity even in the absence of a prescriptive score.

Tenney's theory (called *temporal gestalt analysis*) is based entirely upon the raw experience of listening to a musical form unfold in time. As this experience occurs, the varying sonic characteristics of a succession of sounds (loudness, pitch, timbre, etc.) cause perceptual groupings

---

5   Oliveros, *Sonic Meditations.*

to form in the mind of the listener. It is an analytical method which attempts to reflect the pure experience of listening—temporal gestalt analyses are conducted linearly (from the beginning to the end of a piece) without the global perspective that notated score provides. Each successive sonic element or sectional division is analyzed only in relation to that which immediately preceded it.

First proposed in his speculative 1964 thesis *META+Hodos: A Phenomenology of 20th-Century Musical Materials and an Approach to the Study of Form*[6][7] Tenney eventually refined this theory into an operative method described in the 1980 article "Temporal Gestalt Perception in Music"[8] (co-written with Larry Polansky). Using a musical score, the characteristics of each sound in a piece are quantified so that numerical comparisons can be made between successive sounds and groups of sounds. These comparisons are then used to predict those sounds that will be perceived together as a *temporal gestalt* (formal unit), or *TG*.

The gestalt factors of cohesion and segregation are responsible for the cognitive formation of these temporal gestalten. Tenney identifies two primary factors: 1) the *proximity-factor*, which refers to the relative time between the onset of new sounds (sounds separated by relatively long durations will be less likely to be grouped into TG's than those separated by comparatively short durations), and 2) the *similarity-factor*, which refers to the parametric similarity or dissimilarity between two successive sounds (characteristically similar sounds (loud, soft, high, low, etc.) will be more likely to be perceived as a group than characteristically dissimilar ones). In addition to these two primary factors, Tenney identifies four secondary factors, the first of which is called the factor of *intensity*. The intensity-factor refers to the tendency of parametrically

---

6 James Tenney, "Meta+Hodos: A Phenomenology of 20th-Century Musical Materials and an Approach to the Study of Form" (Master's Thesis, University of Illinois, 1964).

7 James Tenney, *Meta+Hodos and META Meta+Hodos: A Phenomenology of 20th Century Musical Materials and an Approach to the Study of Form*, 2nd ed. (Hanover, NH: Frog Peak Music, 1988).

8 James Tenney and Larry Polansky, "Temporal Gestalt Perception in Music," *Journal of Music Theory*, Vol. 24 No. 2 (Autumn 1980): 205–241.

accented sonic events (i.e. a loud "bang" in an otherwise quiet piece) to cause perceptual segregation and the initiation of a new TG.

The two primary factors (proximity and similarity) plus the secondary intensity-factor are the underlying principles in the operative method of TG-analysis presented in "Temporal Gestalt Perception in Music."[9] By quantifying the characteristics of each sonic event and conducting vector analyses (which mathematically represent the principles of cohesion and segregation), Tenney is able to determine where formal groupings are likely to occur at multiple hierarchical levels of perception, with higher-level TG's encompassing several lower-level TG's, etc.

Temporal gestalt analysis is a useful and refreshing tool in the study of musical form because it shifts the analytical focus away from notated musical elements and instead focuses (as closely as possible) on the role that raw perception plays in formal organization. As such, the analytical method described in "Temporal Gestalt Perception in Music" does not presume or operate upon any one method of harmonic or structural organization, but instead makes the assumption that the individual listener actively constructs formal groupings out of perceived sonic elements. Listening creates form.

Despite this drastic shift in analytical focus, temporal gestalt analysis is still dependent upon the existence of a timeline of quantifiable sonic events that can be objectively compared and analyzed (i.e. a prescriptive score). However, if one supposes that perception is responsible for creating aural-temporal forms, even when none are prescribed, the principles of temporal gestalt formation may lay the foundation for the formal analysis of non-prescriptive, inclusive music.

Without a prescriptive score, it is impossible to determine exactly where points of perceptual segregation may occur, but the three aforementioned factors of segregation (the proximity-, similarity-, and intensity-factors) are no less significant in causing segregation and do manifest themselves in Oliveros' *Sonic Meditations*.

The intensity-factor is explicitly at play in *Meditation VI*, "Sonic Rorschach." In this Meditation, a natural or electronic source of white noise is listened to for a long span of time. At the midpoint of the

---

9   Tenney and Polansky, *Perception*, 205–241.

Meditation, a flash of light or a loud noise is sounded. If a sonic signal is used, it must necessarily be louder than the white noise that preceded and follows it. This results in perceptual segregation because of the greater loudness-intensity of the central noise.

In a more complex example, *Meditation XI*, "Bowl Gong" operates exclusively on the proximity factor and the influence that memory has on the perception of temporal gestalten:

> *Sit in a circle with a Japanese bowl gong in the center. One person, when ready to begin, hands the striker to someone else in the circle. That person strikes the gong. Each person maintains the pitch mentally for as long as possible. If the image is lost, then the person who has lost it hands the striker to someone else in the circle. This person again activates the gong in order to renew the mental pitch image. Continue as long as possible.*[10]

By sustaining the mental pitch-image of the gong, each member of the group maintains the cohesion of the temporal gestalt initiated by the initial gong-strike. When an individual loses the mental pitch-image, perceptual segregation occurs in their mind, which is brought about by the long durational proximity from the previous gong strike. This individual then hands the striker to another member of the group, who sounds the gong again.

For the individual who lost the pitch-image, this initiates a new formal temporal gestalt. However, for all other members of the group, this strike is perceived as a continuation of the TG which they have maintained in their minds between strikes.

A member of the ensemble may also believe that she or he has maintained the pitch-image of the gong, but the new strike reveals that their pitch-image shifted from the actual pitch of the gong. In this instance, the new gong strike initiates a new TG because of the parametric dissimilarity between the pitch-image and reality.

The result of these processes is that each member of the ensemble experiences the form of *Meditation XI* differently, depending on their individual abilities at maintaining a pitch-image. With repetition and

---

10 Oliveros, *Sonic Meditations*.

practice it may be possible to maintain the pitch image for the entire duration of the piece and experience it as a single temporal gestalt.

The proximity-, similarity-, and intensity-factors influence the formation of temporal gestalten because of the unique characteristics of the sounds within a piece, requiring that the analyst have a prescriptive score in order to identify musical forms that are produced as a result of these factors. However in addition to these three primary factors, Tenney identifies (in *META+Hodos*) three other secondary factors which could be used by the analyst even in the absence of a prescriptive/exclusive score. These are the *repetition-factor*, the *objective set*, and the *subjective set.*

Like the long-duration proximity-factors in "Bowl Gong," repetition influences temporal gestalt formation by acting upon memory. A collection of otherwise disparate sounds may come to be heard as a temporal gestalt if the collection is heard several times in succession, simply because each repetition recalls a previous one. The listener may become conditioned through repetition to hear the first sound in the collection as initiating a new temporal gestalt, even if this sound would not necessarily cause perceptual segregation because of the proximity-, similarity-, or intensity-factors.

This is especially true in the case of varied repetition. Changes in the repeated sound-unit might otherwise cause irregular perceptual segregations, but these segregations are less significant because of the cohesion that the repetition provides. *Meditation XII,* "One Word" works upon this principle of varied repetition:

> Choose a word. Listen to it mentally. Slowly and gradually
> begin to voice this word by allowing each tiny part of it to
> sound extremely prolonged. Repeat for a long time.[11]

When performed as a group, this Meditation creates varying perceptual segregations for the different members of the group. When each members' word is heard extremely prolonged, it is often unrecognizable as a word and is only perceived as abstract sounds. The component

11 Oliveros, *Sonic Meditations.*

abstract sounds of each word bring about perceptual groupings through the other factors of segregation.

However, each member is also aware of their own word and hears each iteration of the word as its own temporal gestalt, even if the component sounds of the word would not otherwise cause each iteration to be segregated as such.

The *objective set* is defined by Tenney as "expectations or anticipations during a musical experience which are produced by previous events *within the same piece*."[12] "Set" in this instance refers to a psychological attitude or predisposition towards a certain mode of perception. Altering or influencing perception inherently acts upon the subjective nature of perception and as such, the term "objective set" (confusingly) affects *subjective* temporal-gestalt formation. The term "objective" refers to the fact that these expectations or anticipations are brought about by the musical experience itself, rather than those that we, as listeners bring to the listening experience.

The *subjective set*, by contrast, refers to those forces *outside* of a piece of music which influence our perceptual organization of a piece (including our subjective predispositions, etc.).

After introducing and briefly explaining these three factors in Section II of *META+Hodos*, Tenney largely abandoned them in the later development of temporal gestalt theory. The subjectivity of our perception of repeated musical events (due to the highly personal nature of memory and attention), as well as the factors of the objective set and subjective set make them unwieldy analytical principles in the quest for objective explanations of formal structures. However, these three subjective factors are essential in maintaining formal integrity of a piece of music in the absence of a prescriptive score.

If stipulations (verbal or otherwise) are given which dictate the perceptual interrelationships between sounds or sections within a non-prescriptive, inclusive piece of music, these interrelationships may uphold the integrity of form traditionally maintained by prescribed elements in exclusive music. In exclusive pieces, gestalt groupings that result from the objective factors (the proximity-, similarity-, and

---

12 Tenney, *Meta+Hodos*.

intensity-factors) maintain the aural-temporal form which exists separately from any one performance, since the sonic characteristics of the sounds which cause these gestalt-formations are prescribed, generally by a notated score.

The objective factors are no less active in causing gestalt-formation in inclusive music, but since the particular characteristics of sounds may vary from performance to performance, these factors are less likely to maintain formal structure apart from any temporal experience of the piece. The mechanics of perception affected by the subjective factors (repetition-factor, the objective set, and the subjective set) are more likely to do this.

The types of anticipations or expectations that can be brought about by the objective and subjective sets are numerous, and indeed, it may be impossible to fully identify all of the ways that sounds may influence the perception of other sounds within a piece. However, Tenney does offer a few broad examples, which may be extrapolated in their application to inclusive pieces of music.

The first example of an objective set function is *rhythmic inertia.* The existence (and perceptibility) of a regular meter or pulse creates a kinesthetic framework against which the occurrence of sound events may be contrasted. Those sounds which actively work against the pre-established pulse (i.e. hemiola or syncopation) may be heard as separate formal events simply because of the existence of the regular meter.

Rhythmic inertia functions heavily in Variation C of *Meditation VII,* "Removing the Demon or Getting Your Rocks Off," which is performed outdoors and also borrows the dynamic aural perspective found in *Meditation V,* "Native." In it, the group begins in a close circle, striking rocks together in a uniform tempo. After a time, each member of the group begins to wander away from the circle, though always keeping in audible contact with at least one another member. Eventually, everyone returns to the beginning circle.

The establishment of a regular tempo at the beginning of the Meditation creates the kinesthetic framework for the rest of the piece. As the individual members of the group wander away, they maintain this framework in their mind. However, just like the shifting pitch-images in

"Bowl Gong," the individual members may speed up or slow down, and reinforce a pulse that is out-of-step with the rest of the group. As their wandering, shifting aural perspective brings them in sonic contact with the other performers, a jarring contrast may occur, which can initiate a new perceived formal unit in the listener/performer.

Like rhythmic inertia, other referential norms, such as a central pitch or pitch collection, a pervasive timbre, etc. may also create a standard for comparison which influences gestalt-formation. The most obvious example of this occurs in tonal music—a tonic pitch or chord acts as an overarching "goal" against which other harmonies may be compared or contrasted.

Finally, repeated themes or musical ideas act upon memory to influence temporal gestalt-formation. As with the repetition-factor, the recurrence of a familiar musical idea may cause it to be heard as its own temporal-gestalt, even if its sonic characteristics would not necessarily segregate it as such. (Similarly, Tenney identifies only one possible function of the subjective set which may be useful for analysts—the quotation of or allusion to preexisting pieces of music. Borrowed passages from familiar works may be perceived as their own temporal gestalten simply because they, too, act upon memory in the mind of the listener, rather than being a function of pure perception. While quotation is not a particularly important formative factor in the *Sonic Meditations*, it is very important in much hip-hop and electronic music, which often rely heavily on borrowed samples. Oliveros' use of snippets of Puccini's opera *Madama Butterfly* in her 1965 tape work *Bye Bye Butterfly*[13] is another example of this phenomenon.) In all of these factors of the objective set, the expectations or anticipations brought about by musical elements influence only temporal gestalt-formation—in exclusive music, any interpretation (musical or extramusical) of these musical elements is a function of the subjective set (as it is defined by Tenney).

However, in much inclusive music, the interpretation of sounds in relation to other musical events within the same piece may lead to the generation of new sounds or modes of listening. This may occur because

13 Pauline Oliveros, *Electronic Works 1965–1966*. Paradigm Discs PD04, CD, 1997.

of the tastes or predispositions of the performers (as in free impro-visation) or because of directions given for generation/reaction by a composer or leader. In the latter instance, these directions may lead to predictable objective set factors of formal segregation which preserve an aspect of formal integrity from performance to performance.

Summary and Application

I have chosen to apply these theories to Oliveros' *World Wide Tuning Meditation* (2007), which is exemplary of Deep Listening works and builds heavily upon the earlier *Sonic Meditations*:

> *Begin by taking a deep breath and letting it all the way out with air sound.*
> *Listen with your mind's ear for a tone.*
> *On the next breath using any vowel sound, sing the tone that you have silently perceived on one comfortable breath.*
> *Listen to the whole field of sound the group is making.*
> *Select a voice distant from you and tune as exactly as possible to the tone you are hearing from that voice.*
> *Listen again to the whole field of sound the group is making.*
> *Contribute by singing a new tone that no one else is singing.*
> *Continue by listening then singing a tone of your own or tuning to the tone of another voice alternately.*
> *Commentary:*
> *Always keep the same tone for any single breath.*
> *Change to a new tone on another breath.*
> *Listen for distant partners for tuning*
> *Sound your new tone so that it may be heard distantly.*
> *Communicate with as many difference voices as possible.*
> *Sing warmly!*[14]

The formal analysis of inclusive music is not a study of static structures, but rather a study of the dynamic factors which, like a mathematical function or computer program, filter and create perceived formal units

---

14 Robby Herst, "World Wide Tuning Meditation," *Arthur Magazine Archive,* August 1, 2007, accessed April 30, 2012, http://www.arthurmag .com/2007/08/01/world-wide-tuning-meditation/.

out of indeterminate inputs. Using the aforementioned principles of gestalt-formation, a four-part method is proposed for the analysis of inclusive music:

1.) Determination of possible inputs.

This step is threefold. First, it requires determining those parameters or sounds which are structurally significant in a given piece. In some sense, this a measure of the "degree of inclusivity" of a given work, with highly-inclusive pieces treating all sounds and/or parameters as possibly structurally significant, while other, less inclusive pieces only concentrate on one or two formative parameters. Second, after the formal parameters have been determined, one must identify the source of the input sounds. These may be randomly generated by an ensemble, taken from the environment, produced randomly by a computer, etc. Third, based on the input sounds and the parameters in use, one must consider the range of parametric values in use in a given piece, which may be determined by the parameters themselves or by the capabilities of the input sounds (i.e. the range of the human voice, etc.). Also significant is whether the parametric scales are continuous (i.e. computer-generated glissandi) or measured in discrete intervals (i.e. the pitches on a piano).

In the *World Wide Tuning Meditation*, pitch is the only musical parameter that is structurally significant in maintaining the integrity of form from performance to performance. This is not to say that other parameters are insignificant and may be responsible for perceptual segregation in a particular performance. However, as the Meditation is constructed, we can only assume (based on the directions given) that pitch-based segregations will occur in every performance of this piece.

The sources of the input sounds are the individual voices of each member of the ensemble. Since our voices are capable of producing a virtually infinite number of gradations within our vocal range, the parametric pitch scale can be said to be continuous. The range of parametric values in any performance of the *World Wide Tuning Meditation* is simply the combined vocal ranges of the entire group of performers.

It is also important to note that in a performance of the *World Wide Tuning Meditation,* the pitch of each sustained tone does not change for the length of an entire exhalation. This negates the possibility of perceiving two or more pitches as a melodic unit simply because they are sung in one breath. Each singer's new pitch is separated from the previous one by at least the length of time it takes to inhale.

2.) Determination of the subjective judgments at play on the input sounds.

Once the input sounds of a piece are produced and perceived, the audience and/or performers immediately judge these sounds both objectively and subjectively based on the particular sonic characteristics heard at a given time. The subjective judgments are responsible for the creation of temporal gestalt forms and—in the case of generative music—are also responsible for propelling the piece forward.

In a free improvisation, the subjective judgments used by the performers are most likely a result of their own personal experiences and aesthetic tastes, unless they have discussed goals or guidelines for the improvisation before beginning. In pieces like the *Sonic Meditations*, Pauline Oliveros focuses our attention on a particular sonic characteristic and then ascribes some significance or goal to sounds that exhibit a particular characteristic. Our knowledge of these goals affects our judgments and often, these goals force us to hone our perceptive skills during the course of a Meditation in order to successfully perceive the sounds in a way that informs the next sound we make.

The subjective judgment in the *World Wide Tuning Meditation* is dependent on what point in the form an individual performer currently is in, but always involves trying to perceive all of the individual pitches being sung by the ensemble, rather than hearing a large, dense cloud. The judgment each singer makes based on this set of pitches is binary— "Will the next pitch I sing match a pitch currently being sung by someone else or will I deliberately avoid matching another pitch?" Like many of the *Sonic Meditations,* it involves actively imagining the next sound and comparing it with the sounds currently being produced by the rest of the ensemble.

The *World Wide Tuning Meditation* is cyclical in nature and this binary judgment recurs in the minds of the performers before every new pitch is sung. I have found, however, in my experience performing this Meditation, that my ability to isolate the individual pitches of the ensemble increases as the piece goes on and that I am able to perceive, judge, and perform much more rapidly by the end of the Meditation than the beginning. This creates a dynamism to the piece that could not possibly be evident in any score, since this change occurs entirely cerebrally. This is also a characteristic of Oliveros' *Sonic Meditations,* where the performers are their own audience and cerebral changes that come about through performative decisions critically influence the perception of the work.

3.) Determination of outputs (if any).

In generative music, subjective factor judgments often initiate the creation of new sounds. As before, one must consider both the possible significant parameters of the output and the possible range of parametric values. These may be stipulated by directions based on subjective judgments, or by the source of the outputs themselves. Most often, these generated outputs will become new inputs, themselves subject to subjective judgments. Thus, a loop is created between step 1 and step 3 of the analysis. One must consider whether or not this loop remains static throughout the course of a piece or if the subjective judgments and/or outputs are themselves dynamic.

The "output sounds" in the *World Wide Tuning Meditation* are virtually identical in character to the initial input sounds, but their exact pitch content is determined by the each performer's subjective judgments from step 2 and where in the form the singer is (i.e. whether or not she is trying to match a pitch or deliberately avoid doing so).

When trying to sing a particular pitch that is not present in the harmony sung by the ensemble, the singer will most likely take one of two approaches. She can either try to sing a pitch that is between two pitches being sung by other members of the group (which, depending on the size of the group and the density of the harmonies, may result in very dense, microtonal clusters). Or, depending on her vocal range, she may decide to sing a pitch higher or lower than any of the other pitches in the whole harmonic "cloud." While either is an equally acceptable approach, the perceptual segregation caused by increasing the aggregate range of the group at any moment may be structurally significant.

In the *World Wide Tuning Meditation*, these "output sounds" immediately become new "input sounds," so that a rapid alternation between sounding and listening (judging) is constantly taking place.

4.) Find points of possible perceptual segregation.

Once the possible inputs, judgments, and outputs have been determined for an entire piece, the basic principles of temporal gestalt analysis can be applied to find points of possible segregation through the factors of gestalt-formation. These factors may come into play at any point in the piece—they may be a result of the parametric restrictions of the inputs, the particular subjective judgments at play, or the unique qualities of the outputs. While the subjective factors (repetition-factor, objective set, and subjective set) might be most applicable (if specific parametric values are unavailable) in these analyses, the objective factors (proximity-, similarity-, and intensity-factors) are no less significant and must be taken into account as well, if possible.

In the *World Wide Tuning Meditation*, the onset of each new pitch sung by any member of the ensemble is a possible point of perceptual segregation. The exact points in time where these onsets occur is variable and unpredictable, since the duration of each pitch and the time before the onset of the subsequent pitch is determined by the length of each performer's exhalation and inhalation, respectively. Since, like vocal ranges, lung capacity and breath capabilities vary from performer to performer, these onsets become staggered in performance. It can be safely assumed, however, that a greater number of performers will result in a greater frequency of pitch-onsets and thus more frequent possible points of segregation, though this greater frequency also diminishes the time between onsets, increasing the possibility that several onsets will be grouped as a single temporal gestalt (due to temporal proximity).

The time between each pitch and its subsequent pitch (during which each performer inhales and listens to the surrounding harmonies) is significant because it can help bring about perceptual segregation due to the proximity-factor. Because of the staggering of voice entrances and breaths, there is most often a continuous harmony being sounded at any time. However, this staggering also means that all of the performers (or a large percentage of the performers) can end up taking a breath at the same time, resulting in a jarring silence (or great drop in overall volume) before the next cloud of pitches is sounded.

When this occurs (especially if it occurs only once or twice during a performance), it can cause a very significant perceptual segregation to occur—sometimes one so great that the performers collectively and nonverbally decide to end the piece. This segregation, because it comes about as a result of the duration of time of the silence between events, is a result of the proximity-factor, which is not dependent on any particular musical parameter.

The more frequent perceptual segregations that are likely to occur in a performance of the *World Wide Tuning Meditation* come about as a result of the similarity-factor in the pitch-parameter. As was previously stated, the onset of each new pitch is a possible point of perceptual segregation. Based on the participatory nature of Oliveros' *Sonic Meditations*, where an individual performer's perception is essential in determining the form of the piece, one of two possibilities can occur.

In the first possibility, the performer matches a pitch being sung by another member of the performing group. Like the pitch maintained cerebrally in "Bowl Gong," the performer at this moment is sustaining a perceived pitch-image (though in the *World Wide Tuning Meditation*, she does this audibly, rather than just in her mind). Because of the exact similarity (ideally) in the pitch-parameter, it is much less likely that a new temporal gestalt will be initiated at this point than at others. (This does not negate the possibility of similarity-factor segregation occurring due to other musical parameters, such as loudness or timbre, but since Oliveros' score focuses our attention fully on the pitch-parameter, we cannot assume that these other parameters will help us predict points of structural significance from performance to performance, whereas we can safely make that assumption about the pitch-parameter.)

In the second possibility, the performer deliberately avoids matching any other pitch being sung at a given time. This increases the possibility of perceptual segregation occurring from dissimilarity in the pitch-parameter. However, in order to fully determine whether or not a new pitch causes such segregation, it would be necessary to know relatively how parametrically dissimilar this new pitch is from the pitches that surround it. Such an exact measurement is obviously unknowable when a performance of the *World Wide Tuning Meditation* is considered theoretically, and could only be determined from performance to performance.

The fact that the density of the pitch cloud and the total vocal range of the ensemble are partially a result of the number of performers in the group may provide insights into a possible way of formulating predictions about perceptual segregations within a performance. Density of the pitch cloud becomes significant in regards to the limited number of options a performer has when trying to find a new, different pitch to sing that does not match anyone else in the group. As was previously mentioned, the singer has the option of trying to find a pitch that falls between two other pitches currently being sung (affecting the overall pitch cloud less and causing, presumably less parametric dissimilarity) or to sing a pitch that is above or below the entire cloud of sound (which increases the entire range of the group at any given moment and has a likely greater chance of causing segregation due to parametric dissimilarity than the first possibility). The first possibility becomes increasingly difficult as the density increases and the second possibility is increasingly difficult as the pitches in play at a given time are spread out across a wider vocal range. Because both possibilities are indirectly affected by the number of performers in a group, some correlation could possibly be extrapolated between these two factors of any performance.

Meta-Analysis and Conclusions

Though still in its infancy, this proposed theory of inclusive music, which is based on Tenney's theories of gestalt perception, hopefully demonstrates how many of the musical factors which cause formal segregation do not disappear in the absence of a prescriptive score. These factors are at work during any listening experience, and as such, any listening experience has the potential to be heard as a musical form.

The analysis of this music must necessarily be dynamic and free, since the music to which it is applied is similarly free and unpredictable. If the gestalt factors of cohesion and segregation could be reformulated as series of dynamic if/then statements, they could be used to theoretically represent the formal processes that tie together works of inclusive music. Additionally, this theory would require a statistical approach to analysis, which seeks to determine the *likelihood* that a formal structure will exist at a given point rather than identifying these points in time with black-and-white certainty. The fourth step of my proposed analytical method should involve finding all points of possible perceptual segregation and then mathematically determining the likelihood of such a point occurring at any given time.

If refined and honed, these theories could be expanded to extend our understanding of music outwards into the world so that every sound, when heard deeply, could play a part in the beautiful symphony that plays constantly in the universe.

Negotiating the Space Between: Ramos' *Musica pratica* (1482) and Pauline Oliveros' Challenge to Listeners

JANN PASLER, musicologist, pianist, documentary filmmaker, and professor of music at UC San Diego, has published widely on contemporary American and French music, modernism and post-modernism, interdisciplinarity, intercultural transfer, and cultural life in France and the French colonies. Her article, "The Utility of Musical Instruments in the Racial and Colonial Agendas of Late Nineteenth-Century France," *Journal of the Royal Musical Association* (Spring 2004), won the Colin Slim award from the American Musicological Society for the best article in 2005. Recently she published *Writing through Music: Essays on Music, Culture, and Politics* (Oxford University Press, 2007) and *Composing the Citizen: Music as Public Utility in Third Republic France* (University of California Press, 2009), winning an ASCAP Deems Taylor Award (2010). Forthcoming is *Music, Race, and Colonialism in the French Empire, 1880s-1950s.* She has served on the Board of Directors of the Pauline Oliveros Foundation and is editor of AMS Studies (Oxford University Press). http://www.writingthroughmusic.com

Jann Pasler

LONG IMPORTANT to Pauline Oliveros and the Deep Listening practice she created has been the notion of "being in sound."[1] Consider, for example, the "recipe-like instructions" engaging orchestral players in *Four Meditations for Orchestra* (1996):

> Each performer is responsible for her/his own part within the guidelines given. Since there is no written part to watch, all the performers' attention can be given to sound and invention. . . . The direction is sound-oriented. . . .

---

1 An earlier and much shorter draft of this paper was presented at *Sounding the Margins*, the forty-year retrospective of the works of Pauline Oliveros in San Francisco, June 1, 2002.

> Each sound that each player makes is intended to be unique—
> different from all other sounds in the meditation. . . .
>
> In *Approaches and Departures* each player carries a specific
> pitch which is expressed or implied. Each player invents musi-
> cal approaches and departures to their specific pitch.

Pauline's instructions facilitate "being in sound" through inviting one
to focus on sound in certain ways, that is, to create specific types of
relationship with what one hears through both listening and imagining.

Equally essential in Pauline's music is "being with sound," an awareness of not only one's sound, but also those of others and the dynamic
interplay created through collaboration. In the *Tuning Meditation* (1996),
for example, "players are asked to tune exactly to another player or to
contribute a pitch which no one else is sounding."[2]

But these two notions do not tell the whole story of Pauline Oliveros'
music as well as that of Deep Listeners. What happens to the performer
and to the nature and the notion of music when one is not making the
sound or being in the sound, and one is not being with someone else's
sound, but rather one is somewhere in the middle? Pauline also calls for
awareness of "being between," an attention to the space of waiting. In
her *Sound Fishes* (1992), she refers obliquely to this:

> Listening for what has not yet sounded, like a fisherman wait-
> ing for a nibble or a bite. Pull the sound out of the air like a
> fisherman catching a fish, sensing its size and energy. When
> you hear the sound, play it. Move to another location if there
> are no nibbles or bites. There are sounds in the air like sounds
> in the water.[3]

This is not silence, or non-sounding, but almost like John Cage's music of
4'33", that is, an all-sounding out of which we are challenged to choose
what we attend to. In some ways, "being between" is even more challenging and compositionally important as "being in sound" and "being with

---

2 Pauline Oliveros, *Four Meditations for Orchestra* (Kingston, NY: Deep
  Listening Publications, 1996), Notes.
3 Pauline Oliveros, *Deep Listening: A Composer's Sound Practice* (Lincoln, NE:
  iUniverse, 2005), 50. *Sound Fishes* is available on: Pauline Oliveros, *Pauline
  Oliveros and the University of Michigan Digital Music Ensemble*, directed by
  Stephen Rush. Deep Listening DL-DVD-3, 2010, DVD.

sound." What happens to sound, and to the performer, in between sound acts? Such moments lie at the intersection of perception and thought when the realm of possibilities is not yet defined and choices are not yet being considered, weighed, and decided upon.

Ramos' *Musica pratica* (1482)[4]

The notion of "being between" recalls one of the most wrenching periods of music history when the stakes in the West were among the highest. Western music had long been shackled by *mutatio*, the system of medieval mutation that permitted movement only between three six-note scales (or hexachords) starting on C, F, and G, as depicted on the Guidonian hand. In the late fifteenth century, Bartholomeo Ramos, a Spanish music theorist living in Naples, looked to the Greeks to challenge this system and in doing so laid the foundation for the eight-note scale.

The kind of musical movement implied by *mutatio* required a system of generative change, wherein each mutation is the movement from one self-contained, independent hexachord to another hexachord, each with its own *proprietas* [properties],[5] that is, from one whole to another. To ascend or descend in a piece of music, mutation involved a change of hexachords via the exchange of two syllables on the same pitch. In the mutation from the F hexachord to the G hexachord, however, the syllables *fa mi* do not occur on exactly the same pitch in the different hexachords. To avoid a tritone in ascending or descending lines, performers sing either B flat or B natural. This was called *permutatio*. With the sound space confined to the notes of these hexachords, *permutatio* and the use of *musica ficta* (accidentals) was limited to this situation. Listening to performers, however, convinced Ramos that, in practice, singers used accidentals to avoid tritones in other situations as well, engaging in proto-tonal gestures. This led him to reject the theories of predecessors like Tinctoris and to envisage a new musical system not dependent on

---

4   Johannes Wolf, ed. *Musica pratica Bartolomei Rami de Pareia* (Leipzig: Breitkopf & Härtel, 1901), available at http://www.chmtl.indiana.edu /tml/15th/RAMMP3T2_TEXT.html. All translations here used are my own.

5   The property of each hexachord, whether "hard," "soft," or "natural," was dependent on where and what kind of semitone was involved.

the mutation system. This called for collapsing the distinction between mutation and permutation.[6]

Wishing to initiate a system based on quantitative rather than qualitative differences between the notes, he proposed a new kind of movement, *transitus*. Whereas mutation required a change of focal point, *transitus* implied any movement between two points on the monochord—all pitches, not just those belonging to the hexachords. This eliminated the kind of disjunct movement called for by permutation. In his system, there was only one mutation, at the octave.[7] Both Ramos' new system and *transitus* were much easier for performing musicians to understand and more suited to their concerns than those of the theorists. With the whole string subdivided into parts that kept their same function with regard to the whole string instead of changing from hexachord to hexachord with each mutation, the system was closed rather than open. But every part of the space was now accessible and the notes were of equal value: *ficta* (chromatic notes used to avoid tritones) and *recta* were both acceptable in all kinds of music. Diversity came from the different arrangements of whole-tones and semitones of the different modes. Ramos' innovations opened discussion about which movements were preferable to the ear, qualitative value judgments irrelevant in the older mutation system.

Crucial in Ramos' argument against permutation and the development of his notion of *transitus* was his differentiation between various concepts used to discuss the area between two points, pitches, or syllables. If *intercapedo* is the fixed quantity or distance enclosed by two entities, a difference of physical size and aural proportion, and *spatium* is

---

6 Properly speaking, permutation, rather than mutation, has come to be used in mathematics to designate the act of changing the order of elements arranged in a particular order. This is exactly how Ramos used both mutation and permutation.

7 The change in terminology from a Greek-rooted word, mutation, based on *mu*, to a Roman-rooted word, based on *trans-ire*, is representative of Ramos' revolution in music theory. In modern usage, transition has come to means an "incidental modulation" (*New College Encyclopedia*) or even a "modulation, especially a brief one" (*American Heritage Dictionary*).

the physical extent which makes division of these entities possible, then *intervallum* in Ramos' usage represents the aural differences between the pitches. Intervals, for example, may be alike in sound, such as in the movement from C to D which sounds similarly at various octaves, while their physical sizes on the monochord are very different. Analogous to the measured sound *between* discrete pitches, *intervallum* is also the amount of time *between* the discrete pulses that regulate it. As such, *intervallum* is a notational abbreviation for the motion of sound as well as time, while leaving open the exact nature of how this motion might take place.

Thanks to Ramos' revolutionary notion of *transitus* that permitted composers to move freely and easily in the musical space represented by a monochord, in the early sixteenth century Adrian Willaert was able to traverse the entire musical system through the circle of fifths just as Magellan, in 1519, was circling the globe.[8] But the importance of Ramos' thinking goes beyond how it prepares for the advent of tonality. His preoccupation with the distinction between pitches and the intervals between them foreshadows Schoenberg's *sprechstimme* and much twentieth-century electronic music. Schoenberg's use of x's to indicate pitches on his score of *Pierrot Lunaire* was meant to define the beginning and end points of the singer's gradual musical movement *between* the pitches, rather than the precise and distinct articulation of these pitches. Like Ramos, it was perhaps Schoenberg's interpretation of contemporary singing practices (in cabarets) that led to such a new way to think about music and its notation. Since then, many have found that in moving away from the constraints of fixed pitches, they could liberate Western listeners from the expectations that Ramos' system ironically put into place. Yet, it is in the music of Pauline Oliveros and other deep listeners that I find an even more radical rethinking of the "space between" in music-making.

---

8 For a brilliant, foundational article on this subject and the importance of the octave as compared to the circle, see Edward Lowinsky, "The Concept of Physical and Musical Space in the Renaissance," reprinted in his *Music in the Culture of the Renaissance and Other Essays*, Vol. 1, ed. Bonnie Blackburn (Chicago and London: University of Chicago Press, 1989), 6–18.

Being Between: The Implications

Improvisation as practiced by Oliveros and her Deep Listeners draws attention to the deeply creative nature of how performers and listeners define and negotiate the "space between" in making music. Pauline, Dana Reason, and Philip Gelb, in fact, have used "The Space Between" as the name for their trio, formed in the late 1990s. Here the reference recognizes the differences that must be bridged in both the instruments they play—accordion, piano, and shakuhachi—as well as the tuning systems, with the accordion in just intonation, the piano in equal temperament, and the shakuhachi in its own pentatonic tuning. In the program notes for the premiere of *For Tonight* (2002), Pauline explains the nature of their collaboration as "We negotiate the space between."[9] As with *permutatio*, the challenge is how to move in the musical space when the pitches of one entity are not the same as those of another entity, and the musicians need both (in this case all three) to move forward. Here, betweenness also acknowledges the cultural differences represented by these instruments as well as their musical traditions that traverse time and space, from the middle ages to the nineteenth century and from West to East. As in Pauline's and IONE's play with music and pageantry, *Njinga the Queen King: The Return of a Warrior* (1993),[10] an aesthetic model for intercultural cooperation, the point is not to deny differences, but "to listen and not go in with my ideas of how things have to go."[11] Focus on the "space between" calls for exploring relationships developed through performance. It creates an opportunity for musicians both to push on the limits of identity and, like Ramos, to search for modes of movement and relationship that transcend previous assumptions and the rigid constraints associated with them.

---

9 Program notes for the 2002 San Francisco Oliveros retrospective *Sounding the Margins*, during which the trio performed Oliveros' *For Tonight* (2002).

10 The work was written and directed by IONE, with music and sound by Pauline Oliveros. Pauline Oliveros and IONE, *Njinga the Queen King*, Mode 220, 2010, DVD.

11 Jann Pasler, "Postmodernism, Narrativity, and the Art of Memory," in idem, *Writing through Music: Essays on Music, Culture, and Politics* (New York: Oxford University Press, 2008), 79.

Making the negotiation of the "space between" an important aspect of music also has important social implications. Because the enterprise of creativity is more important to Pauline and deep listeners than compositional ownership, they often use improvisation to break down the distinctions between the musical roles and practices of performers and those of composers. In this tradition, if the composer conceives and articulates only the basic recipe for a work—a kind of call to action, to reflect in a certain way, to behave in a certain way, through sound—it is the performer who considers the implications in the instructions—what is "between" the lines, between the instructions, unspecified in the notation. Performers, as with singers during Ramos' time, make the betweenness in the instructions audible through their choices, the relationships assumed and articulated. Meaning arises from and in this betweenness.

Because of the importance of community to Deep Listeners, these musicians also construe "betweenness" as a space for engaging amateurs as well as professionals. From a certain perspective, deep listening practices can be understood as growing out of the desire to inhabit the betweenness traditionally separating professionals from amateurs—construed as talent, skill, and dedication—and thereby to collapse this space of difference, as Ramos did in doing away with the difference between *permutatio* and *mutatio*. From still another perspective, through their focus on using listening to tune to oneself and others, deep listeners attempt not only to bring more awareness to themselves, but also to bring the self into harmony with others. This entails not collapsing difference, but making something with it, occasionally a relationship transformative for all involved. The vague and malleable nature of the "space between" is therefore very inviting, allowing for the exploration and expression of varied interests and abilities, stimulating (ideally) the development of new interactive skills, and encouraging an awareness of the impact we can have on an environment and the behavior of others. This space of possibility is inclusive, enabling, and empowering because, like Ramos' *intervallum*, its abstract potentiality takes form in the present and how we shape and experience it. In other words, one only inhabits in-betweenness when one grasps and engages in relationship with others.

Several recent authors have used the idea of the "in-between" to discuss anything from the time of transition (e.g. between jobs or marriages) to the place between life and death, recognizing this as characterized by both stress and the possibility of transformational growth. In her essay on Pauline's *Library of Maps*, an opera in many parts, Moira Roth, her collaborator on this project, proposes her own "the Land of the Inbetween." It is the space between physical space and cyberspace, as articulated in the work by children in California and New York who interacted simultaneously in real time as characters in a narrative.[12] Indeed, the ultimate "space between" that Pauline has sought to negotiate in myriad creative ways arises from ever-more discerning increments of contraction and expansion of space itself, not only physical space, bit also cyberspace and imaginative mental space.[13] From 1992 when, to celebrate her forty years of composing, she organized and coordinated videophone performances simultaneously in six places where she had lived (Houston, Oakland, La Jolla,[14] Los Angeles, New York, and Kingston, NY)[15] so that each could interact with the others, to her recent teaching at Mills College (Oakland, CA) and Rensselaer Polytechnic Institute (Troy, NY) via Skype from elsewhere, Pauline has long exploited

---

12 The work, exhibitions, and performances on this opera began in 2001. On October 8, 2003 Roth wrote of this, comparing it to Borges' short text *The Garden of Forking Paths*: "To learn how to chart a series of invisible pathways in order to make (poetically, scientifically, metaphorically . . .) not only more navigable but also more habitable (even, perhaps, more comfortable?) this new "inbetween" world of ours in which (for better or worse) many of us live these days—so that it becomes more than a mere passageway from an unknown point of departure to an unknown point of arrival. . . . In my mind's eye, I see the maps of the Land of the Inbetween and the Garden of Forking Paths superimposed on each other, their inhabitants stumbling back and forth between time and space, looking for places and moments in which to find respite, in which to reflect—as do the thoughtful and imaginative artists in this exhibition." "The Land of the Inbetween and the Library of Maps Series, 2001-2003," accessed September 11, 2011, http://www .picture-projects.com/between/essay.html.

13 I'm grateful to Monique Buzzarté for her contributions to this idea.

14 I directed the San Diego production of this event on November 23, 1992.

15 See the review, Joe Catalano, "Electronia Midwifery: A Videophone Celebration of Pauline Oliveros' Four Decades of Composing and Community," *Leonardo Music Journal* 3 (1994): 29–34.

the musical potential of technology to expand the notion of between-ness as a space of relationship. As she writes, "Making music together makes friends."[16] The most recent emanations of this interest have been the *World Wide Tuning Meditation* (2007)[17] from eight remote locations as well as Damrosch Park, and Telematic performances, beginning in November 2007. As with the previous Videophone event, Telematic concerts have been performed simultaneously in multiple places and involved improvisation.[18] With the globe itself providing the most open and malleable "space between" imaginable, in perhaps her most astounding work in this regard, *Echoes From the Moon*, first performed in Boston in 1987, Salzburg in 1997, and St. Pölten, Austria in 1999, she even construed this space as between earth and the moon.[19] In her vision and far-reaching use of technologies, Pauline has often preceded others by decades. What's next?

---

16 Ibid.

17 Robby Herst, "World Wide Tuning Meditation," *Arthur Magazine Archive*, August 1, 2007, accessed May 8, 2012, http://www.arthurmag.com/2007/08/01/world-wide-tuning-meditation/

18 See the six short papers on this subject, "Telematic Music: Six Perspectives," *Leonardo Music Journal* 19 (2009): 95–96, and Michael Dessen, "New Polyphonies: Score Streams, Improvisation and Telepresence," *Leonardo Music Journal* (2010): 21–23. See also recent activities of Deep Listeners and the Avatar Orchestra Metaverse.

19 Pauline describes the process of playing "aural tennis" with the moon, the sound traveling there and bouncing back: "The antenna has to be large enough to receive the returning signal from the moon. Conditions are constantly changing—sometimes the signal is lost as the moon moves out of range and has to be found again. Sometimes the signal going to the moon gets lost in galactic noise. The delay is around 2 and 1/2 seconds and it seems to shift slightly downward in pitch—a Doppler effect caused by the motion of the moon moving relative to the earth—like the whistle of a train as it rushes past." See Guillermo Galindo, "Listening to Pauline Oliveros," Nature Sounds Society [Newsletter], Spring 1999, accessed January 15, 2012, http://www.galindog.com/pauline_oliveras.html. My thanks to Monique Buzzarté for this reference.

Deep Listening through the Multiverse

Listening at the Top of the Sky: A Memoir of Rose Mountain Deep Listening Retreats 1995–2009

ANNE BOURNE improvises parallel streams of extended cello and voice, and composes chamber music for dance, film, experimental context, digital media, and words. Anne traveled widely with songwriters Jane Siberry, and Loreena McKennitt as an arranger and accompanist on electronics, piano, cello and voice. She has created work with Michael Ondaatje, Andrea Nann, Susie Ibarra, Eve Egoyan, John Oswald, Tom Kuo, Peter Mettler, Fred Frith, and Pauline Oliveros. Anne met Oliveros when invited to perform a distance concert with the Deep Listening Band at The Kitchen in NYC in 1995. From that year on Anne attended the Rose Mountain retreats in New Mexico, where she received one of the first Deep Listening Certificates. Anne performed in the original creation of Oliveros' composition *Primordial/Lift*. Anne is interested in musical expression being a point of departure for the resolution of difference tones, between peoples, landscapes, and individual thresholds of the heart. http://AnneBourneMusic.com/

Anne Bourne

STRAIGHT UP, that's how you had to get there.

— Bare bones, carry only what you need to live.

Bring a tent.

The Plaza Hotel in Las Vegas, New Mexico, had an early-twentieth-century stillness. I woke up rested. In the morning ambience of the lobby I met Tom Dougherty, ready to camp with his black wheeled suitcase, leather jacket, and brilliant mischief. Tom, a researcher in human interface systems, had flown in from the Bay Area. I was a recording artist. I had flown in from Canada, finished with concert touring, an ending that coincided with the death of my father. Nat Gold arrived, distinguished by his wide brim felt hat the color of Mourning Doves. Nat had a sparkle in his smile, and an internal peace in his voice.

275

Tom and I drove with Nat to the Dominguez Ranch to gather with the others and load the trucks. Depending on the forgiveness of rain patterns that summer, we would ride up the carved trails that could serve as streambeds to the higher altitude of Rose Mountain.

Our conversation was paced by the urgency of the road, red sand and ruts left by recent rain. Nat had a history in Manhattan where out of the family apartment on the Upper West Side he assisted young men by listening and helping them find ways to stay out of the Vietnam War. Nat Gold, father of Andy and Heloise.

Andy Gold, with his heart as compass and in league with the natural world, traveled west and claimed Rose Mountain. Heloise, who with the subtlety of a butterfly kiss could raise laughter, danced with the Bolshoi, was drawn west by experimental theater, and immersed herself in the Tao. Visionary improviser and composer, Pauline Oliveros, and IONE, author and dream sentient, settled near the previous Karmapa in upstate New York. From there they could reach the world. Heart lines intersect in Manhattan.

In 1990 Oliveros committed to a ten-year tenure of retreats. Rose Mountain would be a new location to follow the Sonic Meditation research she had begun at the University of California, San Diego. With an infinite sonic landscape to open, Rose Mountain would become a place to refine the Deep Listening retreat.

Driving off road, we parked at the Dominguez Ranch. I spotted Arturo Salinas under his Panama hat, a composer well attuned to the ghost cultures of his beloved Mexico. Among the other participants was Abbie Conant, triumphant and battle-worn from a decade-long ordeal with the Munich Philharmonic,[1] which broached nascent gender law, and significantly heightened both her empathy, and her sense of humor. I soon met among others, Tom Bickley, extended recorder player, of the Smithsonian in DC, holding a library of contemporary music in his heart, and Margrit Schenker, Swiss composer, and accordionist, with a penchant for creating transformative performance art, that integrated

---

1   Malcolm Gladwell, *Blink: The Power of Thinking Without Thinking* (New York: Little, Brown & Co., 2005), 245.

the chant of mystic composer Blessed Hildegard of Bingen, with bear scat, and lamplight. Newfound friends, all in one breath.

Each person carried a story that birthed the desire to climb Rose Mountain, to spend some time in the absence of electricity and technology, in the raucous joy and abundant silence, with renowned composer Pauline Oliveros.

I arrive. I step out of Nat's four-wheel drive. Dry heat stops my breath, lizards move imperceptibly across boulders. Thin air, pure clear light.

Standing on the path, there she is at the top of an incline, in the shade of the tall pines. There is Pauline Oliveros, smiling. From quiet disturbed only subtly by the wings of many Ruby-throated Humming birds nearby, I hear Pauline say my name.

The Kitchen

Rose Mountain was our first meeting in person. I initially met Pauline Oliveros on screen, in 1995. Lauren Pratt had called me to play cello in a distance concert with Oliveros and her Deep Listening Band at The Kitchen in New York. Lauren was gathering a group to improvise with them from a studio in Toronto. We would make contemporary chamber music in a simultaneous improvisation between New York, Toronto, and Paris. The performance would be audible as a whole to the audience in New York.

I asked Lauren what I should know about Oliveros in advance.

Lauren said—Call Jim.[2]

James Tenney and I shared a good conversation on improvisation and distance listening. Tenney gave me a clue, that Oliveros had been known to tune her accordion in two separate courses of just intonation. The key of birds, water falls, prepared piano advocates, Partch violists, Tuvans, and sophisticated electronic musicians.

Our preparation for the distance concert was a process of acceptance of the parameters set by provoking the absolute limit to the technology of the time. The Deep Listening Band was receiving our audio and an audio signal from an ensemble in Paris, but no visual from either remote location. In Toronto we had a clear visual of the Band and of the

---

2   Composer James Tenney (1934–2006).

performance space at The Kitchen, but to Paris we were in contextual deafness, and blind. We could hear audio signal only from New York, and this through a two-channel send that had the obstacles of latency and distortion. It called for intense concentration and imagination to improvise a cohesive piece under these circumstances. The elusive composition we were to make could almost be felt kinesthetically, by intention. Listening through instinct was the only way.[3]

Just before we began to play, the screen sent us a clear visual. Pauline Oliveros, with David Gamper and Stuart Dempster at her shoulders, all three resonant and still, as if sitting for a portrait. I was moved by Pauline's presence.

To test the threshold of dynamic range I glided my fingers down a string on my cello, causing a diaphanous cascade of harmonics, a secret inaudible to all I thought, within the distorted sound field of clarinet, and extended electric readymades.[4]

I heard Pauline's voice respond—Ah the cello.

I soon discovered in Pauline a friend who never asked me to repeat myself. She seemed always to hear me.

I asked Lauren Pratt—Is there a way to meet her?

Lauren sent word.

Pauline responded—Come to New Mexico.

This was not the answer I had expected.

---

3   This was my introduction to telematic performance—using information and communication technology in this case to create collaborative music over distance. Telematic performances now progress and glide across international and imaginary boundaries, with the research Oliveros is engaged in at Rensselaer Polytechnic Institute, and parallel work at McGill and Stanford Universities resulting in emerging dedicated technologies, such as JackTrip, and continued simultaneous global improvisations, in the context of experimental Telepresence.

4   John Gzowski performed on handmade electric instruments, a thirty-one tone Cat's Cradle, and a broomstick cello, reminiscent of Dada deeming everyday objects as art.

Setting Up a Tent in a Lightning Storm

I followed the path up the hill with my duffle bag, to the pine shade side of the mountain. I chose my tent site without hesitation for its secrecy, a little plateau. Heloise nodded. I raised my tent and a clothesline. The air was alpine but desert dry, with chance of sudden downpour. In the morning I awoke to the sound of a soft bell and descended to the outdoor kitchen, for silent tea and writing. I perceived through all senses into the part of the mind that does not name all things. I brushed past plants and people, and no one said anything.

Heloise whispered us a phrase to continually return to—*With each step I receive the earth.* Then we followed her higher up the mountain into the forest. The meditation walk took a well-traveled path. I realized too late we were walking directly towards my tent. We walked slowly past my private space, with a slight detour for the clothesline I had inadvertently strung across the path. Each participant did the limbo in silence.

We began the climb to Moon Meadow. One at a time in single file, stepping heel first, touching the path with our feet listening, sending our heat into the ground, and receiving something through our soles. Distraction overrode intention on some mornings but this day was a clear walk. We stumbled and stilled towards grace, slightly disheveled, in our morning camper clothes.

We stopped along the way to breathe it in. I noticed the leaves in the aspens before me, flickering in the breeze, trunks and limbs, leaves: at once a shimmering, cell-level glance at the vibratory life of these trees, the intrinsic dance of atoms. We resumed our walk. Whatever had floated to consciousness in the night, this morning we loved the ground, the plants, the birds, the atmosphere, the sense of becoming. At this pace we had become angelic ourselves.

As the years progressed, each time I returned more attuned to the locations of activities. I would go higher up the mountain and further into the woods to find a tent site, for the illusion of a solitude shared only with the wild. I also brought more effective tarps and ropes. One year I climbed to my plateau ahead of the others. I was quick to raise lines for a tarp with the growl of thunder rolling in, and a cloud burst just as I tied up the red tarp. Then I set my tent up at heart-pounding pace, underneath the tarp, while lightening bolts flew and the heavens opened. I managed to keep most of my belongings dry. When I returned to the meditation room, I felt rugged, fearless, and damp.

Threshold

Can you imagine the sound of all the times someone has spoken your name?
Can you imagine the echo of all the footsteps you have ever taken?[5]

The exploration of listening, while removed on a mountain, was a context for a deeply physical experience of sound and for an opening to non-consensus reality.[6] I was navigating from an identity that held the orientation of passing through many terminals, to perform in a different city every night, for months at a time, over years. Life *was* a dreamscape.

Listening now became part of an infinite press towards being authentic and living as if each day was the only day and each night a thousand and one nights.

The experience of sitting with Oliveros in silence offered a sense of infinite time.

A silence clocked by noticing the architectural form that natural sound and its interruptions create. I could attend the abstract of being in time and space and notice a relationship to this arising out of listening and connecting to each occurrence, in a continuum of sound and silence.

After a few years, the paradigm of silence deepened when Oliveros asked us to commit to silence from 10 p.m. each evening to 1 p.m. the following afternoon. Take the words out of the way of content. This was

---

5 Pauline Oliveros, *Deep Listening Pieces* (Kingston, NY: Deep Listening Publications, 1990), 22, and Pauline Oliveros, *Software for People: Collected Writings 1963-1980* (Baltimore: Smith Publications, 1984), 189. "Can you imagine. . ." meditations can be found in both these publications. Oliveros continues to add to the questions for memory listening focus, to the extent that she continues to imagine sounds and sensations to imagine.

6 Arnold Mindell, *Quantum Mind: The Edge Between Physics and Psychology* (Portland, OR: Lao Tse Press, 2000), 27. "Favouring 'consensus reality' as the fundamental reality destroys the 'non-consensus reality' sense of feeling connectedness with the world as a whole."

a silence to balance the two hemispheres of the brain and allow what had become the lesser hemisphere, the non-verbal hemisphere, to awaken, and detect its own more subtle interpretations. This was a silence to allow for the detection of new constellations of awareness and sensation, for vulnerability, for respect, for understanding to be an open field, for truth, for kindness, for listening. We could all be simple.

Silence altered the mundane. After Slow Walk in the morning to the meadow, slow run down the mountain—the food angels had already rung the gong. In silence the breakfast table was not quiet. Imagine animated plastic honey bear dancing, carafes of coffee, with and without caffeine, juggled hand to hand. Asking for bagels, green chili salsa, and pieces of fresh fruit to be sorted and passed, through eye contact. Dream imagery from the night before was somehow conveyed with gifts given for dream appearances. Once during silence, I received a line drawing on a piece of birch bark from Steven White, and still have a small piece of a broken branch, with its inner rings colored in bright orange and pink and green pastel, by the undaunted South Dakota cellist Jessica Catron.

A communication was devised as if language had not yet been invented. Hemispheres balanced. Paced by the soft arrivals and departures of disarmingly beautiful cooks bringing clean food, there were waves of laughter, the shared rebellious response to a discipline, evocative of human folly, causing acceptance and quantum poetic breakthroughs. There is no small talk without words.

> Walking in silence find a place where you want to be. Lie on a boulder, breathe with it. Listen to the boulder, across all time stored in its form. Once you know it, sing the sound you are now imagining, what calls your heart to express.[7]

At the sound of Pauline's conch shell trumpet echoing over the mountain we would make our way to the Boulders, a natural theater

---

7 Unless otherwise indicated, indented words in italics indicate my notes from Oliveros' teaching on Rose Mountain, transcribed or in my own words. I have many journals from these years. I opened only the first and the last for this writing.

of rocks assembled by the Ice Age. There we would enter in to her way of listening and create sound pieces that within a simple set of parameters signaled raw voices to circle into a natural harmonic order. Pauline's teaching was experiential. Do as you do, not as I say.

A way of listening without preconception allowed for thought as sound vibration to be noticed. Something in the sea of communication as yet undiscovered could be felt with the acceptance of influence and change—human communication, inter-species communication, relationship on a purely vibratory level, with even what had been perceived as inanimate, and now represented a life form, an intelligence.

Listening was communion with the ground, a boulder, the bees, an opera singer, electric current, an apparition, the wind, the source, the sky, oneself.

At first I experienced the practice as a way of disconnecting from the busy mind and all sonic distraction that life had begun to surround us with. With subtlety Oliveros was giving us repetitions of listening strategies, to train focus parameters and musical dexterity for the mirror neurons of the brain. This specific training of acute listening emerged as a sonic experience of empathy and we began to coalesce as community.

Soon I could not imagine *not* returning to Rose Mountain, to sit with Pauline and to sound, in the way of self-discovery, within the matrix of her distinct compositional sense. Each improvised composition we sounded was rooted in stone, trembled by the breeze, and the visitations of hummingbirds, or the difference tones of many voices, urgent or present in their chaos: all at once discovering a form with its own arc, and an effortless ending.

Pauline's words that took us into *The Tuning Meditation*[8] were a distillation that caused compelling harmonic emergence, an embrace of dissonance held by beauty. These plain words could be understood to trigger a release of all forms of human noise and empathy. Simple strategy made waves of imagining, listening, and sonic merging happen

---

8 Oliveros, *Deep Listening Pieces,* 39. These Deep Listening meditations were a continuation of her *Sonic Meditations,* composed beginning in 1970 as part of the curriculum for "Music In Nature" and for a research project at the Center for Music Experiment at the University of California, San Diego.

inside shared creative expression in an extended choreography that removed hierarchy.

Lie down on the carpet with your heads to the centre, almost touching.
Let your breath caress your vocal chords.

What happens when a person is invited by an artist to sound what they absolutely and passionately discover is the note they must sound with all their heart? It is self-organizing, the sound of equanimity, the sound of seeking consensus. Each person is on the same plateau at an equal distance to the focal point of the space, the center. The sonic array that emerges is what I imagine the world sounds like careening and diving towards peace.

It was my second year at Rose Mountain when an advanced retreat was set to follow the opening retreat. I had registered for both retreats, and I remember the moment when several others decided to spontaneously stay for the second week. We were to become *les six*—the first six certificate holders. In the wake of this enthusiasm and in the ongoing process of distillation and expansion of her materials for transmission, Oliveros established a Deep Listening Certificate program in 1996.

I came for both retreats that year and continued on in this pattern. I desired to *be in it*—to experience Pauline's way of cultivating a creative relationship with all it is possible to listen to. I continued to retreat each summer, to the end of the ten-year commitment to Deep Listening on Rose Mountain—and beyond this, we would meet for incidents of creative music.[9]

---

9   Pauline first invited me to record in David Gamper's studio my initiation into the Expanded Instrument System, an improvised score for the documentary film *Paulina*, released in Havana, acclaimed at Sundance. (Funari, Vicky, Jennifer Maytorena Taylor, and Paulina Cruz Suárez. 1997. *Paulina*. Brooklyn, NY: First Run/Icarus Films). Further to this: a creator and performer in Oliveros' improvised *Lunar Opera: Deep Listening For_Tunes*, Damrosch Park, Lincoln Center Out of Doors Festival, New York, NY, 2000; an ensemble performance at Hallwalls, Buffalo, NY, the first recording of Pauline Oliveros' *Primordial/ Lift*, with Anne Bourne, Tony Conrad, Andrew Deutsch, Alex Gelencser, David Grubbs and Pauline Oliveros, released on

At the end of many sonic explorations and listening meditations, Pauline would ask—Do you feel something?

Liminal

An evening on Rose Mountain flowed as a composition, with each person arriving in silence to the meditation room, assembling in no particular order. We formed a circle like a string of black pearls.

Then we would stand to call the directions. Four Directions, along with the morning meditation walk and afternoon T'ai Chi instruction from Heloise, would complete the three aspects of Deep Listening body awareness and strengthening that we practiced each day.

Four Directions, a compass, an aboriginal shamanic pattern, could be interpreted as an interfaith prayer of gratitude and was here designed as a listening practice. We would face each direction in sequence, and listening with the whole body, identify the qualities of sound and sensory vibration in each named place. Then each person would intend a sensation of becoming open to receive all sonic or vibratory information from that place, as an act of courage and a way to receive all sound through the filters of invocation. This made listening visceral and imaginative.

We would describe the directions with poetic metaphors and geographies of association for each direction, in words, in a gesture of movement, or in sound. Fluidly moving from verbal mind to non-verbal mind, from body to thought, from memory to present. It became a collectively composed improvisation, a dimensional architecture of

---

Table of Elements 53 I, 1991 and Deep Listening DL033, 2010, compact discs; *One Long Peace*, an improvised duet performed by Pauline Oliveros and Anne Bourne, X Avant Festival, Music Gallery, Toronto, 2007; communications producer of *Deep Listening Convergence: a sonic gesture of peace*, an international on-line residency and performance in New York, 2007; ensemble performance for Telematic Concert opening the Guelph Jazz Festival, Canada, 2010; live performance and recording of *Primordial/ Lift* at Issue Project Room, Brooklyn, NY, 2010, to be released by Taiga Records, 33⅓ rpm.

spoken word—by declaration, it was an honoring of all existence and being, as beauty.

> East—*a field of untouched snow. the place where the sun first sparks on the horizon*
> South—*mother's milk, abundance. the mesas. warmth*
> West—*the place where the sun descends. brilliant painted sky. dream time. descent*
> North—*limestone. boulders. glaciers. the wise faces of all whom I have learned from*
> Center—*where the lines of sound from all directions meet, a pillar between earth and sky*

A Dream within a Dream

> *Listen for the beginnings and endings of sounds.*

Quiet gathered on the Persian rug in the evening, a soft bell, and with Pauline's words, the Deep Listening meditation would begin and sustain for what seemed long enough to go somewhere far and return. The focus and the stillness of people's minds became more and more potent. The bell signal to return never seemed too soon. Then, illuminated by starlight, we would begin dream listening.

The sound of IONE's voice flowed like honey. She shared clarity of thought about dreaming and sharing dreams to deepen the subtle layers of dream community. We began to notice our dreams.

> —*to know oneself, to know one's edges, to open a way to creatively affect the collective unconscious, even the events of the day as if they were dream*[10]

IONE would cite anthropological sources of dream sharing over time in parts of Africa, and in the great Iroquois culture of North America. She would describe the techniques of lucid dreaming and recollection and how while listening to the telling of a dream, a brain may be activated in the way it is while one is dreaming. While listening we could experience our own version of another's dream.

---

10 My journal notes from IONE's teaching on Rose Mountain.

We not only shared entire night dreams from intentions written in *hypnagogic state diaries,*[11] we were also encouraged to draw on dream fragments recalled, like holograms or cells that contain the essence of a whole dream. Glimmers that could unfold the dream into our waking lives.

With science engaged to comprehend the physics of inter-dimensional reality, we could imagine entering an alternate dimension as effortlessly as falling asleep with the intention to receive metaphoric and sensory resolve for the impossible.

We would tell each other our dreams, and we would begin to expand, and creatively enhance and activate the dream. We would give each other gifts for sightings in each other's dreams. We would seek dreams in the moment. We would dance the dreams. We would go after healing dreams for each other. On these nights Pauline would drum on a frame drum, a hypnotic pulse of spiral harmonic overtones. And IONE's mellifluous voice would take us under, dropping down to altered slow brain wave states. And some times intention would bring back significant material for the person you were dreaming for. My dreams were vibrant.

I began to draw site-specific graphic scores with spatialization, and imagined the lines of sound from each voice, traveling through the air to hold form as sonic architecture, to create place. Lines of sound sent out to penetrate constructs of time and physical form.

I traced sensations of sonic anatomy. My pieces had maps, lines of geometries, sanctuaries, the shapes of beehive, and *vesica piscis.* They were subtle. Retrieved from memory. Located on boulders, in the bulrushes, in a cathedral of pines, on the edges of cliffs.

> *Again we were asked to gather at the aspen grove. The shade is good, not much talk has happened today, it is later in the afternoon. Whoever had taken on the role of producer, had to contend with programming twenty of us, and still allow for*

11 *Hypnagogic* refers to the transitional state experienced while falling asleep, and here, the journal writing we would do to seed and capture our dreams.

maintaining the drawn pattern of activities for body, listening, sounding and dream. This location was an aberration in time.

The light in the aspens now dappled. The air cool in the shade. All of us seemed to be there when she surprised us from above. Suddenly appearing at the top of the cliff beside the grove, startling beautiful. Folding herself over the cliff edge like water, she descended towards us from a great height, singing the rock face like a score. Her face not visible under her dark hair, her hands guiding and supporting her through each crevasse, her voice sounded the topography, the time stored in stone, and what it was she felt for these rocks, this earth that she was listening to, with her body.[12]

Each time I left the mountain to become urban again, and my voice entered the imaginary landscape of the theater, or the recording studio, my listening traveled well. I found an expanded sense of context, as if I were still on a mountain in New Mexico, singing at the top of the sky.

Return

In 2009, more than ten years on, I got word Pauline was returning to Rose Mountain in August. I had a strong instinct to return. Oliveros had been offering a Deep Listening retreat experience in many places in the world and now she was set to hold a retreat in its place of origin. I flew to Phoenix.

Leaving at dusk, I drove across the desert on an angle north towards New Mexico, Tesuque and the mesas. Two days later I made Rose Mountain.

I climbed the familiar path to the highest most remote tent plateau, on the edge of the mountain. I wanted to get lost in dreams at the end of each day, sink into the ground at night, in the dark and silence, a palette for dreaming. Write it all down at first light. Document the dream departures and arrivals.

---

12 My notes for a site-specific piece created and performed by Sangeeta Laura Biagi, PhD, of Siena, Italy.

The silence was profound this time. In the morning while I reflected by my tent, a young deer walked down the slope into view and stood still, close enough to gaze into my eyes for a very long time.

Listen to the Memory of Listening[13]

Part 1
Listening into the quiet across time

As you listen into the quiet the threshold may change
Listening into the quiet is not about identifying, but opening to all, expanding
to absorb where you are
No matter where you are, you are in the centre of it
Space is not empty, even if there is nothing in it

The human ear is sensitive to 20-20,000 Hz generally
This is individual
The ear takes in vibration involuntarily.
Listening is voluntary

Rather than identify, analyze, judge, criticize, all that your mind wants to do,
open the energy centers of your body
Open the skin, the bones, the whole body, to absorb with heightened awareness,
the vibration of where you are
Choose your listening place
Sense where you are

---

13 My transcription of a Deep Listening meditation transmitted by Pauline Oliveros at the boulders on Rose Mountain, New Mexico, 2009.

Thoughts will arise
Cultivate detachment from the thoughts that arise
Return to the Five Gates—the crown, the palms, the soles of the
feet
The challenge is to let go

Continue to listen to the quiet and to the quiet and to the quiet
so grounding
Rely on the Qi
Sit solidly
Ground level listening

Part II
Mirroring what you perceive

Recall the sounds from Part I
Auralize a mirror
Allow yourself to spontaneously mirror sounds that now attract
your attention with internal auralization
empathy

Part III
Sounding

Sensing sounds, simply allow sound to emerge from yourself
The listening has prepared you for this
The mirroring, becoming part of the soundscape internally, is the
source for sounding
from the memory of imagined sounds
Now spontaneously place sounds into the environment you have
been attending

We are ourselves a complex of time delays

Part IV
Return to listening

Connections: Deep Listening/Singing Masks/Ceremonial Dream Time

NORMAN LOWREY is a mask maker/composer and professor of music at Drew University, Madison, NJ. He holds a PhD in composition from the Eastman School of Music and a Deep Listening Certificate. He is the originator of Singing Masks, ceramic and carved wood incorporating flutes, reeds, ratchets and other sounding devices, each with a unique voice, that have been exhibited in East Coast museums and galleries, including the New Jersey State Museum. Lowrey has presented Singing Mask ceremony/performances in such diverse locations as Plan B and Site Santa Fe in Santa Fe, NM; Roulette and Lincoln Center in New York City; Deep Listening Space in Kingston, NY; and at pictograph caves outside Billings, MT. Recent performances include *Into The Deep (Dreaming)* presented at Drew University with Pauline Oliveros and the Deep Listening Band and *In Whirled (Trance)Formations* presented with the Avatar Orchestra Metaverse online in Second Life. http://users.drew.edu/nlowrey/

Norman Lowrey

This is the great mystery.
Music. Sound. Sounding.
Listen. Listening.
Connecting. Connection.
Dreaming. Dream.

Music Deep Listening Vibrating
Connecting Linking Surrounding
Sounding Dreaming Opening
Revealing Interconnecting
Illuminating Listening Thinking
Feeling Probing Discovering
Words Sound Word Sounds

ARE YOU LISTENING? What are you listening to? How are you listening? Can you hear subtle nuances of sound in the words you are reading: shifts in shape, contour, texture, timbre, pitch, rhythm, loudness? Sound. Music. Listen. Connect. Integrate mind, body, spirit. Actively observe. Your thoughts are interweaving with what you are reading. Spontaneously translate feelings into sounds both internal and external. Sense the connections of everything.

Shift perspective. Listen from a different angle.

Every word and arrangement of words here emerges from the core of my trying to put into practice, and to understand, Deep Listening. These are things I think about all the time. This is essentially a very personal account of how Deep Listening has affected my life and work. I invite you to participate with me in this process and to think of this as a ceremony celebrating the miracle of our being alive. We are reading this together. We are directing our thoughts together. It is the nature of our language to be on a path leading from one place to the next. This is a temporal path. This is our common experience of time. Time past flows into time future through time present. Time past resides in memory. Time future resides in imagination. Time present resides in our awareness. The present is all we have. Let's listen to the eternal present together.

I invite you on a meandering journey. I hope we might stray from the beaten path. I like to wander. Feel free to follow however you are inclined. Or not to follow at all. Strike off on your own. If we get lost, let's just be still and listen wherever we are. Join me if you will.[1]

Spirit Talk, Conversations with the Singing Masks (1998)

In silent awareness, listen for an unknown, unspoken language, heard internally or externally. When you are ready, join in the mystery of conversation with your newly discovered language. You may wish to do so in silence or stillness, in whisper, quiet utterance, or gentle movement. Always maintain openness to the myriads of conversations that are occurring. Any conversation you have with anything else, including with the Singing Masks, need not be in its language; your own tongue, whatever it is, will be heard. Continue until the enveloping Spirit Talk becomes still.

This is a score for one of my Singing Mask ceremonies. My scores are simple invitations to listen from a particular perspective. Several will be a part of our journey now, perhaps creating a labyrinth.

---

1 The reader is invited to participate in any way desired in the following Singing Mask Ceremonies, which appear in italics. For further information see http://www.users.drew.edu/nlowrey.

Deep Listening is conducive to the production of alpha waves, a condition of mind known to be "alive" to creative ideas and in which we are open to information from the subconscious. We are relaxed yet alert.

I first met Pauline Oliveros in 1972 after a concert of Karlheinz Stockhausen's *Zyklus* at the University of California, San Diego. When I was introduced to her she remarked something like "Well that sure was a piece of male bombast!" This was a new thought for me. In subsequent meetings I learned that Pauline had a gift for making "simple" observations or raising provocative questions that would lead to altered awareness. Deep Listening is like that.

From that time in the early 1970s I followed her career with interest. I moved to Missouri, teaching in the Humanities Department at Stephens College. I invited Pauline to visit my classes and to perform. She opened our ears. She later moved from California to New York State. Our paths then crossed rarely for several years. We reconnected in the late 1980s after she began offering Deep Listening workshops. Around that time I had discovered that building sounds into masks could lead to interesting experiences both musical and mythic. I called them Singing Masks. But after a spate of works done with them they ended up resting in my attic. I brought one to that Deep Listening workshop. Pauline recognized its potential and arranged for me to give a mask ceremony workshop. The masks came out of the attic and have been out ever since.

I also met IONE at that Deep Listening workshop. Dreams and dreaming had been important components of my thinking and work previously, but now ceremonial Dream Time entered with gusto.

The masks function as "vehicles of transformation." Their voices and imagery speak to our ancient and primal "one-ness." They may stimulate experiences of (real) alternate imaginal/dream realms.

In Parallel: Dreaming into Alternate Universes (2000)

Just as William Blake suggested that we could "See a World in a Grain of Sand," so too is it possible to hear a universe in each instance of sound. With this in mind, listen to all sounds and select any one in any given instant to follow into its parallel universe. Sound and/or move with your own sense of that universe. Stay within that universe as long as you wish, via memory, imagina-

tion, or any other body/dream/cognitive modality. Remain open to simultaneously occurring universes. Transporting yourself into sounds in this way, go to as many universes as you wish. Or none at all. "Just" listening is ok. The Singing Mask Spirits are guides along your journey. Have fun and bon voyage!

Deep Listening directs our attention toward inter-action. It heightens our sensitivity to our self/world relationship. It raises our awareness of community.

Here we are now. We are listening. We are dreaming. Together. A community of listeners. Dream Listening. What are we doing here? Where are we going? Age-old questions that stimulate our wonderment.

I attended five successive annual Deep Listening Retreats in New Mexico from 1995–2000. I continued to make Singing Masks. After a collaborative project with the Delaware Riverkeeper called "River Sounding" in which Pauline and IONE participated, my Singing Mask work became further involved with ritual, ceremony, myth and dream, remaining always grounded in listening and in connection to all of nature.

Deep Listening results in communal music-making and spontaneous organization of sound. It is rich in sonic textures interspersed with quietude. It is emotionally fecund.

Private Prayers, Public Rituals: for Peace (2005)

Every location, however small or seemingly insignificant, may be thought of as a holographic image containing the whole, a kind of portal into infinity. With this in mind, all present are invited to select a small territory anywhere within the gathering space, to listen intently, and to offer a prayer for peace to/through this portal. This localized, particular place may be thought of as an altar, making connection with everything. Your prayer may consist of simply listening, being silent, or vocalizing in any way you wish. Movement is also welcome. As you pray, Singing Masks will function as resonators, amplifying all prayers into Dream-Time.

Deep Listening offers a direct exploration of sound allowing us to discover unique sounds and combinations of sounds. In this exploration we may also make discoveries about our own self, our abilities, limitations and potentials. Our curiosities are stimulated.

Music	Deep Listening	Vibrating	Connecting
Linking	Surrounding	Sounding	Dreaming
Opening	Revealing	Interconnecting	Illuminating
Listening	Thinking	Feeling	Probing	Discovering

Courage. Change. Courage to change. Facing our fears. Who is there to help us? What can help? I'll tell you this: the Deep Listening community helped save my life. During one of my darkest periods of ill health, members of this community provided unconditional love and support and listened to my needs and responded with accepting wise counsel. Deep Listening offers healing.

Into the Deep (Dreaming) (2006)

take a dive into the deep (dreaming)
take a dive into the (dreaming) deep
take a dive into (dreaming) the deep
take a dive (dreaming) into the deep
take a (dreaming) dive into the deep
take (dreaming) a dive into the deep
(dreaming) take a dive into the deep
sound from these depths whatever emerges
singing masks will be guides into this dreamtime realm

Deep Listening stimulates imagination, opens and heightens awareness, connects with the subconscious and questions pre-conceptions and assumptions.

Most recently I have extended Singing Masks into the virtual realm with the Avatar Orchestra Metaverse, an international community that performs together in real time online in the virtual world of Second Life. We listen to one another over great gulfs of space. We are many becoming one.

OneMany (OM) (2010)

We are One. We are Many. Following the implications of the title *OneMany (OM)*, you are invited to listen and participate in any way you wish to explore that ancient notion of the One and the Many. How does One become Many? How does Many arise from One? Singing Masks will join in exploring the delight of our making spontaneous art together in sound and movement, in silence and stillness, in the One and the Many. OM.

Deep Listening has provided me with a foundation and framework for living, working, and being in the world. More than any other single influence in my life, Deep Listening has contributed to helping me understand why I am alive and what I believe in. The following summary remarks are a direct outgrowth of being introduced to Deep Listening. While specifically related to the Singing Masks, what is suggested as an approach to them is also applicable to listening itself. This is not an ending. Deep Listening is indeed a life practice.

> *I am an unabashed animist. I believe that everything is infused with spirit. There is intelligence at the heart of all matter. Human intelligence is just one peculiar manifestation of this larger ground of being. Other manifestations are radically different, incomprehensible to conventional human sensibilities. Yet all things give voice to the underlying cohering essence, the spirit swirling through cells, molecules, atoms, quarks and superstrings. If we listen carefully we can resonate along with these primary vibrations and receive information, knowledge, altered understanding.*
>
> *This has been the thrust of the teaching by the Singing Masks that I have been making and employing in ceremonial/performances over the past twenty-five years. Their voices and iconographic presences have been continual reminders of connection with that animistic sense of spirit essence in rivers, rocks, sky, trees, as well as among all things animate. They have become guides in all my work into shifting perspectives, into experiencing everything as holy (William Blake), into mythic and oneiric reality.*
>
> *The ceremonial/performance pieces inspired by the Singing Masks are not entertainments in a traditional sense. They are not music, theater or dance meant to tell a story or lead one along a preconceived path. They are more often invitations to*

dive into ineffable richness and chaos even, to discover and explore.

I incorporate state-of-the-art computer technology to loop and pitch-shift the voices of the masks in real-time. I do not hide the technology. Neither do I make much effort to gloss over the sometimes awkward gestures needed to control the devices in my near-blind masked condition. I have an interest in the convergence of the primal and the present, the sacred and the mundane. In the Dream Time presence of the masks, even the most trivial occurrence may be recognized as having its own kind of perfection and beauty.

So how might you approach experiencing the Singing Masks? First of all, you are free to discover your own unique and individual way. I suggest some possibilities here just to nudge us away from habits induced by traditional concert and media formats:

1) Look at a mask for a moment then close your eyes and listen with the image of the mask retained by your inner eye. 2) Squint to defocus your vision while you are listening. What is the aural equivalent of squinting to defocus your listening? 3) Drift off into dreamland. Sleep, though attempt to be aware that you are sleeping and dreaming. 4) Apply no labels. Make no judgments. Or apply labels and judgments, then drop them immediately. 5) Be aware of the passage of time, yet also perceive timelessness. 6) Listen as if you're tuning in to multiple foreign language radio stations. Listen for nuances of timbre, pitch inflection, and rhythm. Go for the sensuousness of the sound rather than the sense of the words. 7) Dream some more.

So it is that we are all interdependently interconnected within the intricate interwoven depths and delights of Deep Listening Dream Time.

Dream. Dreaming.
Connection. Connecting.
Listening. Listen.
Sounding. Sound. Music.
This is the great mystery.[2]

---

2   http://www.users.drew.edu/nlowrey/music/mysterium magnum.html

Deep Listening in Dreams: Opening to Another Dimension of Being

IONE is an author, playwright/ director and improvising word-sound artist. As an educator and counselor she conducts seminars and retreats throughout the world specializing in dreams and the creative process. Ione's international Dream Festival, now approaching its seventeenth year, takes place annually. Her written works include the acclaimed memoir, *Pride of Family Four Generations of American Women of Color*, *Nile Night, Remembered Texts from The Deep, Listening in Dreams* and *This is a Dream!* IONE is playwright and director of *Njinga the Queen King; A Play with Music and Pageantry*, and the dance opera *Io and Her and the Trouble with Him*. She is the director and writer of *The Lunar Opera: Deep Listening For_Tunes*, and the film *Dreams of the Jungfrau*. She is Artistic Director of Deep Listening Institute, Ltd. http://ionedreams.us

IONE

"Every time you ignore sentient, that is generally unrecognized, dream-like perceptions, something inside you goes into a mild form of shock because you have overlooked the spirit of life, your greatest potential power." Arnold Mindell[1]

A Dream Keeper Speaks

IN ADDITION TO BEING a *Dream Keeper* at large, celebrating dreams wherever I go, I've enjoyed being a kind of *Dream Listening* activist for twenty years with the vibrant *Deep Listening Community*, taking up the cause of listening in dreams with the many ear-minded folk and musicians who have attended Retreats and Intensives and who are a part of

---

1 *Dreaming While Awake: Techniques for 24-Hour Lucid Dreaming* (Charlottesville, VA: Hampton Roads Press, 2001), 7.

299

the new *DIY (Do It Yourself) Deep Listening Study Groups*.[2] The Dream *Festival*[3] is an annual international celebration of the creative aspect of dreaming, presented by Deep Listening Institute, Ltd. that is now in its sixteenth year. In order to accommodate dreamers throughout the world, I've had a hand in launching virtual Dream Stations: a *Dream Sack*[4] that receives and gives out dreams randomly 24/7 ("The more that go in the more come out!"); an invitational *Dreamers' Blog*;[5] and with Deep Listening Certificate Holder Sharon Stewart, a budding *Dream Sound Anthology*[6] as well.

Why dreams? Because dreams are our deepest source of creativity—because humans and animals alike dream and all cultures, ages, and classes dream. Whatever their symbolic story content, we can always rely upon them to tell us the truth about our feelings. On this fundamental level they do not disappoint. I lean toward an organic method of dream awareness that brings deeper understanding to the dreamer the more she pays attention. I champion the inclusion of dreaming in our world-view, much as our ancestors and relatives—the indigenous peoples of the Earth—have done for millenia and continue to do to this day. In considering the aforementioned group, it is important to note that there is really no "other" involved, for essentially we discover the deeper we go into our dreaming, that "they" are "us" and "we," "they."

Though dreams have been marginalized in Western cultures for thousands of years, they are still very much in our psyches—and, pun intended—on our minds. Our fascination with dreaming reveals itself in our language, in the plethora of popular and classical songs, and it finds a happy home in our art. I feel that even those who fear and/or dismiss dreams (often one and the same folk) are in fact acknowledging the *power* of dreaming.

---

2 accessed December 23, 2011, https://www.facebook.com/pages /Deep-Listening-Study-Group-Portal/138891889485016.

3 accessed December 23, 2011, http://deeplistening.org/site/content /dream-festival.

4 accessed December 23, 2011, http://deeplistening.org/cgi-bin/dreamsack.cgi.

5 accessed December 23, 2011, http://www.deeplistening.org/site/content /dreamblogaccess.

6 accessed December 23, 2011, http://www.deeplistening.org/site/dsa.

I believe in the freedom of dreams in general, in the sanctity of their multiple meanings, their subtleties and their mysteries. I'm fascinated by all dream phenomena and would like to pass that fascination on to others, particularly those of us who are accustomed to focusing only on *analysis* of dreams. It is a quiet and sneaky revolution I seek. A world in which non-judgmental *Dream Awareness* and sharing reached the highest levels of government would be a very different world indeed. For better and worse, our politicians are a reflection of ourselves, and so let us begin with our own listening.

ΔΔΔ

The Voices of the Gods

When I first approach people on the subject of sound in their dreams, I am most often met with silence and a puzzled look. It is gratifying for to me to find that with a little encouragement, dream sounds begin to emerge for most once they start to pay attention.

Much has been made of the concept that we are primarily a visual society, but it has not always been so with us humans. Our current written emphasis on the visual began with the Greeks. By the fourth century BCE, the verb "to see" was equated with "to know." Greek texts tellingly featured descriptions of "the bright-eyed Athena" and mention her "wide-eyed owl."[7]

As we became more self-aware and at once more separate from nature and the universe around us, a complex shift was occurring in our very relationship to "all there is." A duality that would become our modern plight was making its appearance.

By the first century when Plutarch wrote his famous essay *The Obsolescence of Oracles*, the voices of gods and the way of life that went along with listening to them were fading.[8]

---

7 Jeremy Naydler, "The Restitution of the Ear," in *The Future of the Ancient World: Essays on the History of Consciousness* (Rochester, VT: Inner Traditions, 2009), 9–10.

8 Plutarch, "The Obsolescence of Oracles" (from the *Loeb Classical Library,* V:347–501) available online accessed December 23, 2011, http://penelope .uchicago.edu/Thayer/E/Roman/Texts/Plutarch/Moralia/De_defectu _oraculorum*.html.

For thousands of years prior to this time in history, the ancient Egyptians and Sumerians were *deep listening* societies. For them, listening was equated with heart and with mind. The God Ptah was said to exist in "every heartbeat and in every sound." Those who revered him learned that: "The heart makes of its owner a listener or a non-listener."[9]

During the Old Kingdom in Abydos, Egypt, ca. 2649–2150 BCE there was a ceremony entitled *The Night of the Great Sleep.* The officiating High Priest slept in a special chamber on the sacred grounds and listened in a dream for "The Call" of Osiris before beginning the rites of the Opening of the Mouth for the King's mummy. Outside of the sacred grounds, all music and talking ceased as the people listened in rapt attention for the transmitted Call.[10]

In Mesopotamia, when the Sumerian Goddess of Heaven, Inanna (ca. 4000 to 3100 BCE) made her famed initiatory descent to the Underworld, she "opened her ear to the great below." Enki, the God of Wisdom was said to have his "ear wide open." In Sumerian, the words for "the mind" and "the ear" were identical.[11]

There are many practitioners of ancient practices of sacred sound today, including devotees of Nada Yoga[12] and Dream Yoga such as Chogyal Namkhai Norbu[13] and Tenzin Wangyal Rinpoche,[14] who have brought timeless Tibetan dream teachings to the West. These teachings include visualizations accompanied by sounds that permeate the body/mind spirit prior to and during sleep and dreaming. And the tradition of listening in dreams for one's own sacred sounds and songs continues

---

9 Naydler, 6.

10 R.T. Rundle Clark, *Myth and Symbol in Ancient Egypt* (London: Thames and Hudson, 1978), 130.

11 "Interpretation of Ianna's Descent Myth," accessed December 23, 2011, http://www.halexandria/org/dward387.htm.

12 Swami Janakananda, "Nada Yoga – outer and inner." accessed December 23, 2011, http://www.yogameditation.com/Articles/Issues-of-Bindu/Bindu-10/Nada-Yoga.

13 Chogyal Namkhai Norbu, *Dream Yoga and the Practice of Natural Light* (Ithaca, NY: Snow Lion Publications, 2002).

14 Tenzin Wangyal Rinpoche, *The Tibetan Yogas of Dream and Sleep* (Ithaca, NY: Snow Lion Publications, 1998).

among the Aboriginal and Morai cultures of the Pacific Rim as well as in many of the First World Nations in the Americas.[15]

Today, world-wide listening trends in waking state seem to be gravitating toward louder sounds. Vying with both desirable and non-desirable mechanical external sounds, engrossed in multi-tasking with all the senses including sound, many people seem to be following the faster spin and wobble of our Earth by speeding up everything while also ramping up sonic input. Perhaps we have given up on listening for the gods? Or more likely, perhaps we are unwittingly seeking them in the noise?

Whichever is true, it is perhaps also possible to open our ears to "the great below" of our dreaming where there are rich interior soundscapes just waiting for everyone to pay more attention.

For Deep Listeners accustomed to an inclusive, rather than an exclusive form of listening, the "voices of the gods" might be heard in music—soft or loud. They could be received in nature, as well as in machines, in highway traffic, at construction sites and other surprising sonic locations.

For "gods," we might substitute the concept of listening for our own connection to the divine—or our own connection to the source of our deepest being, the seat of our creativity, our very existence.

ΔΔΔ

A Few Examples of Dream Listening Phenomena

Over time I have observed several forms of Listening in Dreams. The reader may wish to add to this list with her or his own observations:

1. Direct listening to recognizable voices (friends, family—particularly recently deceased close relatives and friends—grandparents are particularly vocal)
2. Direct listening to a spiritual being's voice
3. Listening to unknown voices—often an impartial speaker— shortly before rising (in the sleeping to waking hypnopompic state)

15 Donald Bahr, "Native American Dream Songs, Myth, Memory and Improvisation," *Journal de la Société des Américanistes*, 80 (1994): 73–93.

4. Listening to conversations within a dream story context
5. Listening to the sound of one's own voice speaking or crying out (sometimes these are moans as the dreamer attempts to speak or cry out, but cannot get the full sound out)
6. Receiving the information of people conversing—as if by a form of "sonic telepathy"
7. Listening to "Ear Worms" (pesky, pre-existent songs, compositions that spin round in the head during sleep and waking)
8. Composing or receiving new music while dreaming or upon awakening in hypnopompic state
9. Seeking and receiving or spontaneously receiving a spiritual song, sound, mantra or important life message
10. Having the *memory* of sounds within the dream
11. Listening to external sounds entering the dream—often taking on and blending with one's own story content
12. Listening to sounds gleaned from written texts in dreams
13. Listening to the sound of one's own *thinking* in the waking to sleeping hypnogogic state as well as the sleeping to waking hypnopompic states
14. Having a visual of sounds with or without the actual sounds
15. Listening to and speaking a foreign language (an existing language or a dream-invented language) unknown to the dreamer and understanding it perfectly
16. Hearing and speaking multilingual words in the languages that the dreamer speaks and understands
17. Singing in dreams and finding that the singing spontaneously continues in waking state

ΔΔΔ

A Dream Listening Experiment

I recently conducted an informal study on listening in dreams, asking a few colleagues to spend a few nights paying close attention to sound in their dreams.

My own methodology simply involved writing down my intention in my journal and saying to myself just before settling into to sleep, "*I will pay attention to sound in my dreams tonight.*" I include here some of my dreams and those of another dreamer, with my short commentary following each of the dreams.

IONE'S Listening Experiment

DREAM 1:

Toward waking I hear my own voice saying, "I am listening," there is a pause and I hear another voice responding, "Yes, but you are asleep. . . I am awake!"

Commentary:

On awaking fully I am a bit startled by this exchange! Who, I wonder is the owner of the other voice? Later on I have some ideas that these voices belong to my (somewhat more judgmental) "awake" left brain speaking to my still sleeping right brain.

DREAM 2:

I am aware during the night of sounds of my own breathing—coming to me in pleasurable tonalities and harmonies.

Commentary:

This was an enhanced kind of listening to the breath—truly Deep Listening. I am reminded of Tibetan lama Tenzin Wangyal's powerful Dream Yoga teachings on breath or Prana as an integral part of clearing and focus leading to dreams of clarity.[16]

DREAM 3:

I am preparing to perform—actually it is a rehearsal—I am wearing a red dress. I peruse the words/lyrics—on a sheet of paper—I've done this before—but I feel a bit nervous—what is the melody? I can't seem to recall. I begin to realize that I will create it (improvise) in the moment.

I awaken with sounds and melodies in my head—a song my mother used to play and sing at the piano, "I've got an island in the Pacific. And every thing about it is terrific. . ."

Commentary:

This dream is a "listening" variation on the classic performance anxiety dream. One layer of this dream is my own performance anxiety

---

16 Tenzin Wangyal Rinpoche, *The Tibetan Yogas of Dream and Sleep*, 38, 90–92.

re: listening in the dream. (Noticing the other aspects of the dream—I also have the ability to access my linear mind enough to read in a dream—not always easy. In the dream I do see the words, but do not "recall" them on waking. They are hiding, lingering and encoded in the right brain. This is a code the left brain can no longer decipher once I'm awake. Are they the words to the song in my head in the morning?)

DREAM 5:

I'm walking in front of a woman who is carrying a baby—her husband behind her—she also has groceries and it is clear the baby is getting heavy for her to carry. I wonder why the husband doesn't help and I am aware of my voice building up. Then finally I say to him, very loud and bold: "Why don't you help her? Why don't you carry the baby?" He points to his stomach as if some sickness prevents him from assisting. I am conscious of my own voice and boldness as I speak to him. I offer to carry the baby, and the woman gives it to me. I'm very aware. I know how to do this. The baby feels unusually light as I hold it—I am however, enjoying the familiar feeling.

Commentary:

Such energy in my voice, pushing up through the (dream) vocal chords in this dream with feminist "overtones." (Does the man have no "stomach" for holding a baby?) And there's also my own nostalgia for baby holding. There is a consciousness of the sound of my voice and my own boldness breaking through. I could have remained silent. But I didn't. During the course of this experiment my voice seems to want to get louder—as if wanting to please and get my attention.

Ximena Alarcón's Listening Experiment

DREAM 1: Voice of Consultation

I am writing an e-mail and on the subject I write: "Presidente Estados Unidos de America." I wonder if I should write this in Spanish or in English. In the dream I think that in Spanish it sounds pretentious and offensive at the same time (why?). *I read it in my mind and hear it* and think about the language connotations.

Commentary:

Ximena often dreams in Spanish and in English, her dreams reflecting her relationships to these languages in waking state. There seems to be a kinship between some dream sound phenomena to the sounds that move through our consciousness when we are reading words, or reading music."[17]

DREAM 2: *Hazaña*

I am with Ron on a trip, which is a kind of adventure, we are sort of heroes of a movie, people are watching us, we are resting, and while Ron lies on the bed I am sitting on the floor organizing some cables, and their connections. We are in a room with friends. They are watching TV, *I can hear the TV.* We are next to a sea or lake, and there is a boat. . .The boat detaches from the dock, and Ron jumps into the water (as a hero), to rescue the boat. Then I am in the boat, it is mysterious and rusty, *I can hear the "quick, quick" of the rusty metal that moves with the wind and the movement of the boat in the water.* Like in a film, I see Ron in a room in the boat, with black painting on his face, two Gothic young women enter in his room.

Commentary:

Movement and water and an adventure, as in a film. The sound of rusty metal and wind add to the mystery of the journey of relationship in this dream.

DREAM 3: Jealous Soul

I am with Ron in a cinema. I arrive first and select two seats. The seats are very tight. Other women are coming to sit next to us, I recognize they are schoolmates. Ron is in his wedding suit, one woman comes and says something to him touching his hands. I stare her directly in her eyes saying *"I don't like that." Ron is calm, happy and innocent. I woke up listening to one love song (Cuban love song). The words are: "Yo vengo aquí, yo vengo aquí, para cantar, para cantar. . . eres mi adoración. . ."*

---

17 "The sound of words is a memory (echo) of their physical shape—space of letters printed or drawn, of spaces between them; shape itself a memory (echo) of their sound." Stephen Ratcliffe, *Listening to Reading* (Albany: State University of New York, 2000), 8.

Commentary:

Ximena has many images that are film like or related to films in her dreams. . . an ongoing theme. Her dream song expresses deep underlying feelings.

All in all, I am pleased with the results of this simple listening experiment, indicating both the responsiveness of dreams to our desire to listen to them, and the subtlety and humor that they can bring forth for our listening edification.

ΔΔΔ

Right Brain - Left Brain

We know that during dreams, the right hemisphere of our brains is extremely active, with the left brain passively observing. This situation reverses itself several times during sleep. Just as there is hemispheric oscillation during the night, this balancing activity takes place during the day as well. The two cerebral hemispheres oscillate in activity every ninety to one hundred minutes and are 180 degrees out of phase both day and night. The cycle corresponds to changes in cognitive efficiency, the appearance of daydreams, REM (dream sleep), and, conversely, N-REM (dreamless) sleep. When the right brain is at its peak, the left is at its nadir and vice versa.

These interactions are also responsible for another curious phenomenon. We dream backwards in response to our external sounds. We've all experienced the entry of external sounds into our dreaming, and experienced them somehow becoming a part of our story. So for example, the sound of a clock alarm while you are sleeping may enter your dreams as a complex story that eventually leads up to your entering a contest in which a game show buzzer goes off when you touch it with your hands.

Researchers have discovered that a curious function of right hemisphere dreaming causes us to dream backwards! The story around the dream seems to precede the buzzer/clock sound, but in truth it is developed and dreamed backwards in response to the sound. This is the unique property of the language of the right hemisphere during sleep (as well as amygdale action) that makes up the story around the sound of the bell in order to explain it.[18]

Does the eardrum respond to Dream Sounds, much as the eyes respond to visual dream stimuli? (Our Rapid Eye Movements during sleep, REM Sleep, are associated with 80% of our dreaming time.) The answer appears to be yes. Middle ear muscle activity (MEMA) begins just before or at the onset of rapid eye movement, and the MEMA activity though not always simultaneous, continues in patterns resembling that of REM sleep. *While we are sleeping our ears are listening to the sounds of our dreams as well as to external sounds.*

In 1976, R.I.P. Hayman participated in the studies of sound perception in sleep at New York's Montefiore Medical Center. MEMA were monitored, assessing the feedback response of the nerve endings on the tympanic tensor muscles of the eardrum.[19]

Using a system in which a pressure-strain gauge was embedded in a custom plastic ear mold fitted next to the tympanic membrane, the movement of the muscles was registered on a polygram, alongside REM and brainwave readings from electrodes. The MEMA was registered at sub-audio frequencies, which exhibited surprisingly dynamic variations. The subjectively estimated sounds were loud—85 decibels and over. Subsequently, an attempt was made to record sounds emanating from R.I.P's eardrum; though many sounds were recorded during six hours of sleep in an audio studio, the results were blurred by the interference of the sounds of breathing and circulatory systems. Since this 1976 experiment, scientists have been refining research on MEMA, making particular advances related to middle ear function in subjects with mental illness. Most related to R.I.P's endeavor is the startling research that is allowing scientists to "read thoughts" of patients with

---

18 Rhawn Joseph, *Neuropsychology, neuropsychiatry, and behavioral neurology* (NY: Plenum Press, 1990), 32. See also: http://brainmind.com/Dreaming.html.
19 R.I.P. Hayman, "Listening to Dreams: Project for Middle Ear Muscle Activity Audio Level Telemetry" in *Current Research in Arts Medicine: A Compendium of the Medart International 1992 World Congress on Arts and Medicine*, ed. Fadi J. Bejjani (Pennington, NJ: A Capella Books, 1993), 463–464.

implanted electrodes.[20] This is giving the expectation that one day—not too far away—we will be able to record actual dream content. All seem to be in the visual realm thus far, with no mention made of the audio in those dreams. Can listening and recording the real time sounds of our dreams be far behind?

Dream researchers are moving in new directions that are showing that dreams are not only responses to or reflections of our waking states, but can have their own integrity. Ursula Voss and Karin Schermelleh-Engel at the University of Bonn in Germany, Inka Turin at the Centre for the Research and Rehabilitation of Hereditary Ataxias, Holguín, Cuba , and Alan Hobson of Harvard Medical School in Boston collected dream reports from participants who were born deaf and did not speak, as well as those born with paraplegia.[21] Able-bodied participants acted as controls. To the researchers' surprise, about 80% of the deaf participants dreamed that they could hear. Similarly the paraplegic volunteers dreamed of being able to walk and run. Among the deaf participants, beautiful sonic dreams were reported in which the participants felt much emotion at being able to listen to loved ones and speak with them. No mention of measurement of MEMA in this study as of yet. Could there somehow be measurable sound in the dreams of the deaf?

The authors of the study suggest that during REM sleep babies in the womb are practicing for all the future functions of their bodies. They feel that the dreaming brains of the participants in their study were tapping into the brain's genetic ability to mimic life functions.

ΔΔΔ

Can we approach the expanded relationship to the universe that the ancients had? Can we recover from the steady inroads of our society's

---

20 Moran Cerf and Michael Mackay, "Studying Consciousness Using Direct Recording from Single Neurons in the Human Brain" in Stanislas Dehaene and Yves Christen, *Characterizing consciousness: from cognition to the clinic?* (New York: Springer, 2011), 133–146.

21 Ursula Voss, Inka Tuin, Karin Schermelleh-Engel, and Allan Hobson, "Waking and Dreaming: Related but Structurally Independent. Dream Reports of Congenitally Paraplegic and Deaf-Mute Persons," in *Consciousness and Cognition* 20.3 (2011): 673–687.

linear left brain emphasis and recover a bit more of the sense of our own "be-ing"?

While we do not wish to replicate the conditions of the ancient mind, we might begin to reclaim the best of our right brains. Music is generally associated with the right brain—but not exclusively so. Rhythm and the phenomenon of perfect pitch for example tend to access the left brain. It is a re-balancing that we seek.

Albert Einstein summed it up well in the following statement: "The intuitive mind is a sacred gift and the rational mind is a faithful servant. We have created a society that honors the servant and has forgotten the gift."[22] Reclaiming our dreams and particularly accessing more of the sound and music that floats through them can certainly be a big part of a renaissance of human well-being.

I've selected two healing dreams by members of the Deep Listening Community and one poem by a deeply listening child. Each takes us into a profound realm of listening and also illustrates both a literal and figurative harmony that seems healing for the dreamer as well as for the dreaming community as a whole.

ΔΔΔ

Rachel's Dream

My cat, Isis, wanted to be taken to the ocean, so I held her and brought her there and she made it clear to me that she wanted to go in the sea. I waded in with her in my arms, and she leapt into the waves, which were a beautiful icy green, like her eyes. I saw her moving in the waves and felt concerned, and suddenly there appeared a giant blue whale. It came very near her. The whale began to sing, and Isis sang with the whale. The sound was so beautiful, they knew how to make mysterious harmonies together and it was very healing and mystical to listen to, and the surf was strong so the waves were as if percussion, and sometimes their sound included bubbling, which strangely I could hear, as if I were underwater. I just stood there, amazed and listening. I wondered how

---

22 Attributed by numerous sources to Albert Einstein, e.g., http://www .goodreads.com/quotes/show/7090.

Isis knew that it was the moment to go to the sea, I wondered if they had communed telepathically, had they made a date?[23]

Monique's Dream

Last night in my dreams I heard, listened, and played (the trombone) quite a bit in a variety of situations. Eventually in the shifting sonic dreaming scenes I dreamed that I was listening to a group's musical sounding. I was somewhere nearby, not actually in the room where this was taking place. The exquisite beauty of this sounding grew in my consciousness into awareness, and a desire to draw closer. I followed the sounds through various hallways within the structure until I was led to the doorway where I listened some more from a few paces back, and finally inside where I listened and watched.

The doorway—a threshold and frame but no door—was set into a corner of a very large almost square room of white. There was a short row of perhaps seven, eight, or nine Deep Listening certificate holders sitting in the center of the long axis of the room, and behind them a larger number of Deep Listeners were also sitting in rows—perhaps forty or fifty people in all.

The sounding was a kind of vocal call-and-response in the sense that the row of certificate holders would sound for a while, and then the larger group would answer them. The elision between the two musical forces felt like standing in that spot in the ocean where the surf pushes in while it also pulls out. The larger Deep Listener group's answer to the certificate holder's call would shift into its own call which the certificate holders would answer, and so on, cyclically, into a time beyond time.

There was an extremely strong sense of cohesion from all those present, a solid and stable group energy that was also very dense. The interconnection and interweaving within the improvisations were fluent, and the fluidity of the sounding reflected a great mastery of intent from all present. The sounds were incredibly beautiful.

I did not recognize anyone there in this room—it seemed a different time than the one now, a time in the future. I listened and listened, listening into the sound, becoming the sound, and then later I woke.

---

23 Rachael Koenig's dream, described in email from dreamer to author, July 11, 2011.

The sense of loss upon awaking—of being here now in this time instead of there then—was so great that I went back into the sleep sounding over again and again, until finally I was able to slip back into this time without feeling attached to the other. Without that attachment there was no loss; instead a feeling of empty peace.[24]

A Third Grader's Dream Poem

The wind isn't really the wind
It's a woman saying some of her golden dreams.
She breates [*sic*] every second.
Her dreams never end
One of her dreams blows away—
And it comes true.
And her secrets never end
Her dreams are stuck in a cloud—
And fall with some snow
And she catches it.
And she lives as if she was God.[25]

ΔΔΔ

I invite you to listen deeply, this very night.

---

24 IONE, "Dream of Monique Buzzarté," *Listening in Dreams: A Compendium of Sound Dreams, Meditations, and Rituals for Deep Dreamers* (New York: iUniverse, 2005), 10–12; *This is a Dream! A Handbook for Deep Dreamers* (New York: iUniverse, 2001), 10.
25 Anonymous child poet ca. 1986, culled during the author's residency as a professional poet teaching in a New York City school.

Editorial Team for the Anthology of Essays on Deep Listening

Editors:

Monique Buzzarté, trombonist/composer, is a leading proponent of contemporary music who was selected by Meet the Composer as a "Soloist Champion" in recognition of her long history of commissioning and premiering new works. Her recordings on the Deep Listening label include *Fluctuations* with Ellen Fullman, *Holding Patterns* as Zanana, and *Dreaming Wide Awake* with the New Circle Five. The past Co-Chair of GRIME International (Gender Research in Music Education) 2009-2011, as Vice President of the International Alliance for Women in Music in 1997 she led world-wide advocacy efforts resulting in the admission of women members into the Vienna Philharmonic. Buzzarté holds BA and BM degrees from the University of Washington where she was a student of Stuart Dempster, along with a MM from the Manhattan School of Music. Pauline Oliveros' *Red Shifts* (2000) for trombone, four oscillators, and noise and *The Gender of Now: There But Not There* (2005) for trombone and piano were both written for Buzzarté, who also contributed the Midword for Oliveros' *Sounding the Margins: Collected Writings 1992-2009*, served on the Deep Listening Institute's Board of Directors, and is certified to teach the meditative improvisation practices of Deep Listening. http://www.buzzarte.org

Tom Bickley is a composer/performer/teacher exploring the sound-scape and contemplative practice. He grew up in Houston, sojourned in Washington, DC (studying plainchant with Ruth Steiner, recorder with Scott Reiss, music librarianship with Neil Ratliff and working at the Smithsonian

Institution Libraries). He came to California as a composer in residence at Mills College in 2000. He holds a BM from University of Houston, an MA in musicology from the American University, an MDiv from Wesley Theological Seminary, and an MSLIS from the Catholic University of America. Through study with Pauline Oliveros, IONE, and Heloise Gold, he earned the Certificate in Deep Listening. He is a member of the library faculty at CSU East Bay and the music faculty at the Bay Area Center for Waldorf Teacher Training, and chairs the Public Services Committee for the Music Library Association. He performs with shakuhachi player Nancy Beckman as Gusty Winds May Exist and co-founded and directs the Cornelius Cardew Choir. http://about.me/tombickley

Layout Editor

Joseph Zitt is an author, composer, and improviser. His book *Surprise Me With Beauty: the Music of Human Systems,* as well as much of his other work in music, focuses on enabling people with varied skills and experience to do their best in situations without leaders or conventional political or organizational structures. His other books include *19th Nervous Breakdown: Making Human Connections in the Landscape of Commerce, Shekhinah: the Presence,* and *The Book of Voices.* He has coordinated Silence, the Internet's John Cage mailing list since founding it in 1994. He performed at Lincoln Center in *The Lunar Opera* by Pauline Oliveros. He has formed ensembles and created performance works in several cities, and composed for and performed in the ensembles Comma, Gray Code, and the Cornelius Cardew Choir with Tom Bickley. His compositions have been performed by orchestras and other ensembles throughout the US. http://www.josephzitt.com

Index

Index of Names of People, and Titles of Scores, Recordings, Books, Ensembles and Festivals

This is an index to the main text of this book, and does not cover authors' biographies or footnotes.

9 781889 471181